Your Child Abroad

A TRAVEL HEALTH GUIDE

PUBLISHER'S FOREWORD

The first Bradt travel guide was written in 1974 by George and Hilary Bradt on a river barge floating down a tributary of the Amazon. In the 1980s and '90s the focus shifted away from hiking to broader-based guides to new destinations – usually the first to be published on these places. In the 21st century Bradt continues to publish these ground-breaking guides, along with other guides to established holiday destinations, incorporating in-depth information on culture and natural history alongside the nuts and bolts of where to stay and what to see.

Bradt authors support responsible travel, with advice not only on minimum impact but also on how to give something back through local charities. Thus a true synergy is achieved between the traveller and local communities.

*

I have known Jane Wilson-Howarth for over 20 years, first as an expedition leader, then as a doctor specialising in travel medicine, and finally as a trekking companion in the Himalayas with her two young sons in tow. Seven-year-old Alexander skipped ahead with his father, involving himself in every aspect of Nepalese life, while three-year-old Sebastian rode in a specially designed basket carried by a porter, or trotted along the trail admiring flowers and insects. This was the first time I had travelled with children, and I was delighted to see how easily the kids coped with the rigours of an arduous (to me) trek. It was clear from Jane's calm demeanour that any illness or accident would be no more of a problem here than at home – if you know what to do. And so the idea of this book was born.

Hilary Bradt

Hilary Bradt

19 High Street, Chalfont St Peter, Bucks SL9 9QE, England
Tel: 01753 893444; fax: 01753 892333
Email: info@bradtguides.com
Web: www.bradtguides.com

Your Child Abroad

A TRAVEL HEALTH GUIDE

Second Edition

Dr Jane Wilson-Howarth
Dr Matthew Ellis

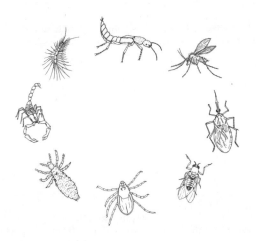

Bradt Travel Guides Ltd, UK
The Globe Pequot Press Inc, USA

Second edition 2005
First published 1998

Bradt Travel Guides Ltd
19 High Street, Chalfont St Peter, Bucks SL9 9QE, England
Published in the USA by The Globe Pequot Press Inc, 246 Goose Lane,
PO Box 480, Guilford, Connecticut 06437-0480

British Library Cataloguing in Publication Data
A catalogue record for this book is available from the British Library

ISBN-10: 1 84162 120 X
ISBN-13: 978 1 84162 120 3

Cover photographs
Top left Sebastian Howarth and Som Bahadur (Hilary Bradt), *top right* Quin, and *bottom right* Quin and Carole (Hallam Murray), *bottom left* Catherine (Tricia Hayne)

Illustrations Betty Levene

Typeset from the authors' disc by Wakewing
Printed and bound in Italy by Legoprint SpA, Trento

Authors

Dr Jane Wilson-Howarth BSc, MSc, BM, DCH, DCCH, FRSTMH, DFFP has lived in Asia for 11 years while she has worked on child health projects in Ladakh, Madagascar, Peru, Sri Lanka, Pakistan, Bangladesh and Nepal. Her three sons all went abroad in their early months. The family has enjoyed a dozen treks in Nepal including four to over 11,000ft with children from three months of age upwards.

She first studied zoology, then parasitology. Since qualifying as a medical doctor, she trained in paediatrics (DCH 1990; DCCH 1990) and has worked as a paediatrician in Oxford. She has been general practitioner to expatriate families living in Pakistan and Indonesia. In Nepal she worked on child survival programmes, and gave health briefings to US Peace Corps volunteers and VSOs and medical advice to the British School, Kathmandu. Now settled in England again, she works as a GP and teaches on travel health for the London School of Hygiene and Tropical Medicine, at travel shows and at the University of Cambridge. Her other books are *Bugs, Bites and Bowels*, *Shitting Pretty* and *Lemurs of the Lost World*; she contributes regular medical features to *Wanderlust* and *BBC Wildlife* magazines, and has written health chapters in a number of Bradt guides.

Dr Matthew Ellis MA, PhD, MBChB, MRCP, DCH, MRCPCH is a paediatrician and father of two who started his family whilst leading a child health research project in Nepal. He trained first in social anthropology and then went to work amongst the Ashaninka Indians of the Peruvian Amazon. Since qualifying as a doctor of medicine he has practised in the UK, Sudan, conflict-ridden southern Ethiopia and in Humla at 11,000ft in a remote corner of Nepal. For three years he was a clinical research fellow based in Kathmandu for the Institute of Child Health, Great Ormond Street, London. He continues his international child health activities from Bristol where he now lives and practises. He also examines for the London School of Hygiene and Tropical Medicine and has advised the World Health Organisation, Geneva.

Contents

Acknowledgements

We have received lots of encouragement and suggestions from many people especially Hallam and Carole Murray, Dr Alison Bolam, Mel Roche, RGN, RM, Dr Sue Holmes and Anne Tiede. Technical information was supplied by Dr Vaughan Southgate (bilharzia), Dr Richard Lane (sandfly precautions), Dr Anne Denning (eye problems), Jean Sinclair (diabetes), Mary Kedward (vaccines), Lynn Poole (American drug names), Sally Crook (malaria), Christian Turner (dental problems) and Carmen Devlin (resuscitation). Dr Colin Morley gave advice and also permission to reproduce a shortened version of *Baby Check*. Dr Mark Howarth, Dr Jill Sutcliffe, Dr Mary Styles, Dr Roly Blumberg, Catherine Hayne and Dr David Shlim also commented. Many well-travelled parents have been kind in sharing their thoughts, especially Dea Birkett, Dr Deborah Mills, Kerry Moran, Sheilagh Stewart, Sally Cox, Veronique McConnell, Dr Bill Pigott, Chrissie Dobbs, Sue Spencer, Lesley Thomas, Lorna and John Howell, Henriette ter Heegde and other parents of children at the British School in Kathmandu. Mariko Iizuka provided the Japanese, Monica Verano the Spanish and German, and Dr Izhar Fihir the Indonesian translations.

Hilary Bradt has done a great deal to encourage Jane's forays into writing about travel medicine and has been a great friend and inspiration for many years. Tricia Hayne, also of Bradt Travel Guides, has given a great deal of sound editorial help based upon her experiences both in publishing and in travelling, as well as helping keep Jane sane. Janice Booth and Adrian Dixon made numerous gentle suggestions to improve the text, and Janet Mears at Bradt has worked tirelessly.

Special thanks should go to Alexander and Sebastian Howarth for providing rich experience and inadvertent collections of various parasites that have provided insights on the pleasures and challenges of travelling with children; and little David, who only travelled with Jane for a couple of years but who cheered her children up with his carefree chuckling. Matthew's daughters Harriet and Kate have similarly been an inspiration. Finally Jane owes her husband, Simon, a big thank-you for encouraging her to embark upon trips she hesitated to attempt, and for entertaining the children during critical phases in writing this book.

Introduction

It had been a strenuous day: 1,500m of climbing. From the flimsy bamboo bridge across the river, the ascent had been steep. But the children had enjoyed it. Alexander and Andrew were on some fantasy ascent of Everest, where they were high-altitude Sherpas shooting the occasional yeti and looking after Katharine who was the queen, revelling in being able to ride in a huge basket slung from a Sherpa porter's headband; she and Sebastian sang to each other as they were carried up, or listened to Lorna (who seemed to have a lot more spare breath than me) tell stories or lead the singing. We walked up (the children snacking frequently) through terraces, then forests, out into alpine meadows then finally on to the ridge at 3,000m where, amongst pine forest twittering with birds, we looked out to the glistening clean snow on Dudh Kundha glacier and Gauri Shankar himal. We camped by the gompa and in the morning the lama let us inside where he encouraged Sebastian and the older children to beat the huge drums used during worship. We were in no rush to move on; the children helped the wife of the lama feed her fluffy twin yak calves and the dads gave the kids rides in the gompa wheelbarrow. Alexander said 'Why don't we stay here for ever?'

To some, having children may seem as conducive to travelling as having your feet set in concrete. Travel with children is undoubtedly more of an effort and needs more planning, but life does not stop when we become parents. Indeed more and more of us are choosing to travel with our children and that's why you have bought this book. Children are great diplomats and have led us into innumerable delightful encounters with people we otherwise would never have met. Traditional societies are child-friendly and there are baby-sitters everywhere; it is a delight to mingle in these family-centred cultures where you won't feel like apologising for your child all the time. But you don't have to go to Timbuktu to experience this – our European neighbours will almost certainly make you and your children welcome. How though do you organise and cope with the daunting responsibilities of travelling with a young family? This book will help you plan and will reassure you while abroad. It is aimed at anyone leaving home with children whether they are heading for Southend, Spain, Singapore or Santiago. It concentrates on prevention of illness and advises you what to do if your child seems off colour or unwell. Since medical problems are at the front of many travelling parents' minds we have covered all illnesses likely to worry or assail you wherever you end up: whether in Makalu, Machu Picchu, Vanuatu, Timbuktu or Corfu.

We assume no medical knowledge and, for those of you going further afield, presume that there may be no competent medical help within a day or two of wherever you find yourselves. We tell you how to manage the full range of possible medical problems so that you can either treat illness yourself – if that is what you have to do – or you can use the book as a second opinion to give you confidence in an unfamiliar doctor. This then will help you in London, LA, Lima or Lhasa. Where there is some debate about the 'best' treatment of a condition we have supplied information so you can make your own judgements. However, most parents, indeed most travellers, worry more about health matters than they need. Travelling families are unlikely to get struck down by horrendous tropical pox and the few real risks are highlighted and precautions for avoidance given. Throughout the book we have included case histories to illustrate the medical points; but one of the problems we have had is to accumulate good juicy scare-stories, since travelling families generally don't get into much trouble!

DISTRESSED ABOUT DENGUE

An expatriate friend phoned me from a remote village at the other end of Nepal. Little Luke (aged 15 months) had a high fever; there was that dengue epidemic in India; could he have dengue? The boy's temperature had been over 39°C for 24 hours.

'Is Luke eating, drinking and playing? Is he off colour? Any rash?'

'No he's eating fine, playing outside, and no there's no rash.'

'It sounds as if he is not too ill; dengue fever seems unlikely, but malaria is possible. Try giving him some *paracetamol* and see if the temperature comes down. If the temperature stays up you should get the local hospital to check his blood for malaria. Phone me again if you're worried.'

A couple of weeks later I bumped into the family – they were up in Kathmandu shopping and I asked 'What happened to Luke's dengue?'

'What? Oh that: the fever settled after 12 hours. We didn't need to take him to the hospital. I expect it was just a touch of flu!'

This kind of story is common amongst travelling families; one symptom naturally makes parents start worrying about all manner of lurid exotic afflictions which turn out to be the usual childhood trivia.

Many people are concerned about the risks of tropical diseases or snakebite when travelling far, but it is accidents that kill and injure most travellers, young and old alike. Moving around inevitably exposes families to the risk of transport accidents and in developing countries safety standards may be poor. Vehicle maintenance is not always a high priority: spares are expensive or unobtainable, repairs take time and thus lose the driver earnings and in some countries there is little or no legal control over the state vehicles are in. Whether or not the brakes work is up to the driver. Travellers have less control: you may not speak the language and are unfamiliar with the local way of doing things. This is paradoxically why so many of us enjoy travelling – the lack of control, the novelty and the unexpected are very much part of the experience. It is important to become more safety conscious when travelling and the book details how to reduce the risks. To get the best out of this book, read the prevention advice in *Chapter 5* before you travel, find out if your destination is malarious and, if it is, pack repellents and bed nets (*Chapter 2*, pages 19-22), and browse the chapter on accidents and emergencies since knowing what to do in an emergency makes it easier to stay calm. Have fun!

PUKING

Rory awoke saying he didn't feel well and promptly puked all over the floor beside his bed, but only the once. They'd spent the previous day beside the pool but seven-year-old Rory had been messing about with some other kids, slipped on the poolside and hit the back of his head on the tiles. Rory was a pretty stoical kid but the bang was hard enough to make him cry for quite a while afterwards. His Dad had a vague idea in his head that vomiting could be a sign of concussion or even bleeding into the brain. Dad got worried and asked his son if he had a headache. Rory said he did. And when questioned he also said the light hurt his eyes and he felt dizzy. The hotel staff told Dad of an international clinic close by. He phoned the clinic, described the symptoms and the doctor was alarmed. On attending the clinic though it turned out that Rory did not have concussion but just a touch of travellers' tummy. In retrospect Dad realised that he'd planted the symptoms in Rory's consciousness and he was just saying yes to them to be helpful because his Dad had looked worried. Beware of suggesting symptoms.

Children chuck readily and an occasional vomit in a child who otherwise seems cheerful should not alarm parents unduly. Parents of babies are often worried when their baby or toddler vomits a stomachful in the morning. Often the child has a cold and mucus has been swallowed in the night, and is rejected by the stomach in the morning. Once the mucus is cleared the child will then tuck into a hearty breakfast.

Bradt Travel Guides

Africa by Road Charlie Shackell/Illya Bracht
Albania Gillian Gloyer
Amazon, The Roger Harris/Peter Hutchison
Antarctica: A Guide to the Wildlife
Tony Soper/Dafila Scott
Arctic: A Guide to Coastal Wildlife
Tony Soper/Dan Powell
Armenia with Nagorno Karabagh Nicholas Holding
Azores David Sayers
Baghdad City Guide Catherine Arnold
Baltic Capitals: Tallinn, Riga, Vilnius, Kaliningrad
Neil Taylor et al
Bosnia & Herzegovina Tim Clancy
Botswana: Okavango, Chobe, Northern Kalahari
Chris McIntyre
British Isles: Wildlife of Coastal Waters
Tony Soper/Dan Powell
Budapest City Guide Adrian Phillips/
Jo Scotchmer
Cambodia Anita Sach
Cameroon Ben West
Canada: North – Yukon, Northwest Territories,
Nunavut Geoffrey Roy
Canary Islands Lucy Corne
Cape Verde Islands Aisling Irwin/Colum Wilson
Cayman Islands Tricia Hayne
Chile & Argentina: Trekking Guide
Tim Burford
China: Yunnan Province Stephen Mansfield
Cork City Guide Linda Fallon
Croatia Piers Letcher
Cyprus see *North Cyprus*
Dubrovnik City Guide Piers Letcher
East & Southern Africa: The Backpacker's Manual
Philip Briggs
Eccentric America Jan Friedman
Eccentric Britain Benedict le Vay
Eccentric Edinburgh Benedict le Vay
Eccentric France Piers Letcher
Eccentric London Benedict le Vay
Eccentric Oxford Benedict le Vay
Ecuador: Climbing & Hiking
Rob Rachowiecki/Mark Thurber
Ecuador, Peru & Bolivia: The Backpacker's Manual
Kathy Jarvis
Eritrea Edward Denison/Edward Paice
Estonia Neil Taylor
Ethiopia Philip Briggs
Falkland Islands Will Wagstaff
Faroe Islands James Proctor
Gabon, São Tome & Príncipe Sophie Warne
Galápagos Wildlife David Horwell/Pete Oxford
Gambia, The Craig Emms/Linda Barnett
Georgia Tim Burford
Ghana Philip Briggs
Iran Patricia L Baker
Iraq Karen Dabrowska
Kabul Mini Guide Dominic Medley/
Jude Barrand

Kenya Claire Foottit
Kiev City Guide Andrew Evans
Latvia Stephen Baister/Chris Patrick
Lille City Guide Laurence Phillips
Lithuania Gordon McLachlan
Ljubljana Robin and Jenny McKelvie
London, In the Footsteps of the Famous
Nicholas Best
Macedonia Thammy Evans
Madagascar Hilary Bradt
Madagascar Wildlife Nick Garbutt/
Hilary Bradt/Derek Schuurman
Malawi Philip Briggs
Maldives Royston Ellis
Mali Ross Velton
Mauritius, Rodrigues & Réunion Royston Ellis/
Alex Richards/Derek Schuurman
Mongolia Jane Blunden
Montenegro Annalisa Rellie
Mozambique Philip Briggs/Ross Velton
Namibia Chris McIntyre
Nigeria Lizzie Williams
North Cyprus Diana Darke
North Korea Robert Willoughby
Palestine, with Jerusalem Henry Stedman
Panama Sarah Woods
Paris, Lille & Brussels: Eurostar Cities
Laurence Phillips
Peru & Bolivia: Backpacking and Trekking
Hilary Bradt/Kathy Jarvis
Riga City Guide Stephen Baister/Chris Patrick
River Thames, In the Footsteps of the Famous
Paul Goldsack
Rwanda Janice Booth/Philip Briggs
St Helena, Ascension, Tristan da Cunha
Sue Steiner
Serbia Laurence Mitchell
Seychelles Lyn Mair/Lynnath Beckley
Singapore John Nichol/Adrian Phillips/
Isobel Dorling
Slovenia Robin and Jenny Kelvie
South Africa: Budget Travel Guide Paul Ash
Southern African Wildlife Mike Unwin
Sudan Paul Clammer
Svalbard Andreas Umbreit
Sri Lanka Royston Ellis
Switzerland: Rail, Road, Lake Anthony Lambert
Tallinn City Guide Neil Taylor
Tanzania Philip Briggs
Tasmania Matthew Brace
Tibet Michael Buckley
Uganda Philip Briggs
Ukraine Andrew Evans
USA by Rail John Pitt
Venezuela Hilary Dunsterville Branch
Your Child Abroad: A Travel Health Guide
Dr Jane Wilson-Howarth/Dr Matthew Ellis
Zambia Chris McIntyre
Zanzibar David Else

Bradt Travel Guides, 19 High Street, Chalfont St Peter, Bucks SL9 9QE, England
Tel: 01753 893444   Fax: 01753 892333
Email: info@bradtguides.com   www.bradtguides.com

Part One

Planning:
Disease Prevention

Don't get bitten, get BEN'S®

Whether it's France or Florida, the Maldives or Majorca, make sure Ben's insect repellent goes on holiday with you.

Choose from four presentations containing DEET – recognised as the most effective repellent available – or new chemical-free Ben's Natural, recommended for children from 12 months upwards.

Call **0800 1957 400** for your nearest stockist,
or order online at **www.afterbite.co.uk**

Planning

Preparing to leave home with children takes more planning than the journeys you will have made alone or with adult companions. Involving children in the planning is a key to successful, enjoyable travel, although the amount and kind of involvement will depend upon the age and temperament of the children.

EARLY DECISIONS
Where shall we go?
Air travel is so quick, easy and cheap now that those of us wanting travel and adventure are spoilt for choice. Yet some travel agents present a rather unbalanced image of what will greet you. Belize is promoted as a beach and tropical rainforest paradise, but literature rather glosses over the steaming heat and wonderful array of parasites. Does anyone highlight the risk of malaria for visitors to Kenya? And do brochures bill Peru and Nepal as diarrhoea hot-spots? Is a jungle adventure going to end in an encounter with dangerous wildlife? What should influence your choice of destination? Why do you want to travel? What are your interests? Do you go for architecture, archaeology, scenery, mountains or jungle; are you a wildlife enthusiast or do you just want to laze on the beach or mooch around markets? Think about places you will enjoy, will feel relaxed and comfortable in. Then consider whether there will be scope for the children to have fun too. You'll also enjoy the trip more if you do some background research – everyone can get involved in that.

Reading about your destination
Whether travelling long- or short-term, to work or to explore, you will need a good idea of the conditions to be faced. What kinds of temperature ranges can you expect? If you're in the tropics with a year-round temperature over 30°C, are you likely to climb a mountain or volcano where it may be cold? Do you know what clothes are comfortable in clammy monsoon conditions? How are you going to keep the sun off the back of the toddler's neck when he refuses to wear a hat? Are there any particular health hazards in the country you are visiting in the season you plan to visit? What supplies do you or don't you need to carry with you? What foods will and will not be available? If you expect to take all meals in restaurants, are they open when your child wants to eat? Can you buy nappies? What are the local medical services like? Might you be able to meet someone from the country you will be visiting before you go? Will the children do some reading too? In *Appendix 2* there are some suggested books

for younger children; older children may well design their own projects using the internet, reference books or libraries.

Something for everyone?

Children need lots of entertainment and diversity to prevent them whining and whinging. The ideal trip offers variety and lots of choice.

While your family is young you may find you all have a relaxing time at a holiday centre where there are clubs, activities, supervision and baby-sitters for the children, and the parents will be able to read, relax or party.

Pacing

Accommodating the tastes of everyone in the family will make for the best possible trip; yet a hectic see-it-all holiday will probably end in frustration because allowing time is also important.

Even if you have the luxury of a longer trip, don't try to do and see everything – that risks overload and you are likely to find the children harder to handle. Allowing more time for them to potter about on a river beach, collect stones, play hide-and-seek in hollow trees or scramble around on rocks will let you relax too; and you'll reap unexpected pleasures, especially encounters with new friends, colourful locals and rare wildlife.

How much shall we spend?

You may wish to use budget accommodation but some families will find cheap hotels awfully cramped, and extra beds or mattresses (if available) may limit floor-space for children to potter. Expensive hotels are not necessarily the best; kitchens in international-quality hotels everywhere are notoriously unhygienic but staff are more likely to know some English. Small, family-run accommodation (like Indonesian *losmen*) can be good for a travelling family; often the owners can appreciate family needs because they also have children, who may sometimes become playmates for yours. Self-catering accommodation or camping are easy and flexible enough for most families. Bed and breakfast can be good although you have a problem wondering where the toddler will have his afternoon sleep.

Travelling routines

It seems that the kinds of families who take well to travelling are busy and sociable ones (so that the children are not fazed by strangers), whose home life is either rather unstructured or with normal routines which can be adapted and made more flexible when travelling. Regular bedtimes can be allowed to drift if something interesting is happening; yet there still needs to be a secure base of reassuring daily rituals, like the bedtime story. Depending upon whether story books and a torch/flashlight can be found, this is read or made up: something based on the things we've seen during the day, or an adventure of a hero who does amazing things, like *Tintin in Tibet* rescuing people in the Himalayas. This story routine and other rituals are invaluable in winding children down from the excitements of the day. Bedtime baths are wonderfully calming but were not an option on many of the adventurous trips our children have enjoyed. If there is hot water, it won't be in a bath but more likely sploshed from a bucket with a mug, and sometimes in a very cold and draughty shack or outside toilet. The middle of the day can be a good time for bathing when the water or weather is cold.

What can we cope with?

The size of your family will influence what you can manage and what you will enjoy. If you have more than one small child per parent you may find a destination in northern Europe difficult since these can be rather child-unfriendly areas where children are not always welcome in hotels. In southern Europe and the less industrialised world, however, people will flock to help, children will be safely whisked up flights of stairs, luggage will be carried. North America offers the advantages of better-organised children's entertainments, inexpensive family rooms in hotels and startlingly rapid service in restaurants. There is now an ever-expanding pool of information available to help guide your choice (see websites, *Appendix 1*).

Part of the appeal of travel is that it is exciting because life is different and perhaps a little out of control, but the secret of pleasurable travel with children is to ensure you are within your own limits of coping. Start gently and you will enjoy it more, see more, learn more. And allow plenty of time.

Culture shock

Will beggars make you feel guilty? Your first few trips to the developing world can be quite a culture shock and it is worth considering what you are comfortable with. First tastes of the seemingly unbridgeable gulf between the rich and the desperately poor can be an overwhelming and life-changing experience. Many people will be racked by guilt which may be only slightly softened by making a contribution to some worthy charity – Save the Children and Action Aid are amongst the many who do excellent work. The countries of the Indian subcontinent are dirty, especially in the cities where you first arrive. Southeast Asia, North Africa or South America are gentler places to start, with better infrastructure, and problems which are less obvious.

People cope differently with the reality of poverty. Some manage to convince themselves that the poor are living naturally without our Western cares. The fact is that the majority of the world's population is struggling; sensitive travellers will realise this and try to avoid adding to their burdens. Tourism is a big income-generator, though, and your visit will probably contribute to the local economy. And seeing some of the problems may promote understanding and a move to change inequalities.

Unreal expectations make for an unhappy trip. Many people go to Kathmandu, for example, with starry-eyed images of a Himalayan Shangri-La: they cannot cope with the concrete development, emaciated beggars, air pollution, stinking drains, piles of rotting rubbish and other even more unpleasant deposits which assault the nose and eyes; where the diarrhoea risk is high, and people do not seem to appreciate the need to flush toilets. This, perhaps, is not the place for your first exotic trip with the children. Nor is it a great region to visit if pregnancy has heightened your sense of smell.

Children puzzled by people living in squalor ask why they don't wash or wear shoes. If the poverty horrifies you, you'll find it hard to explain to your

NO TURNING BACK!
Our first family trek was with boys aged three and three months. We planned to be away for three weeks, heading towards Muktinath at 12,500ft on the far side of the Himalayan watershed. My husband Simon, being a Himalayan veteran, was enthusiastic, but I was sure I'd want to give up after a few days. We discussed this. It was only three months since my caesarean section and, although I knew this would not be a problem, it was a good enough excuse to get Simon to agree in principle that I might catch a plane back from the halfway point. Yet within a couple of days, we had worked out a rhythm and routine for the trek; Alexander enjoyed playing hide-and-seek as we walked; and I completely forgot my reluctance: so that we took a longer route back to lengthen our time away.

child. Many major cities in both developing and developed countries have their unsightly quarters. Yet they also have many charms, and the well-informed visitor will be able to cope better, enjoy more fully and answer children's questions constructively.

Manners and sense of personal space differ greatly in other cultures and backgrounds. Sometimes locals seem to take liberties like removing a baby from your arms, or roughly tweaking children's cheeks, or giving them snacks or sweets without asking first. In many places you may be the subject of unabashed stares; either because you are dressed inappropriately or because you're the best entertainment that there's been in the village for decades. It can be a bit much especially if you are tired and cannot ask why. Plan a leisurely schedule so that you are relaxed and well rested and you will enjoy being the centre of attention.

Second thoughts

When you start thinking about your first trip with your child, it is natural to wonder whether it will be 'all right'. Other parents may imply that you are crazy. Are you really being reckless or foolish? Will it be a nightmare from start to finish? If you are planning your trip with dread, stop and take stock of what is worrying you and see whether you can prepare yourself and the children a little better before you go; reassure yourself that you will cope (the children certainly will) and that you won't want to turn back. As departure time approaches keep in mind that it's not a disaster to turn back; and plan a route so that you can stop partway and go home if necessary. If you know you can stop, you won't want to.

PRACTICAL CONCERNS
Is your destination safe?

The two biggest health issues to consider when planning a trip are security and malaria. Is your destination safe? Has war just broken out there? A trip to a travel clinic should give you information on possible civil unrest as well as health risks: most have links to an expert information source, but you could also check with government sources for security advice (see page 191). Wherever you plan to go, remember that dangerous (including cerebral) malaria is on the increase worldwide and children are especially susceptible to it. Much of Africa would therefore be crossed off my list of possible pleasure trips with small children. In India, Rajasthan and Orissa are places to contract dangerous forms of malaria. That does not mean that travel is completely out of the question. Clearly parents going abroad for work have different reasons and motivations, but also budding expatriates are able to exercise better control over their home environment and can limit risks more effectively. Take specialist advice and make sure you know all about avoiding mosquito bites (see pages 19–22).

Insurance and contingencies

Crises happen when insufficient thought is given to contingencies and possible escape routes if things go wrong. There is little point in taking out insurance for helicopter rescue if you can't summon a helicopter if you need one. Sensible route planning is the most important aspect of safe travel and is an insurance in itself; a three-week trek may mean you are weeks away from help when disaster strikes.

The insurance you buy will depend upon how often and how long you travel and, perhaps, your destination and what you intend to do. Frequent travellers will be well advised to check out the very competitive annual holiday insurance market; sometimes an extension of your household insurance is all that is needed. American-based MEDEX provide services which will appeal to longer-term travellers and expatriates. Shop around to find the best scheme for your particular needs and ensure that your insurance covers rescue from where you plan to go as well as evacuation to a good hospital, perhaps in a neighbouring country. Always declare any medical problems since failure to admit the existence of a pre-existing medical condition may invalidate your insurance and leave you stranded. If your child suffers from any kind of long-standing condition the appropriate charity often can direct you to a sympathetic insurer.

Arranging medical treatment in the European Union

British residents can generally obtain emergency treatment (either free or at reduced cost) from the state services in EU countries, on presentation of a completed form E111. This form is included in the booklet *Health Advice for Travellers Anywhere in the World* (Department of Health, Central Office of Information, HMSO). The booklet (leaflet T6 note '75') is available free from post offices and doctors' surgeries, or via the Health Literature Line, tel: 0800 555777 or at www.doh.gov.uk/hat.

How soon? How young?

Is it risky to fly at a very early age? Airlines will probably refuse to carry a baby who is less than 48 hours old, as well as older infants with undiagnosed or unstable conditions. The only real issue is the lower oxygen pressure with associated expansion of gas by 20% at altitude and in the cabin. The blood of the newborn baby contains foetal haemoglobin which is designed to function at low partial pressures of oxygen. Very young babies will therefore cope well with a flight, unless they have some underlying medical problem (see also page 41). It is possible that very small or premature infants could get into trouble if they fly when unwell even with the snuffles or a cold. Most babies will have a routine medical check at four to six weeks of age and can then fly if declared fit. Once on the aircraft small babies need a little more attention to ensure that they are fed regularly and so stay well hydrated, and that they don't get too hot. Remove hats and extra clothing from a very sweaty baby or one whose stomach feels hot.

The first couple of months is a good age to travel (if the parents are up for it) because this is when the infant is at the eating and sleeping phase. The exclusively breast-fed infant is also protected from all the many diarrhoeal diseases (see *Chapter 6*). The risks of becoming ill increase once weaning begins and then trouble really starts when the child gets mobile. This is usually when he learns to crawl at around the age of eight or nine months. From this time until the end of the terrible twos (and the onset of possible bribery) travelling is challenging. If the family is thinking about going somewhere remote and exotic with children between the ages of eight months and three years, then think again. It might be best to stick to places you already know well or to gentler destinations.

Children with continuing medical conditions

A few children suffer from a continuing illness which may have some influence on the family's travel plans. Only the commonest important problems and medicaments are mentioned here, but clearly any doubts or questions should be aired with the child's own doctor. Carry a clinical summary (written by the family doctor or hospital) and notes of any routine medicines (with their *generic* names) and doses; notes on medicines are found in *Chapter 3*, page 33 onwards. A MedicAlert bracelet or neck pendant would also be a sensible precaution (MedicAlert UK; tel: 020 7833 3034) if your child has some ongoing problem. Make sure that you know your child's approximate weight in kilograms so that you can calculate required doses of medicines; some doses are calculated as mg per kg of the child's bodyweight (this is also useful information if you need to buy disposable nappies whilst away). If you are used to thinking in kilos and going to the US, also knowing your babe's weight in pounds will allow you to buy the correct size of nappies/diapers.

Asthma

In this condition the small airways of the lungs are over-sensitive so that infections, pollen, the cold or other trigger factors make them constrict, causing breathlessness. Asthma is common, affecting 15–20% of British children; perhaps half grow out of it. It is unpredictable; travel can make it better or worse. Those with pollen allergies will often feel healthier at the coast, but others meet new trigger factors and suffer more; polluted big cities may make asthmatics worse. Travelling parents need to know a little more than average to manage an attack abroad. Any child who has been admitted to hospital with asthma should travel with a course of steroid tablets as well as his usual inhalers; parents must know the differences between 'first aid'-type and preventative-type inhalers. It is permitted to carry inhalers on aircraft. Peak flow meters are useful in deciding if the child needs extra treatment. Large spacing devices are easiest to use, especially if the child is having a severe attack, but disc devices are less bulky and easier to travel with. Discuss it all with your child's doctor before travel. The UK National Asthma Campaign Helpline (tel: 01345 010203) can also give advice.

Hay fever and problems with other airborne allergens

Older children often suffer from sneezing and runny noses when particular pollens are in the air. Like asthma the problem may disappear when arriving in a destination with clear air. Hay fever is more likely in children who suffer from asthma and/or eczema and in children with close relatives who suffer. Hay fever can also make asthma more difficult to control. The symptoms are a runny nose for longer than the usual week or so for a common cold. There can also be itchy eyes. Antihistamine syrups and tablets work well for this and *sodium cromoglicate* eye drops also help if the eye symptoms are the main problem. Nasal sprays are also good if the nose symptoms are troublesome. The herbal treatment butterbur has been shown to be as effective as antihistamines.

Skin problems

Eczema is a very common dry-skin condition which may get better or worse in hot climates. It is more likely to improve in sunshine if you continue to apply plenty of moisturisers. Remember that the itching is worst when the skin is hot, and that scratching exacerbates itching and leads to infection. Cool baggy 100%-cotton clothes are essential; and pack adequate moisturisers, hypoallergenic suncreams (which you already know suit your child) and a steroid cream in case of a flare-up. The 1% *hydrocortisone* cream that can be bought across the counter in the UK will probably not be strong enough to control a bad exacerbation so ask the child's doctor for some advice. Ensure also that you can tell when the rash becomes infected: weeping, increase in itching, spreading redness and/or fever may indicate skin infection. Half of babies with eczema grow out of it by the age of two.

Psoriasis affects 1.5% of Europeans and is a continuing skin problem; it usually improves in sunlight but taking *chloroquine* antimalarials can make it worse.

Cold sores are aggravated by strong tropical sunlight so if anyone in the family suffers from them pack *aciclovir* cream as well as some physical barriers to sun exposure (eg: hats). *Aciclovir* works best when applied as soon as the child feels that the cold sore is about to erupt; it is much less effective once the sore is visible.

Severe allergic reactions

A severe allergic reaction means difficulty breathing, swelling of the face or collapse after taking certain foods (especially nuts), an insect sting, etc. The parents of any child who has experienced such symptoms should discuss with the family doctor whether they need carry an *adrenaline* (*epinephrine* in the US) injection or 'EpiPen' autoinjector; this can be administered by a parent in case of a repeat anaphylactic reaction. You may need a letter from your doctor in order to be allowed to carry it on to a plane. The US website www.foodallergy.org/ offers a sample letter to present to your doctor to sign. The alternative way of taking *adrenaline* is by inhaling it (eg: Medihaler-Epi), but this is not so effective. Milder food allergies are discussed in *Chapter 5*, page 63–4.

Diabetes

One in 500 British children suffer from diabetes and most manage to reorganise their lives so that their regular injections and slight dietary restrictions do not intrude upon them. It is important to realise, though, that travel involves changes in the routines which are so important to good diabetic control; additional exercise, different diet and any infection all upset the balance. Hot climates tend to reduce the amount of insulin needed, making low blood sugars, a 'hypo' or hypoglycaemia, more likely. Low blood sugar can also make children with diabetes illogical and unwilling to take emergency, high-energy foods when required. It is important always to have a high-calorie, quick-acting snack in case of low blood sugar; and also plenty of needles, syringes and spare insulin in case luggage gets lost or a pen injector gets left behind. Insulin is quite robust and should remain active for a month at normal room temperatures. Shelf lives vary between preparations though (manufacturers will advise). Generally, clear fast-acting insulins are most robust, and can survive freezing while cloudy medium-to long-acting and bimodal insulins are more delicate and are best kept cool. Ideally though protect from heat or freezing in an unbreakable vacuum flask or in a plastic pot that can be stored in a hotel fridge. Find out how long your child's particular insulin survives at the kinds of temperatures you expect to encounter. Useful websites include www.diabetes-travel.co.uk and www.scottish-internet.co.uk/clinents/diabetestravel/home/htm.

Epilepsy

If your child suffers from fits and is on medication make sure you have adequate supplies to last the trip and allow for bottles forgotten in hotel rooms as well as lost luggage. Ask your doctor for some emergency anti-fit medicine before you go. *Diazepam* rectal tubes (Stesolid 5mg for under threes, 10mg for children over three years given up into the rectum) and *lorazepam* buccal preparations (dissolve in the cheek) are very useful and easy to give. If your child suffers with febrile seizures (fits triggered by fever) he is probably not on any regular medicine. Remember to be vigilant with temperature control measures and you may also find it reassuring to travel with rectal *diazepam*. The *Epilepsy Passport* published by the British Epilepsy Association is a useful multi-lingual handbook (address in *Appendix 1*, page 195).

IMMUNISATIONS AND OTHER PREPARATIONS

Immunising injections are important – both those given routinely to all children and also those given to protect travellers. In addition sun-protection (pages 22–4) is essential and it is important to consider precautions against biting insects and the diseases they spread.

Malaria prevention (prophylaxis)

About 300 children a year are treated for malaria in Britain, having brought the parasite back as an unwanted souvenir. Most of these ill children will have taken nothing to protect them against malaria. Sometimes this is because of misconceptions about risks. The choices and sources of information are growing though so it is easier to protect children than it has ever been. There is now some choice of prophylactics suitable for children but whatever you pick it should be decided with expert advice. It should be possible to find a suitable preparation which you can consistently succeed in getting the kids to swallow, then this protection can be further boosted by other measures to avoid being bitten (these are reviewed in the next chapter; pages 19–22). Good bite protection comes with the added extra benefit that it protects from other mosquito-borne diseases.

Find out what are the best antimalarials for your destination; don't just buy the over-the-counter option. The easiest source of expert advice to access is www.fitfortravel.scot.nhs.uk. Otherwise the Malaria Reference Centre at the London School of Hygiene and Tropical Medicine, tel: 020 7388 9600 (premium rate) gives information by country on risks and precautions. Or, probably best of all, go to one of the many specialist travel clinics who can advise face to face.

It will be easiest to remember to take the tablets if the whole family is using the same prophylaxis, whether weekly or daily.

Antimalarial potions

Antimalarial medicines do not afford complete protection, even if you are always successful in getting children to take them. Nor does prophylaxis protect them from other mosquito-borne diseases. Malarone and Lariam give over 90% protection so are usually the best choices; *chloroquine* and *proguanil* these days give only about 40% protection and are unpleasant to take.

Lariam (*mefloquine*) is licensed in the UK as a prophylactic for children over the age of three months or weighing over 5kg. In effect this means that almost any child can take it as long as he or she is able to swallow the pills. The tablets are scored and can easily be cracked into quarters to give small people small doses. Most British prescribers will follow the guidelines developed by the expert committee on malaria, as given below, although these differ somewhat from the doses given in the packet insert:

Age	Child's weight	Dose
up to 3 years	up to 16kg	¼ tablet
4–7 years	16–24.9kg	½ tablet
8–12 years	25–44.9kg	¾ tablet
over 12 years	over 45kg	1 tablet (adult dose)

Weight rather than age is a better guide to required dose and different prescribers may have slightly different recommendations about what proportion of the tablet is needed. Children don't seem to experience the weird feelings, mood changes and psychedelic dreams that disturb some adult takers, although it may rarely happen and needs to be watched for.

Generally though it seems to be a very useful option for children old enough to manage swallowing bits of tablets. Lariam is probably safe to take during pregnancy but it is not suitable for people with epilepsy or for anyone who has had a fit. This seems to be one of those medicines that either suits or it doesn't, and if you are one of the 75% who experience no side effects then it is an excellent option. Most prescribers will suggest taking the tablets for two or three weeks before travel since most side effects will announce themselves in this initial period and so a more suitable option can be identified before departure.

Lariam tip Tablets crack into halves and quarters quite easily when held between finger and thumb. Attempting to cut them with a knife will result in the tablet shattering into pieces, unless this is done on a soft surface, such as on a napkin, handkerchief, folded tissues or kitchen towel.

Malarone is a combination of *proguanil* with *atovaquone* and can be taken by anyone weighing more than 11kg. There is a version for children which is easy to administer. The tablets can be crushed and mixed with food if necessary. The child takes his first dose 48 hours before arriving in a malarial region; it is then taken daily (with food) and for a week after leaving the risk region. The

HOMEOPATHIC PROPHYLAXIS AND IMMUNISATION

Dr Grant Hutchison, consultant anaesthetist, Dundee; from a letter published in 'Wanderlust' Oct/Nov 2001

Homeopathy provides a welcome array of choices when considering which remedy to use to treat particular symptoms and a good range of products is available over the counter in Britain, Europe and North America. The founding principle of homeopathy is to 'treat like with like': so only when a patient has symptoms can the practitioner apply homeopathic principles to choose a remedy.

It's unusual to see practitioners of conventional and alternative medicine united, but both groups would condemn use of 'homeopathic malaria prophylaxis' as potentially lethal. Such unanimity comes from the fact that 'homeopathic prophylaxis' is actually a contradiction in terms. Someone who is completely fit and well provides the homeopath with no information on which to base a treatment plan.

I was so worried about this issue that I phoned the Homeopathic Hospital in Glasgow and spoke to Dr Bob Leckridge, who is president of the Faculty of Homeopathy. He told me, 'There is no place for notions of "prophylactic treatment" or "vaccination" in homeopathy. Such ideas do not fit into homeopathic theory at all. In fact, there are now a number of reports of people who have developed malaria after relying on supposed 'homeopathy' for protection.'

Conventional antimalarials are admittedly unpleasant to take, but the homeopathic alternative is not an alternative at all.

ON SAFARI

I had been itching for years to take the family to Africa but feared malaria and delayed my plans until my youngest was seven. By then he was open to bribery (to put on long clothes at dusk) and he was also able to give a good account of any health problems he noticed. We started taking Lariam three weeks before flying out to the Kruger; each week the seven-year-old took half, the 12-year-old three-quarters and the adults one tablet. We noticed no side effects whatsoever. We had evening suits of long clothes that we had sprayed with *permethrin*. After a shower at around 5.30 each evening, we changed into these clothes, and the small amount of skin that remained we sprayed with repellent. We had a great time – apart from the two robberies.

commonest side effects are nausea, abdominal pain and reduced appetite – especially if it is taken on an empty stomach. It may cause mouth ulcers in some takers. Generally though the tablets are well tolerated and Malarone's main disadvantage is price. Currently prescribers are also reluctant to give it for more than three months, even if the family is rich enough to pay for it.

Deltaprim (Maloprim) is not licensed for use in children but some experts will prescribe it and it can be given from the age of three months or in those weighing over 6kg. The British formulation which was known as Maloprim was withdrawn on December 31 2002.

Doxycycline is an alternative medicine which can be given to children over 12 years; it is not recommended for younger children and should not be taken during pregnancy or when planning a pregnancy.

Chloroquine is given weekly; it is the only antimalarial medicine which comes in syrup form, but it is unpleasant to take. It is so penetratingly bitter and the bitterness so persistent, you can even taste it in a bowl of baby rice. If *chloroquine* is suggested, coated tablets (Nivaquine is the most palatable form of *chloroquine*) are pleasanter to take if the child can manage them.

Some clinics still recommend children taking both *chloroquine* tablets and *proguanil* (**Paludrine**), for which there is no paediatric preparation. The unpalatability of the former and the unswallowability of the latter mean that this option is not going to be popular with young children and furthermore, this combination is rarely good enough for malarious regions.

We want to stress that children under the age of five (and also pregnant women) are highly susceptible to death by malaria. Children must be meticulously protected from mosquito bites between dusk and dawn. Journeys to a region with a high risk of malaria (like much of sub-Saharan Africa) must be seriously reconsidered in the light of the special risks to children. Indeed it is important to consider whether the journey is necessary at all. The highest-risk areas are most of lowland sub-Saharan Africa and a selection of parts of Southeast Asia,

Papua New Guinea and Irian Jaya, the Solomon Islands, Vanuatu, etc. Check before your trip with a regularly updated source like a travel clinic. Bite prevention advice and repellents are reviewed on pages 19–22.

Immunisations

Some immunisations need a course spread over 6–12 weeks and some cannot be given at the same time as others, so make an appointment with a travel clinic about three months before you go. If you don't have that much time then 'accelerated schedules' are often possible, but try to go early.

Frequent travellers can get in a bit of a state about immunisations, but jabs will trouble children less if parents can seem relaxed about them: calm parents = calm kids. And there's no harm in a little chocolate afterwards. Immunisers can use anaesthetising EMLA cream before injections although personally I think that chocolate seems to work better as an anaesthetic. Parents occasionally express concerns about what repeated immunisations may do to a child; there is a fear that the body might only have a certain amount of immune potential which could get 'used up'. In fact the reverse is true: the more the immune system is used the fitter it gets, and the better practice it gets at fighting infection. Indeed the 'Hygiene Hypothesis' speculates that early infectious disease exposure may even help protect children from problems like asthma.

Immunisation gives people 'disease experience' without having to suffer from a disease and without the risks of complications of that disease. Some immunisations even give some cross-protection to other illnesses: Japanese encephalitis immunisation, for example, partially protects against dengue fever.

The timescale of your proposed trip has some influence both on what immunisations are required and on risk. Confusingly, immunisation schedules vary according to the nationality of the immuniser. Go to a specialist travel clinic (some addresses are in *Appendix 1*, page 191) for at least some of your immunisations. Many travel clinics are linked to databases which are updated daily with information on new disease outbreaks and changing immunisation requirements. Most will give a personalised printout which has been tailored to the particular region of the country you plan to visit, and which will give seasonal risks and any risks related to your personal arrangements. These clinics are in the business of selling immunisations, though, so a few notes on the pros and cons of what you might be offered may help you plan. Note also that once UK residents have their list of immunisation requirements, some can be done free or for less money (but maybe more hassle) on the National Health Service.

In Britain and North America, the first routine childhood immunisation is usually given at six weeks or two months. It is probably best to pick a schedule and stick to it; many families will follow the schedules advised by their GP or clinic at home if they can be fitted in with travel plans. Don't worry over-much about the various choices. They are all protective and the most important thing is that your child is immunised. It is worth noting that American authorities are more prescriptive than European, and European families who are going to live in the US will need to be fully immunised before attendance at school or college is permitted.

IMMUNISATIONS EVERY CHILD SHOULD HAVE WHETHER TRAVELLING OR NOT

UK residents		US residents	
Age due	**Immunisations offered**	**Age due**	**Immunisations offered**
Birth	BCG and/or hepatitis B in some children	Birth	Hepatitis B in some children
2 mths	Diphtheria, tetanus, acellular whooping cough (pertussis), haemophilus influenzae B (Hib), inactivated polio (IPV), meningococcus C	2 mths	DaPT: diphtheria, acellular whooping cough (pertussis) and tetanus, Hib, IPV, pneumococcus
3 mths	Diphtheria, tetanus, acellular whooping cough (pertussis), haemophilus influenzae B (Hib), IPV, meningococcus C	4 mths	DaPT, Hib, IPV, pneumococcus
4 mths	Diphtheria, tetanus, acellular whooping cough (pertussis), haemophilus influenzae B (Hib), IPV, meningococcus C	6 mths	DaPT, Hib, pneumococcus
		6–18 mths	IPV, influenza
12–18 mths	Measles, mumps, rubella (1st MMR)	12–15 mths	Hib, MMR, varicella
		15–18 mths	DaPT
3–5 yrs	2nd MMR, diphtheria, tetanus, acellular whooping cough (pertussis), polio booster (IPV)	4–6 yrs	DaPT, IPV, MMR
10–14 yrs	BCG after Heaf test unless previously	11–12 yrs	Hepatitis B, MMR, varicella
14 yrs	Tetanus, IPV, diphtheria booster	11–16 yrs	Tetanus, diphtheria

Many immunisations cause some soreness at the injection site and sometimes a mild fever which makes children a bit irritable for a few hours; in exchange for these minor transient upsets they are protected from serious illness. Vaccines are carefully safety-tested and risks of serious side effects are very, very rare and must be weighed against the chances of death or disability arising from the immunisable diseases. Having practised in countries where immunisation is not readily available and having daily seen children disabled by polio and encountered communities devastated by infectious disease, we are convinced of the necessity and good sense of immunisation. Because most children in the developed world are immunised, there is less risk of infectious disease for the whole community. Travelling children are not protected in this way and full immunisation is especially important for them.

Immunisations most children will need for travel to a developing country

The length of time you will be away will influence what protection is needed; a trip of more than 2–3 months or frequent trips to less developed countries requires good cover against hepatitis A and rabies, also hepatitis B.

Tetanus, polio and diphtheria are in the routine childhood immunisation schedules so most people have some immunity but boosters are recommended for any teenagers prior to travelling if they have not already received them in secondary school and ten years have elapsed since previous immunisation. **Tetanus** is a valuable vaccine for all since it protects against a killer disease acquired through deep, dirty wounds. In the UK until 2004 **polio** immunisation was by drops containing live virus on the tongue but now the inactivated antigen is injected. **Diphtheria** is given as a special low-dose preparation in anyone over the age of ten years. It can be difficult to get diphtheria vaccine in Italy, for example, so if you are going to live in southern Europe it may be best to get as many immunisations completed as possible before departure. All three give protection for ten years.

Typhoid is an immunisation which is given to more people than really need it. Since the vaccine is only about 60% effective, it is wise also to ensure you know how to avoid getting this nasty little pathogen inside your insides (see *Chapter 6*). Children under a year of age are at low risk and need not be immunised; otherwise it is sensible to be immunised if going to the Indian subcontinent (including Nepal) or Mexico or to tropical South America (Peru, Ecuador, Bolivia). In Africa and Southeast Asia, however, the risk of contracting typhoid is little higher than in south and eastern Europe. There are two kinds of injections available; the newer Vi kind gives less of a sore arm. Intradermal (rather than subcutaneous or intramuscular) injection of the old 'whole cell' vaccine reduces side effects too. Immunising injections need boosting every three years.

Hepatitis A is very common amongst travellers in the developing world, especially in the countries mentioned as high-risk for typhoid. Hepatitis can make children unwell for some weeks and immunisation is probably worth having if you are travelling to the subcontinent, Central or South America or are living in the developing world. It can be given from the age of one year although few children will actually need it before their second birthdays. A single dose gives protection for at least 12 months and a booster dose 6–12 months later confers protection for ten years. Gamma globulin is cheaper but protects for only about three months.

Rabies is a risk in many countries and rampant in the developing world, and as soon as children can walk they are at risk of bites to the face by rabid dogs. The incubation period of the disease and the length of time you have to seek treatment before it becomes untreatable and invariably fatal depends on its severity and on the distance of the bite from the brain. Bites anywhere on the head (which is where toddlers often get bitten) must be treated immediately. We think that all children over a year of age should be immunised if they are travelling to a developing country; safe post-bite treatment can be difficult to find in some developing countries so pre-travel cover is safest. The primary course is on days 0, 7 and 28 with boosters every 2–3 years.

BCG (Bacille Calmette-Guérin) protects against tuberculosis (TB). It is required once only and if you plan to travel a great deal there is wisdom in kids being immunised. Americans have a policy of not giving BCG, since they feel it confuses diagnosis of TB, but British doctors consider it is a good thing, especially for children travelling to the subcontinent and other well-populated developing countries because it protects against the very dangerous forms of TB including TB meningitis. It can be given from the first day of life.

Immunisations recommended for certain geographical areas or situations

Meningococcus immunisation against meningococcus type C is now offered routinely to British children and adolescents. A further injection covers other types that are commoner overseas and are responsible for epidemics of bacterial meningitis in Central Africa, Saudi Arabia and parts of South Asia. These epidemics cause many deaths. Meningococcus immunisation does not protect against all forms of meningitis: in Britain, for example, meningococcus type B or viral meningitis are commonest and there are no immunisations for these.

Any child over three months may be immunised against meningococcus. In Africa epidemics start in December and are terminated by the rains in May–June. In Nepal and north India the meningitis season starts from November and lasts through until April. Vaccine-induced immunity lasts about five years in older children and adults, but only about two years in younger children.

Yellow fever immunisation is a statutory requirement when entering most tropical African countries and some Central and South American countries (including Panama, and Brazil down as far south as Bolivia). It is not recommended in infants under the age of nine months, and protects for ten years.

PILFERED PAMPERS

We took three-month-old Harriet on an eight-day family trek through the middle hills of Nepal. The first drops of inauspicious rain fell as we helped the porters distribute the loads. At the first camp in the misty and damp late afternoon we discovered that a (rare) rogue porter had run off with his load, including Harriet's sleeping bag and all of the disposable nappies. He must have been disappointed in the cache of nappies and tossed the bag into a ravine! Our senior porter tracked them down on a hillside in the darkness and also recovered the all-important baby sleeping bag. Our troubles continued and unseasonal rainclouds clung to our forested ridge unremittingly; Harriet was kept dry under a poncho draped over her basket but still developed a cough. Halfway we reached the road, baled out and at home Harriet recovered from her mild attack of bronchiolitis – and we were reminded that you always need a back-up plan when travelling off the beaten track with small children.   *ME*

Japanese encephalitis is rare in travellers but might possibly be a risk to families living in rural South and Southeast Asia and the Far East; in some regions it is highly seasonal and peaks during and just after the monsoon (June–September) but close to the Equator it occurs throughout the year. Travel clinics can advise. The infection is commonest amongst people who grow rice, keep pigs and sleep close to their pigs; the disease is acquired from night-biting mosquitoes (so think about bite prevention). Up to 30% of people catching Japanese encephalitis die from it and one-third of the survivors suffer some permanent brain damage, so consult a specialist travel clinic to help you weigh up the particular risks for your family. Protection lasts for at least two years.

Tick-borne encephalitis is a risk in temperate zones of eastern Europe and across to the Pacific coast of Asia; immunisation is a good idea for summer walkers and campers

Hepatitis B immunisation would be wise for expatriate children and long-term exotic travellers; this infection may be acquired during medical treatment in clinics where sterilisation procedures are poor, or from a blood transfusion after an accident, or even from a haircut. It is worth being protected since this is a serious persistent disease which is very common in the tropics, especially in Southeast Asia and Africa. Protection lasts at least five years.

Cholera immunisation is not required anywhere but a new fruit-flavoured vaccine, Dukoral, is now available in the UK and Canada, and it gives some protection against travellers' diarrhoea.

What to Take

PACKING

Finding a pair of socks, underwear or the suncream when the whole family's possessions are thrown into one or two suitcases or rucksacks can be a nightmare and it can be difficult to check that key items (like an idolised cuddly toy) have been packed. Try to design a packing system where each person's belongings are physically separated in different coloured bags; also have a separate bag for dirty clothes, as well as a small bag or bags of special activities. These can be packed into one or two larger rucksacks, kit-bags or cases. Get the children to pack their own bags and encourage them to bring only what they can carry. Children's trolley cases keep the brood involved and make them feel very grown up.

What will you pack? This chapter should give you some ideas. At the end of the section is a checklist. What you need to take will be influenced by what is available at your destination, the type of activities you plan, the climate and your personal preferences. Your mode of transport will dictate how much you can take and how many kilograms you want to lug about; travelling by car or narrow-boat allows you to transport more clutter and weight. Air travellers should check allowances: some airlines measure by weight and others by volume. Remember that infants have no allowance.

The equipment suggestions are biased towards babies but include items useful for older children too.

PROTECTIVE ITEMS
Stopping biters biting – avoiding mosquitoes
Insect repellent

A good insect repellent is probably the most important item you will pack; it avoids the misery of bites which itch for days and, when properly applied, will considerably reduce the chances of contracting insect-borne disease, including malaria.

If the family is venturing into high-risk regions for malaria – sub-Saharan Africa for example – it is crucial to prevent bites, and the gold-standard repellent is still *diethyl toluamide*, DEET. This is best used in association with wearing long clothes so that the amount of repellent that needs to be applied to the skin is kept to a minimum. There are many DEET formulations on the market, but most physicians will suggest using low concentrations for small children: 10% if you can find it. As the child grows, higher concentrations are fine. The newer, slow-release preparations should be the least irritating and are said to repel effectively with less exposure to DEET. Products include a 6.2% time-release DEET preparation for children, marketed in the US as Skedaddle, and 31.5% DEET, marketed as 3M Ultrathon, which costs £10 for 59ml from Nomad, UK. My recommendation for school-age kids would be Ben's 30% DEET since this comes with a rather neat, non-spill pad for delivering repellent; it costs £4.99. Ben's also now market DEET wipes (£4.99 for 15) which we found very convenient to use. Otherwise there is the newish Ben's family insect repellent cream containing 30% DEET. It is much nicer to use than other DEET preparations which have a somewhat unpleasant smell, tend to be oily and are cosmetically unattractive. Ben's family cream smells OK (and it is not too perfumed so won't offend boys) and it feels fine on the skin. It comes in a convenient spill-proof 125ml tube although you still need to be careful with it because, like all DEET-based products, it destroys plastics, synthetics and varnishes. As with all repellents, it needs to be reapplied frequently to be effective; treat the claim that it gives up to eight hours protection with caution. Ben's products are available from chemists, Tescos and via freephone 0800 1957 400.

DEET should probably not be used on pregnant women or on children under a year old. There are rather theoretical concerns about applying DEET in quantity to small babies who (because of their large surface-to-volume ratio) will absorb the chemical, although it is passed out of the body again unchanged. If babies are taken to highly malarious regions, the solution is to look at other ways of keeping biters away, such as a *permethrin*-impregnated cot-net (see below).

In addition to a net, much of the skin can be protected with long clothes so that the area of skin exposed is small, and the amount of repellent required minimal. A related product, *diethylbenzamide*, marketed as Odomos, is available in India and Nepal; it claims to be safe for babies and is supposedly less irritant, but Jane would only use it occasionally and sparingly on small babies if nothing else was available. She wrote to the manufacturers (twice) but received no response to her enquiries about the safety tests they had performed. Apply the same cautions as for DEET.

DEET was first developed in the US in 1951 and is now estimated to be used by 200 million people worldwide each year, with very few problems. However DEET products will be uncomfortable in anyone with broken (or sunburned) skin and in some with sensitive skins, so in these cases an alternative may need to be found. Mijex Extra or Jungle Formula (containing synthetic Merck 3535) are about as effective as 30–60% DEET and are the next-best preparations. There are other less effective but gentler products including Autan and those based on natural oils. There is good evidence that biting insects are repelled by many aromatic natural oils including neem, tea tree, eucalyptus and even garlic (which – at a pinch – you could rub all over!) but the important issue is to balance the risk of dying of cerebral malaria in Africa, say, with the effectiveness of the repellent used. We tend to use natural oil products in midgey Scotland and also during the day in malarious regions and then don long clothes and apply Ben's or Jungle Formula at dusk or retire to an air-conditioned hotel room.

Is it toxic? The few cases of problems with the toxicity of DEET seem to have come about through parents applying high concentrations over much of the body, long-term, or from people swallowing the stuff. Either toddlers have mistaken it for something nice, or adolescents have made a suicide gesture. It may come as some surprise to learn that natural oils when swallowed are also poisonous. Accidental swallowing of any of these products would be less likely if wipes, roll-on or stick-type preparations were used.

The market leader in natural alternatives to chemical repellents is Mosi-guard, which comes in stick, spray and roll-on preparations costing about £6. In 2004 Ben's launched Ben's Natural in the UK. The active ingredient is PMD, which is said to be the best 'natural' around. PMD is the main active compound in citriodiol so Ben's Natural will be comparable with Mosi-guard. Whatever repellent you buy, try it out before you travel to ensure it doesn't cause itching. Insect repellent sticks are least messy (as well as safer) and best for travelling. These two natural repellents seem reasonably effective against the most important biters: the night-biting mosquitoes which attack from dusk until dawn. Suppliers are listed on page 193.

Vitamin B preparations are not effective as repellents despite claims.

Repellent clothes

Clothes sprayed with *permethrin* solution and then dried in the open remain repellent to ticks, mosquitoes, and other biters for two weeks and through a couple of washes. On a short trip – or a trip when you are passing through a malarious region – wearing *permethrin*-treated long clothes further minimises the amount of repellent that needs to be applied directly to your child's skin. And it doesn't sweat off. Nomad (www.nomadtravel.co.uk) originally won the licence to sell *permethrin* for this use in Britain and sell it as 'Bug Proof' for £6; Cotswold shops also sell it. Sprays are designed for proofing one adult outfit and I found that it was sufficient for two small boys. HealthGuard AM1 (costing £9.99 for 250ml or enough to treat the equivalent of perhaps six adult garments) can also be sprayed on to the child's normal clothes and it renders them repellent for three months or 30 washes. Newly relaunched HealthGuard (www.HealthGuardTM.com) treated clothing – currently sold by Mountain Equipment, Berghaus and Life Systems – is a welcome addition to the armoury, although there are few garments for children at present. HealthGuard-treated cloth has *permethrin* bound to the fabric and so it also retains repellancy for more than 30 washes. Nosquito clothing also uses this clever technology.

Bed-nets and cot-nets

Bed- and cot-nets are excellent in protecting children from the misery of bites and they are essential in malarious destinations – especially if travelling with an infant. Cot-nets can be difficult to find in non-malarious countries but may be available at your destination, or you could get a local tailor to make one that you can proof with *permethrin* (kits from www.nomadtravel.co.uk). Otherwise you might like to look at buying a Travel Bed which will accommodate a child up to about five months in a bug-proof nest for £29, or a LittleLife Packlite Travel Cot for up to three-year-olds for £89; both are available through www.youngexplorers.co.uk or by phone, 01789 414791 (new parenthood is all about acquiring new gear). A bed-net for an older child can be suspended from a single hanging point centrally placed above the cot or bed. Otherwise a cot-net can be slung over the cot and the cot-sides will support it. Tuck the net in as much as possible so that it does not trail on the ground otherwise scorpions and venomous centipedes can climb into bed with your child and *Mansonia* mosquitoes (which spread elephantiasis) can squeeze under the net. When putting the child to bed make sure that there are no mosquitoes inside the net. The risk of contracting malaria is particularly high on the African mainland and research on bed-nets in the Gambia and Mozambique proves without doubt that even the tattiest bed-net gives much improved protection if treated with *permethrin*. Indeed bites are reduced considerably by proofing room curtains with *permethrin* and also by surrounding the bed with a curtain of treated cloth or frill of old sacking that has been impregnated. Treating bed-nets with *permethrin* also protects those who roll against the mesh: mosquitoes find the insecticide unpleasant and will not feed through it. It also keeps out minute biters (sandflies) which otherwise will squeeze through the mesh. Nets need to be re-treated every six months (and after washing), but you can usually re-treat more than one with one batch of insecticide, depending on net sizes. bed-net treatment kits are inexpensive at £3.75 from Nomad. Suppliers of treatment kits and various nets are listed on page 193.

Vapour

Vaporising an insecticide within a room also deters mosquitoes. Once lit, pyrethrum coils smoulder for about eight hours and give off smoke which repels mosquitoes or sedates them. Coils are fine for occasional short-term use in places where the electricity supply is absent or intermittent. Mosquito coils reduce biting rates but do not completely protect and there is a theoretical health risk (similar to that of passive smoking) from inhaling their smoke. They cost £2–2.50 if bought in the UK but they break easily during travel; they are often available in Third World destinations. Little electrical hot-plates, which vaporise insecticide from impregnated mats, are safer and those containing bioallethrin have been cleared as safe by the British Health and Safety Executive. They cost about £9 plus £3 for the mats or 'tablets' from Cotswold. Electric 'mosquito-destroyers', mats and coils, are also usually available cheaply in-country. One mat is effective for 10–12 hours (so longer than a coil) in a room of about 1,200ft³ or 34m³; use two hot-plates plus mats for larger rooms.

Sunscreens

Caucasian families are spending more time globe-trotting and soaking up tropical sun so the incidence of skin cancer is rising fast; children who spend a lot of time in the tropics or subtropics are at particularly high risk. It is important to keep children out of the sun during the hottest part of the day (11.00–15.00): see what in-the-shade activities you can plan, and encourage them to wear long loose clothing. Pack some good sun-screening products from home unless you are travelling to Australia where the range is better: there are even fun face-paint screens. It may be difficult to buy sunscreen at your destination if the locals are brown, unless it is a very touristy spot.

SUN WORSHIP

High rates of skin cancer in Australia are a direct result of their glorious weather. Sunbathing is now known to be bad for the health and for the complexion – and if the sun is bad for us, it is even worse for our children. If an Australian moves to cloudy Britain when he is 20 he will retain his Australian risk of skin cancer, and if a Brit migrates to Australia at 20 he retains his lower skin cancer risk: we need to protect the children. Another part of the sun-protection armoury are sunblock suits (and legionnaires' hats) which have been in vogue in Australia for years. Made out of dense-weave Lycra which gives an SPF of up to 80 (a cotton shirt gives about 15), they are light, cooler than normal swimwear and quick to dry. UV-protective clothing is also widely available now but tends to be synthetic and therefore sweaty; children's suits from Young Explorers for example cost £37–39.

There are two kinds of sunlight radiation that reach the earth's surface and damage the skin: Ultraviolet A or UVA radiation and UVB radiation. Only UVB causes sunburn, but both UVA and UVB cause skin cancer and skin ageing, and there is a worry that, if you sunbathe using a very high protection factor sunscreen, you will expose yourself to enough radiation to cause skin cancer before sunburn warns you that you are 'overdone'. The Sun Protection Factor (SPF) ratings of sunscreen give an approximate guide to the amount of protection afforded against burning; that is UVB protection: an SPF of 20 will allow you to stay in the sun 20 times longer before you burn. SPFs are not properly standardised, but higher SPF ratings (above 25) are to be avoided because although children will not burn, they are still being exposed to harmful rays which contribute to skin cancer and premature ageing; children should probably use SPF ratings around 15–20, but with a preparation containing titanium dioxide crystals, 'microfined' to a whitish sparkly paste, or zinc oxide, both of which reflect radiation and so protect against UVA too; a star rating of three or four stars implies good UVA protection. Sunscreen containing microfined titanium dioxide crystals seems to be more irritant when rubbed into the eyes (as babies are particularly wont to do) so you need to weigh up the pros of using a very effective sunscreen against the pains of a miserable child; you can usually arrange good protection with the right clothes and an umbrella, although beware of sun reflected up off water. Sun reflected up off snow too could result in sunburn in places you might miss putting sunscreen on like the nostrils and bottom lip. The alternative to creams is a sunblock suit. See box.

Some suggested brands

Boots (in the UK) make a range of babies' and children's Shady Monster sunscreens, eg: Baby Soltan; Mothercare have their own brand and there are Maws (expensive) children's sun lotions. Coppertone (from the US) also market a good range of suitable sunscreens. Remember that sunscreens (and repellents) have a shelf life so the one you used last year may not be suitable any more.

Sunglasses conforming to British Standard 2724 or equivalent should protect eyes against sun damage that is thought to speed cataract formation and degeneration of the retina. Babybanz and Kidsbanz are good ones which have a soft, adjustable neoprene strap to secure the frame to the baby or child's head.

It is easy to burn whilst swimming. If your child doesn't have an all-over swimsuit, insist on T-shirt-wearing when kids are playing on the beach and in the sea. This is even more important when snorkelling because the back, back of the thighs and even the calves get burnt. Long bermuda shorts are recommended.

Clothing

Clothes will protect the family from the sun (or the cold). In the tropics and subtropics natural fabrics are the only fabrics to wear. Mixtures of manmade fabrics with cotton – even mixtures containing 70% cotton or synthetic/cotton mixtures marketed by various outdoor specialists tend to be hot and encourage problems like prickly heat. The wearer sweats more and hot clammy children are often whingy children. The garments you choose for the child walking out in the tropics should also be loose and should cover much of the body. Polo shirts are best since they have a small floppy collar and do not really need ironing. T-shirts are not so good since they do not protect the back of the neck and the cloth is thick, hot and clingy. Even so some are useful as vests (if you unexpectedly get cold and wet) or pyjamas, and also help keep the sun off while swimming. Dark colours attract malaria mosquitoes and, since black or navy absorbs more sunlight radiation, they are hotter than pastel shades. Blues attract tsetse flies.

Large colourful cotton neckerchiefs will double to protect your child's neck from strong sunshine when you have forgotten the suncream; you can make a game of dressing up as a cowboy while you tie a neckerchief on, and stop further burning. A neckerchief or large handkerchief dipped in water and slung around the neck will cool a hot and grumpy toddler effectively; will stop mosquitoes dive-bombing the neck space and getting inside your child's shirt; and finally can be used to mop up various things which children produce or spill in places you would rather they had not. Pack lots!

If it is going to be cold, a woolly or fleece hat will be needed, and for both warm hats and sunhats you may need to do some pre-trip training to get younger children used to wearing them; most who have not worn hats from an early age will throw them off in seconds. Similarly children may not be impressed by parental suggestions that they wear shoes, yet shoes worn in unfamiliar terrain will reduce injury, parasites, bites and stings. Umbrellas are useful sunscreens, especially if they will clip on to the backpack or buggy.

Children's clothes will be on sale in all countries and often they will be a fraction of the price they are at home, but certain styles may not suit your needs. Nylon and mixed synthetic materials are more hard-wearing than pure cotton and in many developing countries (even sometimes those that grow cotton) cotton clothes, and especially cotton socks, may be difficult to find.

The right kind of dress can reduce hassle too. Older girls who dress immodestly in some orthodox countries (where their contemporaries may be married by the age of ten or 12) will be misunderstood and may experience sexual harassment at rather too early an age; even boys and young men who walk the streets in shorts may be considered vulgar, undignified or even provocative. Several layers are warmer and more flexible than one or two thick garments. Think about packing clothes which will be good for a range of temperatures. Short trips on small boats can get surprisingly cold, even in the tropics, if there is a bit of a swell and sea breeze and the sun is going down. Sea spray plus wind is a chilling combination even at the Equator. Monsoon downpours can make you all feel cold too; waterproofs may be worth packing.

USEFUL EQUIPMENT FOR INFANTS AND SMALL CHILDREN
Clothing
All-in-one sleep-suits are good to cover up baby and child and help reduce insect bites. Woolly tights make a good extra layer in cold weather. Make sure all clothes allow quick and easy nappy-changing in difficult conditions. Small children grow fast and if you are travelling for more than three weeks they may need bigger clothes! Sleep-suits and baby clothes that wrap up the bottom are not popular in many tropical countries where babies and toddlers go bare-bummed, so you may not be able to buy familiar baby garments. Pram shoes or good leather shoes may not be available either. Pack lots of bibs.

Hats Peaked caps leave the tips of the ears exposed to the sun; this area is a common site for skin cancer. Bush hats protect this vulnerable area and also help protect the back of the neck which is so easily burned. In Australia there are excellent hats with a protective neck-flap. For babies take a sunhat which ties on (sew on some tapes or elastic) and pack a spare.

Gloves These need ties around the wrists, and preferably should be connected to each other with a long string which goes inside the coat and ensures they never get lost.

Shoes Is your child likely to start walking whilst you are away? The average age to begin walking is 13 months but some children start as early as eight months. Sturdy shoes are useful for travelling with toddlers; this is a clumsy age when the child is learning about mobility. Keeping shoes on will protect her from injuring her feet, and from treading on broken glass, weever fish, hairy caterpillars, bees, etc. 'Jellies', neoprene beach shoes or some kind of light sandals are needed on the beach or for frolicking in mountain streams. New shoes may be uncomfortable, rub or cause blisters.

Eating and drinking
Milk Breast-fed infants need no equipment or supplies except mum for the first four to six months. Formula milk is readily available in cities and towns all over the world, but less so in villages; local milks may be sweeter than your baby is used to at home.

Bottles are difficult to clean and you should pack a brush to help with the process, or try the inexpensive Platex disposable bottle liners which means you need only wash the teat. Training cups are the ideal next step; they are easier to clean and thus safer than bottles (so encourage your baby to use one); and they reduce mess when older children want a drink whilst bouncing around on a bus, aeroplane, boat, taxi or elephant. It is worth looking at a range of training cups and non-spill beakers since some close better than others, some need more suck and others are difficult to clean so are unsuitable if your child drinks a lot of milk; also consider whether the volume is sufficient to satisfy your thirsty child in a hot climate. Remember that toddlers chew through soft spouts so take plenty.

Hot water A vacuum or Thermos flask is essential equipment and it is probably worth buying an all-metal one (eg: Tiger brand, which look like bombs) so that it will not smash when dropped. Hotels will supply boiling water which can be used later to scald utensils, make up formula milk and reconstitute baby-foods. If you are travelling in places with electricity and not too many power cuts, a little immersion heater which can be used to boil a cup of water is very useful; but check that it's of the correct voltage. Ones set at 220v don't work well in the US, for example.

Baby food Once the baby is weaned on to solids, travelling becomes more complicated, and it's probably worth packing at least some expensive and heavy tinned or bottled baby-foods, in case of delayed flights, a long bus journey or arriving too late to arrange suitable food. Powdered baby-food which can be reconstituted in hot water (from your Thermos flask) is also useful and lighter than ready-to-eat foods; rice is popular with many children especially if cooked to a slop with milk or coconut. Bananas, papaya and in the Americas avocados are excellent and safe weaning foods. Life becomes easier again when your baby can snack on bread, crackers and biscuits too.

Bowls and spoons It is useful to carry at least one plastic bowl and a teaspoon since, although hotels will have suitable utensils, they can sometimes be inordinately slow in bringing them and your child may not appreciate the wait; if the bowl has a lid it can be useful for storing foods in the hotel fridge overnight. A set of Tommy Tippee 'travelling baby cutlery' comprising two little plastic spoons and a fork in a plastic box is useful since it can rattle around in the bottom of a rucksack without getting dirty. A folding high chair or clip-on chair might be worth considering if you are driving to your destination.

Storage bag A soft, zip-up, plastic-lined bag (made by Thermos, measuring 8x12x12 inches, capacity around 15 litres) is great for transporting all food and related items. Draw-string bags designed for trips to swimming pools would also be good. Such bags help keep insects out and spilt food is easy to clean off.

Sterilising utensils

If you are going to live abroad you may consider taking a steam steriliser. It makes cleaning and storing bottles, beakers, cups and cutlery easy; Avent make a good one costing about £40 from www.kiddicare.com. Fizzing chlorine tablets such as those made by Milton can be useful, although such cold chemical 'disinfection' is not as good as thoroughly washing and scrubbing in hot soapy water! After 'disinfection' with Milton or the like it is not necessary to wash out in copious quantities of boiled water; shake out the excess and rinse around with a dribble, and ensure that the teat is free from the bleach.

Nappies (diapers)

Disposable or cloth nappies? Disposables are easy and are obtainable in many foreign cities, but they are expensive: in Kathmandu, for example, they cost about twice as much as in the UK; and in Cuenca, Ecuador, it costs as much to keep one child in nappies as to rent a small house. Used nappies are unsightly blowing around the streets: many developing countries have no effective solid waste disposal system and modern nappies do not burn even if you pour kerosene on them! Using a mixture of disposables and terry nappies saves money and gives some flexibility if nappy use increases because of diarrhoea; terry nappies which have only caught urine can be quickly rinsed through and hung on the back of a rucksack to dry. Fabric conditioner put in the final rinse from time to time stops terry nappies going hard and crisp when dried in unforgiving tropical sun. Disposable nappy liners are invaluable and allow easy disposal of poo into a toilet; if liners are only wet with urine, they may be rinsed and re-used. They are rather indestructible and are efficient blockers of toilets and drains, however. Terry nappies are sold by Boots and branches of John Lewis in the UK. There are also many excellent washable 'nappy systems' which are easier to use than terries. If you are concerned about the environment and want to use disposables then take with you Moltex-eco nappies which use only a small amount of gel and are made with unbleached cellulose. They come from Germany but are widely available in the UK (and via mail order). **Barrier/bottom cream** is essential since, with routines disrupted by travel, your child is more likely to get nappy rash. Sudocrem is the best but almost any greasy product is fine. A **potty** can be useful for even older children to use if the toilet is too far, or too smelly.

Plastic changing mat This can be very useful both for nappy changes and to lay a baby down in a scratchy, prickly or not-too-clean environment. There are models which fold to the size of a sheet of A4 paper. Otherwise a large towel, a lightweight groundsheet or a Karrimat will do instead.

Nappy bag A sturdy plastic-lined bag is useful to store all the changing equipment; a few plastic shopping bags are good for carrying the dirties until you can dispose of them.

Getting about

Push-chairs/strollers When are push-chairs useful? They are good on city holidays or trips to big shopping malls. And on journeys when there is more than one small child per adult, particularly long-haul flights. Push-chairs are carried free on airlines but check how easily they collapse and whether you can fold one single-handed whilst holding a baby. A light 'umbrella' style push-chair or buggy can be very useful, but you may want one that allows the baby to lie flat to sleep. A buggy can also be used to feed and/or restrain a child in a busy airport. Can you fit a sun-shade or will you need a plastic cover for the push-chair if you expect tropical downpours? When buying, think about the weather, the need for a raincover or sun-shade, whether you'll need to navigate rough paths or need the buggy to fold down easily to negotiate the underground.

Push-chairs can be a liability in many developing countries where the pavements or sidewalks are non-existent or at best uneven and pot-holed. They are a pain when getting on and off buses and on the metro/subway/ underground: you haven't enough hands to collapse the contraption, restrain the toddler and hold the baby. European trams, however, allow you to just roll a buggy on board from the little platform; families with push-chairs go free in Helsinki too. Even so, carriers are often better but are more tiring, especially if you only delivered the baby a few weeks before.

A **backpack** is the best option for many holidays, for children from about four months to up to four years; those with clip-on sun-shades are good for summers and hot climates. Free-standing backpacks are easier to get on and off and if the child falls asleep they can be 'parked' anywhere without waking her. A zip-up pocket is an added benefit. A well-padded waist-strap has the advantage of being able to take some weight off the shoulders, but even so the shoulders need to be well-padded too. The Gerry has all these features. There is also a backpack made by Tomy which is recommended by many parents. The 'Bushbaby' made by MacPac, Australia, is also good and comes with a sun-shade and raincover; it has a 25-litre-capacity pocket and is designed to carry children up to four years of age (from www.fieldandtrek.com). It must be said, however, that you have to be strong and fit to be able to carry even a malnourished two-year-old very far.

Some kind of head support will help the baby sleep properly whilst you are walking and reduce head-lolling; use an inflatable C-shaped pillow or pad the child with a sweater, or tie a piece of cloth around him and your shoulders.

Front carriers are for younger babies; supposedly they are designed for babies up to six months, but the sooner you can move the baby on to your back the less back-strain it will cause. None of us did much more than all-day walks with a baby carried in front. If mum is the porter remember that, if the baby is less than six weeks old, too much exercise will increase uterine bleeding again. Try the carrier at home before setting out. Most babies can cope with a backpack from three or four months. The Wilkinet Baby Carrier (£37.50 plus postage from PO Box 20, Cardigan SA23 1JB, UK; tel: 0800 1383 400; www.wilkinet.co.uk) is a comfortable model (although jolly complicated to put on) and can be used on the back as the child gets older; however, such compromises are never as good as models designed for use as backpacks. The Baby Björn is easier to put on than the Wilkinet since it fastens with clips rather than ties and is also very comfortable.

Washing

Your baby will probably need plenty of baths since travelling is a messy occupation. Soap is rarely needed except for hand-washing, but non-sting baby shampoo is an essential for many families. Most places where you stay will be able to provide a bucket or large plastic bowl and hot water for an

EQUIPMENT CHECKLIST
Protection
- Insect repellent
- bed-net(s) treated with *permethrin*; see *Appendix 1* for sources
- Sunscreen, waterproof for the beach or a pool; SPF 15–25
- Sunhat with a brim; peaked caps must have flaps to protect the back of the neck and tops of ears; good hats and sunscreens are available in Australia
- Sunglasses complying to British Standard 2724 or equivalent
- Iodine water sterilisation tablets/liquid (see *Chapter 6*, pages 75–6)
- Medical kit (see *Chapter 3*, pages 31–2)

Eating and drinking
- A Thermos or vacuum flask or miniature immersion heater for hot water (to scald cups and plates and to make drinks or instant snacks)
- At least one leak-proof water bottle
- A small knife for peeling and cutting up fruit
- Plastic or enamel unbreakable mug or cup (useful for bathing too), and bowl

Washing
- A large green towel; green sun-dries fastest
- Wet wipes: for nappy changes, cleaning up before eating and in the aftermath
- Flannel and/or muslin squares for mopping up, washing, etc

Miscellaneous
- Nail scissors/clippers; nails (and hair) grow faster in hot climates but hardly at all in the Arctic, so pack these if you are going somewhere hot. Long nails increase the damage caused by scratching insect bites so keep them short
- Torches/flashlights
- Baby alarm/monitor: useful even with older children who might wake while you are out of the hotel room having supper
- Gaffa tape to bodge-repair all kinds of things
- A selection of resealable plastic bags and containers, or twisties to seal bags
- Cotton cloths: useful as extra sun protection (tied on like a scarf if you lose a hat) and for spills; terry nappies or face cloths are also useful for messes
- Bicycle padlock: for securing luggage on the roof of a bus, while you are asleep on an overnight train, or to lock luggage into an unstealable heap
- A lightweight groundsheet for picnics and for crawling children to romp on
- Plastic bags for wet, dirty or oozy things

improvised baby bath, or you can use a hotel sink (but check that it is firmly attached to the wall). Otherwise you can lay a small baby on a changing mat on the floor of a shower room and mop her down with a face cloth or tip mugs of water on her. Your large bath-towel can double as a changing mat, or a place to lay the baby in a scratchy or dusty environment. Up to the age of about two and a half your child will fit into an ordinary (five imperial gallon or 25-litre) bucket and will probably enjoy the novelty of sitting upright in a 'bath'. Older children will need to be sploshed down with a mug dipped into a bucket of warm water. A face cloth and plastic or enamel mug make this process easier.

Sleeping

Investigate the range of pop-up and inflatable travel beds and baby hammocks to see what will suit your needs. Be aware that some travel cots are heavy and bulky to transport, but may be worth using if you are staying in one place, or if you are travelling by car or boat. Most reasonable hotels will have cots, but book ahead if you can. For the smallest babies, a bed can be improvised by pushing two armchairs together. Otherwise put beds together and up against a wall, or use pillows to stop your baby rolling out. A mattress or Karrimat on the floor is another easy option. If your child likes to sleep on a sheepskin or has a particular cuddly toy, pack these to make an unfamiliar environment and routine feel friendlier.

A **baby monitor** allows parents to escape from the hotel room to have supper in the restaurant. Most models can be run on the mains electricity supply (with the right adapter), and many also use a rechargeable battery. Some also use non-rechargeable batteries. Think about the electricity supply type and reliability at your destination and also the maximum distance there can be between baby and parent; with some models this can be as little as 50 metres. Many children will feel happier if you can leave a night-light on, and a glowing plug can be helpful if you expect a predictable power supply; but check the voltage is correct.

Bedding can be a problem in colder climates since infants usually kick it off and then wake up because they are cold. A small sleeping bag can get around this problem. Grobags sold by www.bumpto3.com are excellent baby sleeping bags for indoor use. A shawl makes a useful additional layer for bedding and also can be used for discreet breast-feeding.

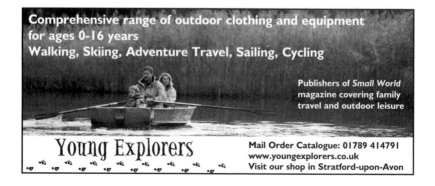

Medical Kit and Treatment

The more we travel the less we take. Medicines and dressings are available in most medium-sized towns in most countries, and many other items will probably be available over the counter. Clearly if you are travelling to very remote areas or to certain badly supplied regions you may need to pack more. Most people take far too much. The size of the kit will depend to some extent on the length of the trip. For trips longer than a month, pack the child's growth chart and any medical summaries including details of medicines taken regularly. Know your child's weight in kilograms.

MEDICAL KIT
Essential items
We have never been this well prepared, but our ideal essential medical kit would contain:

- *Paracetamol* syrup (eg: Calpol) or dispersible tablets; it is called *acetaminophen* or Tylenol in North America
- A drying antiseptic like iodine or potassium permanganate crystals (see below); antiseptic **creams** are not good in the tropics
- A small amount of cotton wool in a resealable plastic bag
- Water-resistant suncream SPF 15–20
- Insect repellent; test for sensitivity before travel (page 19)
- A few packets of oral rehydration salts (ORS)
- A water bottle of the right volume to make up ORS
- Antimalarial medicines (including a curative course) if necessary (pages 11 and 56)
- Pointed tweezers
- A paperclip to release blood under a nail (see page 126)
- Non-stick dressings (eg: Melolin) and micropore tape
- Scissors
- Cotton buds (10 is plenty) useful when bits get in eyes (*Chapter 8*, page 124)
- Steristrips
- Sticking-plasters/Band-aids, the fancy (pictorial) kind
- Crêpe bandage – for sprains, useful in case of severe bleeding (*Chapter 8*, page 112) or snakebite (page 90)
- Travel-sickness pills if your child is susceptible; or 'Sea Bands' (*Chapter 4*, pages 50–232)

- A handful of plastic bags to wrap the various oozy creams, or very dirty wet clothes, etc

Useful additions

In remote places we might also take:

- Antiseptic wipes
- Antibiotic cream such as *fucidic acid* or *mupirocin*; many people like using *neomycin* powder which is also good in monsoon conditions and for oozy wounds
- Antifungal cream (eg: Canesten) for athlete's foot, nappy rash and mum's thrush
- *Co-amoxiclav*, 5-day course (*amoxicillin* will be as good in most infections, eg: ear, sinus, chest, throat, urine, and is cheaper but is not good for dental or deep skin infections and infected animal bites). Both are *penicillins* so do not give to *penicillin*-allergic children; use *erythromycin* instead.
- *Nalidixic acid* (or *ciprofloxacin*; 3-day course) for severe diarrhoea or dysentery or urine infections. Such antibiotics may be easier and cheaper to buy abroad over the counter than to acquire from your family doctor, but syrups may not be available; your doctor will be able to give you information about times when they should be used with caution. Notes on taking medicines are below, page 33
- Teething gel or a dental first-aid kit
- Eye and ear drops (antibiotic)
- Sore-throat pastilles
- A fine-toothed metal nit comb
- *Aciclovir* (Zovirax in the UK & US; Cyclovir in India) cream if anyone suffers from cold sores
- An antihistamine and, if a child suffers ear or sinus pain during flights, a decongestant (see below)

A **thermometer** may be useful, particularly if travelling with an infant or using *Baby Check* (see pages 145–7); a low-reading thermometer may be useful if going to high altitudes or cold climates, otherwise read the section in *Chapter 7* on diagnosing hypothermia. However, clinical thermometers containing mercury cannot be carried on aircraft. Use a digital thermometer. (See also page 130.)

Ointments and lotions are often messy and inconvenient to carry when travelling, but *calamine* lotion can do a lot to ease the discomfort of insect bites and other itchy skin conditions; *calamine* mixed with any oily preparation will be less effective, if easier to carry. A greasy healing bottom-cream such as Sudocrem is essential if you have babies on board. Whether aluminium or plastic, tubes of creams seem to travel less well than good sealable plastic bottles.

TREATMENT ABROAD

Consultation styles vary from country to country and in many developing countries doctors are not used to discussing issues with patients or parents of patients. Some doctors will assume that if you have consulted them you will expect a medicine or even several medicines. In less developed parts of Asia I have heard patients complain, 'I went to the doctor and he gave me some pills but no treatment – no injections!' If you consult a doctor then you may wish to try to discuss what treatment he or she proposes. Drugs given by mouth are safest, and for most illnesses syrups or tablets will be effective treatments; it may be necessary to give medicines by other routes if a child is seriously ill but in this case he will probably be admitted to hospital. As a general rule, intramuscular injections should be avoided if possible.

In the West doctors are trained to institute treatment compatible with curing the disease that they have diagnosed. Generally one diagnosis requires one treatment, plus *paracetamol*, perhaps. In some developing countries this process may not necessarily be followed and the doctor may try the blunderbuss approach and give a range of medicines to ensure a rapid cure. This often gives a quick fix but it may cause side effects; and if the scattergun does not work it may be difficult to decide what to try next. On many occasions in Nepal patients have asked for my help after having taken 15 or 20 kinds of tablets and had several injections by which time they are so drugged and confused that they can't distinguish side effects from symptoms of the original disease!

In many countries you will be able to buy antibiotics and other prescription-only medicines over the counter and in some cases it may be easier to do just this rather than find a doctor. Ask to speak to the pharmacist (rather than one of the shop assistants) since they are experts in drug side effects and are full of good advice. In many regions pharmacists are excellent sources of advice on treating locally common illnesses; but view all advice with scepticism for although some people who sell medicines are highly trained, others are not. Prescribing for your family has its dangers too though; so read on carefully before you treat your child. Notes about doses and particular aspects of common medicines are given below.

Medicines
Names
Throughout this book we have used generic (international non-proprietary) names of medicines which are in *italics*. Generic names suggest chemical composition and, while the drug-company name of any medicine will vary from country to country, generic names stay fairly consistent. If your child is on any regular medical treatment ensure that you know the generic name in case you run out or lose your supply.

Quality
Control of medicine manufacture may not be as good as it is at home. Medicines may be very cheap, but quality is not always guaranteed. *Paracetamol* syrup brought from home may be better, for example, because local equivalents often leak once open. You will also find it easier to find sugar-free preparations at home, so buy in advance if this is an issue for you. There have now been at least two 'outbreaks' (in Bangladesh and in Haiti) of lethal poisoning of children taking contaminated *paracetamol*. It is likely that you will avoid buying poor-quality or dangerous medicines by buying known brands or medicines made by a drug company whose name you recognise.

VOLUME
1,000 millilitres = 1 litre = 1³/₄ pints = 35 fluid ounces
A standard teaspoon is 5ml

WEIGHT
1,000mcg or μg (micrograms) = 1mg (milligram)
1,000mg (milligrams) = 1g (gram)
1,000g (grams) = 1kg (kilogram) = 2¹/₄lb (pounds)

Doses/how much medicine?

Most paediatricians calculate what dose of medicine is required by knowing how many milligrams should be given per kilogram of the child's bodyweight, so you should know roughly how much your child weighs in kilograms; dose information is often given in literature provided with the medicine. Wherever we have suggested a medicine we have tried to give examples of the range of doses you may need to give. If your child is especially small or large for his age it is more likely that mg/kg dosages are closer to the required dose than by-age doses. Most medicines have wide safety margins and there is no need to work out doses to the last 25mg, but many are dangerous in overdose so never double the dose or give extra doses without expert guidance.

Doses can be confusing especially for children's medicines which come in syrup form. Have you confused milligrams (mg) which are units of weight with millilitres (ml) which are units of volume? Most bottles of children's medicines will say how many milligrams of medicine each 5ml (one teaspoon) contains; check so as not to confuse mg with ml. Check the dose according to the label on the bottle too. The box above should help.

The dose for similar medicines may differ; for example 250mg of *flucloxacillin* is equivalent to 500mg of *cloxacillin*. This does not mean that one medicine is stronger than another but just that their chemical constituents are different. For any antibiotic or medicine you give, check that the dose is right for the child's age.

Kinds of preparations

It is often difficult to find syrups and formulations which small children will take. With some medicines you can crush the half or quarter tablet between two teaspoons and mix with sugar or jam. This works fine for *nalidixic acid* and *paracetamol*, but antibiotics such as *penicillin* are bitter if taken out of their gelatine capsules. There is thus some sense in travelling with your own medical kit. Dissolvable tablets are lighter and less bulky than bottles of syrup.

Which medicine?

Antiseptics

Clean even the smallest wound promptly or infection is likely to set in. In hot moist climates antiseptic creams are not so good and a drying antiseptic solution will aid healing best. Dilute iodine, Betadine or potassium permanganate crystals dissolved in water or gentian violet are all good. The

DOSES OF PARACETAMOL (ACETAMINOPHEN)
Up to 9 months old – 60mg
9–12 months old – 120mg
1–5 years old – 120–250mg
6–12 years old – 250–500mg
Children over 12 take the adult dose of 500mg–1g every four to six hours.

Do not give more than four doses in 24 hours.
The number of millilitres depends upon the preparation, but many 'infant suspensions' contain 125mg in 5ml.

advantage of these is that you have plenty of fluid to wash wounds thoroughly. In the UK Savlon Dry aerosol spray is fine (if expensive at about £4 for 50ml) and in Chile there is a good antiseptic solution sold as Lastomon. Antiseptic wipes are most convenient for short-term travel or when you are moving base frequently and have trivial scratches to deal with.

Pain and fever
It has been clinically proven that dropping a sugary solution on the tongue of newborn babies reduces distress when they are having unpleasant things done to them in hospital; little naughty sweet treats seem to cheer up children very effectively after a tumble and Jane is a great believer in occasional chocolate therapy. If that doesn't work, *paracetamol* (Calpol) which is called *acetaminophen* (Tylenol) in the US is excellent treatment for pain, inflammation and fever. A melt-in-the-mouth formulation is available in the US but not in Europe.

Paracetamol may be given safely from the age of two months and is recommended after the first immunisation at this age. Generally children with some trivial problem like a cold will get considerably better 30 minutes after a dose of *paracetamol*; if they do not perk up, seek medical advice. Children can also be given *ibuprofen* instead, or with *paracetamol* if symptoms are severe. *Ibuprofen* can make children with asthma more breathless. *Aspirin* is not a good drug to give children except when prescribed for some special problems like juvenile arthritis.

Severe pain, such as that from a broken bone, will need stronger medicine such as *codeine phosphate*; this is widely available and can be given safely to any child over one year. Start with 1mg/kg every six hours. The main side effects are constipation and drowsiness.

Antibiotics
When a doctor prescribes an antibiotic for a bacterial infection, her decision about which is likely to work best is based upon her knowing first the range of bacteria most likely to cause a particular symptom and secondly what medicines are most likely to eradicate the local bacteria. It is hard to give advice to travellers since the resistance to antibiotics varies geographically and so does the range of possible bacteria. Doctors usually prescribe their best-guess antibiotic (suggestions are in the medical chapters in *Part Two*) and wait for 36

ANTIBIOTIC DOSES

amoxicillin	up to ten years 125mg; over ten 250mg every eight hours
co-amoxiclav	combination drug; doses as plain *amoxicillin*
penicillin	up to one year 62.5mg; 1–5 years 125mg; 6–12 years 250mg every six hours
flucloxacillin	under two years 62.5mg; 2–10 years 125mg; over ten years 250mg every six hours, at least 30 minutes before food; for skin infections
cloxacillin	under two years 125mg; 2–10 years 250mg; over ten years 250mg every six hours, at least 30 minutes before food; for skin infections
erythromycin	under two years 125mg; 2–8 years 250mg; for anyone over eight years 500mg every six hours; do not give with the antihistamines *terfenadine* or *astemizole*
clarithromycin	under one year (less than 8kg) calculate dose as 7.5 mg/kg bodyweight; 1–2 years 62.5mg; 3–6 years 125mg; 7–9 years 187.5mg; 10–12 years 250mg, twice daily; do not give with the antihistamines *terfenadine* or *astemizole*
trimethoprim	2–5 months 25mg; 6 months–5 years 50mg; 6–12 years 100mg twice daily; good for urine and chest infections
nalidixic acid	50mg/kg/day which means a 10kg one-year-old needs 125mg; a 20kg five-year-old needs 250mg and a 12-year-old 500mg four times daily. In India a syrup is available called GramoNeg 'oral suspension'.

hours to see if the fever subsides and the symptoms improve. If there is no obvious response after 36–48 hours a second antibiotic will usually be given. Since self-prescribing is not ideal, the suggested antibiotics cover the first best guess for the common ailments of travelling children. If your child is so ill that you have decided to self-prescribe you should be well on your way to a doctor for a second opinion by the time you are thinking that a second antibiotic might be needed. In the notes we have offered alternative suggestions of antibiotics since availability varies. Unless stated otherwise a course of antibiotics is for five days.

Although there are theoretical controls over sales of antibiotics, in practice many are available over the counter in most countries. It is especially important to understand the cautions, advantages and disadvantages of taking these medicines. The most useful broad-spectrum (wide-ranging) antibiotic for children is *amoxicillin*; this is usually excellent for treating ear, sinus, chest and urine infections; it will probably also clear quite a lot of skin and throat infections too. Treat a throat infection with *penicillin*, particularly in children over ten, since if the throat infection is caused by glandular fever there will be an unpleasant skin reaction if the child takes *amoxicillin*. *Penicillin* is also excellent for dental infections, and works for many of the infections covered by *amoxicillin*. *Co-amoxiclav* contains *amoxicillin* but is more effective since it also includes *clavulanic acid* which makes *amoxicillin* effective against many more bacteria. *Co-amoxiclav, amoxicillin, penicillin, flucloxacillin* and *cloxacillin* are all *penicillins* and the very few children who are allergic to *penicillin* will be allergic to this whole group of antibiotics. *Erythromycin* is the usual alternative for *penicillin*-allergic people, but it often causes nausea. *Clarithromycin* is more expensive but has fewer side effects than *erythromycin*.

Nalidixic acid, norfloxacin and *ciprofloxacin* are excellent for treating many of the microbes which cause severe diarrhoea or dysentery. *Nalidixic acid* is also effective for urine infections. A three-day course is required.

Allergy to a medicine

Many people think they are allergic to a medicine because it made them vomit or gave them a touch of diarrhoea. These are not true allergic reactions but are common side effects of many medicines. An allergic reaction is not a side-effect of the medicine but an over-sensitivity in certain people. It almost always involves a rash and in more serious cases there is swelling, especially around the face and mouth. In serious cases the airways may get tight causing sudden wheezing, breathing difficulties and collapse. This usually begins within minutes of starting the medicine. Rarely a widespread blistering rash may develop over a few hours or a day or so. If someone who is allergic to a medicine takes it again, the reaction may be worse than before. The *penicillin* family of antibiotics are the most common sources of drug allergy, but it is possible to be allergic to all sorts of medicines.

The symptoms of allergy are variable and unpredictable but if you think your child is experiencing an allergic reaction to a medicine, stop giving that medicine at once and, if there is any swelling of the face, wheezing or widespread blistering of the skin, you should seek immediate medical advice. The treatment of serious anaphylactic allergic reactions is a shot of *adrenaline* which will be available in any pharmacy or clinic. Antihistamine tablets or syrup will help settle the rash and itching. A course of steroids may prove necessary for continuing skin problems.

Penicillin allergy is estimated to affect about one in 50 people prescribed antibiotics. Fortunately, although allergy is common, severe and life-threatening manifestations are uncommon (around one in 4,000 of all people treated, and it is commoner in adults than children). Severe reactions are also less likely and less severe after taking tablets or syrups rather than antibiotics given by injection.

Sulphonamides were amongst the first antibiotics to be developed. They have been very useful and continue to be widely used in developing countries mainly because they are cheap. It is now realised that they do have a slightly higher risk of serious side effects than the newer antibiotics described above. The commonest sulphonamide formulation is *cotrimoxazole* which also contains *trimethoprim*. It is safe enough to remain the first-choice drug for serious infections like pneumonia or *Cyclospora* in much of the developing world. We would have no hesitation in using it on our children if there were no choice.

Medicines for the bowel

Many people think their children need medicines for diarrhoea and constipation. Usually they do not. Specific advice is given on pages 134 and 158 but 'bunging up' agents (such as Lomotil) for diarrhoea should be avoided (see pages 136 and 159).

Steroids

These are a class of medicines which suppress the inflammatory reactions of the body and skin. They are commonly used to treat asthma. Prednesol is fast acting and palatable. Since long-term use in the wrong doses can reduce the body's ability to fight infection, it is best to use them only under medical supervision if treatment goes beyond seven days and it is also not good for children to have repeated courses at short intervals. Creams containing steroid in dilute form are used to treat eczema; there are no concerns about long-term use as long as they are applied as advised by your doctor.

Decongestants and antihistamines

Syrups containing a decongestant such as *pseudoephedrine, ephedrine* or *phenylephrine* can be useful if your child has a very congesting cold, is going to fly and might suffer from the pressure changes. A sedating antihistamine (eg: *hydroxyzine, diphenhydramine, promethazine, chlorphenamine* or *triprolidine*) is good when itchy bites might deprive children of a night's sleep; these are also useful if eczema or chickenpox are driving a child to distraction. Combinations of decongestants and antihistamines are available in preparations such as Actifed, Boots Catarrh Syrup for Children and Benylin Cough and Congestion Syrup. Sudafed, Actifed and Drixoral (in the US) contain *pseudoephedrine*. There are innumerable non-sedating antihistamines; *cetirizine* (Zirtek) and *loratidine* are good. Do not take the antihistamines *terfenadine* (Triludan, Seldane) or *astemizole* (Hismanal) at the same time as the antibiotics *erythromycin* or *clarithromycin*. Medicines for motion sickness are listed on pages 50–1.

Ears and eyes

Conjunctivitis and infections of the external ear canal are common and you can often find antibiotic drops or ointment which can be used in either site. You can put almost any medicament in the ear (although suppositories can cause temporary reversible deafness!). You must be careful what you drop or smear into a child's eyes. Never apply strong steroids to the eye, or near to the eye; 0.5% *hydrocortisone* ointment or cream is mild enough for applying to the eyelids or near the eyes in the case of eczema. *Sodium cromoglicate* drops are harmless and useful in case of red itchy eyes from hay fever.

RULES TO CONSIDER WHEN PRESCRIBING MEDICINES FOR YOUR FAMILY

Check that whatever you take has not expired. Old medicines are unlikely to be dangerous, but they may not work.

Avoid combinations of more than one drug in a tablet or syrup, unless it is something familiar like *paracetamol/acetaminophen*. Indonesia and Thailand are two countries where it can be surprisingly difficult to buy the single medicine you require. Combinations may be popular in many places, but generally it is best to take one medicine at a time; if your child needs two or three, use separate preparations so that you can give exact dosages of the medicine required. The more medicines a person takes the greater chance there is of side effects and problems.

Some over-the-counter drugs can be dangerous, particularly in children. Beware of any unfamiliar drug. Some are effective but may have serious side effects; others are useless as well as hazardous.

Warnings

- *Aspirin* and *ibuprofen* can make asthmatics wheezier.
- Avoid *chloramphenicol* in the form of tablets, syrup or injections; trade names include Chloromycetin, Catilan and Enteromycetin. This can have nasty side effects, so competent doctors reserve it for treating meningitis, septicaemia and often typhoid. It is sometimes offered to treat simple travellers' diarrhoea; it works very well for this but there is a slight risk of fatal damage to the immunity-providing blood cells. It is simply not worth taking this risk when treating such a mild disease. This is a good example of the kind of simple risk:benefit analysis that wise doctors make each time they prescribe a medicine.
- 'Blocking' medicines (eg: *loperamide*, Imodium, *codeine* or Lomotil) are dangerous in young children and in anyone with dysentery.
- Avoid Enterovioform, Clioquinol, Iodoquinol, Mexaform and Intestopan; these products may cure travellers' diarrhoea but the risks of serious side effects are unacceptably high.
- *Tetracycline* should not be given to children under the age of 12 years, nor to pregnant or breast-feeding women except as eye or ear drops.
- *Aspirin* is also not good for children under 16 years unless it is prescribed by a doctor for some special condition like arthritis. *Paracetamol* and/or *ibuprofen* are the safe alternatives.
- Avoid intramuscular injections when your child is ill; medicines are usually best given by mouth, or in severe illness intravenously.
- Encourage your child's medical adviser or the pharmacist to prescribe only one or at most two drugs; avoid combinations of more than one medicine in a single preparation if possible.
- If taking advice from a drug store or medicine shop see if you can talk to a qualified pharmacist rather than a shop assistant.
- Thailand Disento tablets, which may be offered to cure diarrhoea, contain *diiodohydroxyquin* (a close relative of Enterovioform *iodochlorohydroxy-quinoline*, banned because it can cause brainrot), *furazolidone* which cures some diarrhoeas, *neomycin* which can cause diarrhoea, *phthalylsulfathiazole* which can cause an unpleasant, long-lasting rash, and *kaolin*: a 'blocker' which is dangerous in dysentery. Such combination treatments, which sometimes contain dodgy components, are the vogue in many countries.

Journeys

GETTING THERE
Which airline?

Before you book your flight, find out what different airlines are likely to provide. Airlines from richer countries generally offer quite a lot of extras to entertain and feed children; there are films, and some provide snack boxes, amusement packs or a toy, but they are often less child-friendly and you may need to remind the busy crew. No-frills companies and airlines from countries with less money will give you little beyond the bare minimum. In that case, think about what you need to take on the flight to entertain, distract and feed the brood.

The airline you choose – as well as the timing of the flights – will influence how relaxed a journey you have. Two American mothers independently told us that American air-hostesses are the worst. Some European parents find that air-hostesses from northern Europe lack any appreciation of how difficult travelling with children can be, although others are excellent. Safety records are good though. Asian and South American airlines are generally wonderful and Thai even have special air-crew assigned to help parents; they also have some clever little puzzles and sticker scenes which will occupy children from four years for up to a couple of hours. While airlines from less prosperous countries have less to offer materially (Royal Nepal, for example, have no toys and no films and sometimes no bassinet/sky-cot facilities on their 14-hour flights to Europe), the air-hostesses are attentive.

Fit to fly?

Airlines have strict rules on who may fly although fortunately the normal child in rude good health should have no problems. However, if your child is unwell with an infectious disease – such as chickenpox – flying is forbidden. If she has an ear infection flying will be unwise since the pressure changes may cause pain, particularly on descent. Pregnant women are not usually allowed to fly close to their due date but rules on this vary with the length of the flight, the airline, whether there are twins due or any other complications. The box highlights conditions that may prevent flying. Some may need a GP letter, others may need medical clearance by the airline. Finally, note that with increased security following the terrorist attacks on September 11 2001, travellers carrying an EpiPen or any other sharp object for medical reasons may be wise to carry a note from their GP explaining its use and the need to keep it in the carry-on bag.

CONDITIONS THAT MIGHT PRECLUDE FLYING
- Newborns – in their first 48 hours of life or if there are complications
- Any infectious disease during the infectious stage
- Ear infection* – recent or ongoing, unless grommets are in place
- Severe congestion, even from a common cold – it may hurt especially on descent*
- Recent severe sinusitis
- Tonsillectomy in previous week
- An operation within the previous 10 days – including appendicectomy
- Sickle crisis within the previous 10 days
- Grand Mal epileptic fit within the previous 24 hours
- Fractures in plaster within 48 hours – unless the plaster is split in two
- Jaw wired (dangerous in case of vomiting)
- Unstable medical conditions of any sort
- Pregnant women after the 36th week
- Women pregnant with twins or other complications after 32nd week

*Flying though will not cause any permanent damage to the ear

This list is not comprehensive; if there are any medical conditions consult your specialist.
For further information visit www.britishairways.com/health

Seating and sky-cots

Ensure that you book any special meals before departure, and if you have a small baby pre-book the cot too; it can be a great relief to stow a baby in a sky-cot or bassinet. Never assume that because you have bought a ticket for a one-month-old the cot will be booked automatically. Some airlines do not have them; others are over-subscribed. Sky-cots are designed for small babies, but even if you have an 18-month-old you may like to put her in it after she's fallen asleep – you can either bend up her legs or they can dangle over the end of the cot: at least it will give you a break from having a child on your lap for hour upon hour. On long-haul flights you may decide to pay for a child seat (usually 50–67% of the adult fare) so that you all have more space and leg-room. You cannot usually have both a seat and a sky-cot for one child, though.

If you are unable to book a cot ahead, check in early to ensure a bulkhead seat which accommodates the cot. Even if there is no sky-cot, bulkhead seats are more convenient with children, and there is also room for children to sleep on the floor. All children, whether in a sky-cot or sleeping on the floor, have to be on a lap or in their seats with seat belts on for take-off, landing, and during turbulence; this means that a sleeping child may need to be disturbed, so it may be better to get children to sleep sitting up, belted up. Air-hostesses should provide small pillows and a blanket. A few airlines provide infant seat belts for securing the baby whilst on a parental lap.

At the airport
Before departure
Once your luggage is checked in and through security, you need not rush through into the departure lounge; although sometimes (eg: at Heathrow, Gatwick, Amsterdam, Singapore and Abu Dhabi) it is much less crowded and better served with restaurants and shops. At other airports, often the older international ones (such as at Pisa, Phuket or Quito), and in domestic terminals, it can be far more crowded and there is hardly anywhere to sit, eat or shop. If you are being seen off by doting, gullible relatives, engage their help for as long as possible in entertaining the children. Airports are often fascinating places for young travellers: even the hand-dryers will amuse them for a while so make use of all the flashing lights and stimulation to tire them out before you board. You will have to be extremely alert since it is all too easy to mislay a child in a busy international airport! A harness or wrist-'lead' may be a good way of controlling mobile children up to the age of about three. It is sensible to ensure that your child is carrying a card bearing his name, address and destination so that there is a chance of reconnecting with him if he does wander off. Any such labels should not be visible to the casual passer-by though.

If your child is in nappies, make use of the changing facilities in the toilets before you get on the plane: on-board toilets are cramped and are unlikely to be so clean. As boarding time approaches, it may be wise to resist normal airline policy of boarding families first. Board at the last possible moment unless you need to butter up the crew to organise a change of seats. You will have a hard enough time entertaining the children while you are in the air without an extra 20 minutes sitting waiting to get airborne.

Waiting around in transit
If your schedule involves a long wait at a foreign airport you may want to keep familiar sleeping-bags or a shawl or cuddlies with you so that the children will settle to sleep. Keeping the push-chair with you may also be wise; you can use it to lull a child to sleep or give her tours of the airport and also you can carry some extras for the children on it. Children in transit will need some project to entertain them and keep you all sane; many smaller children love playing with little cars and airports can provide some interesting 'roads' to race toy vehicles along, or you could keep one of those folding 'maps' for the cars to run on. Other children will be happy to do some colouring, or just exploring. Some airports have the air conditioning set too high so that you all – in your tropical beach attire – feel uncomfortably cold. There is a normal drop in body temperature at night so that you feel chillier if you are awake in the small hours. Spare sweaters in the hand-luggage are therefore useful, even during tropical travel.

During the flight
Comfort/entertainment
Children are messy on long flights. Training beakers reduce spills even in children who drink out of a cup competently when not travelling; some children may be amused at returning to a training beaker though others will

be deeply insulted. Keep a change of clothes in the cabin bag. Long flights are dehydrating so ensure the children get plenty to drink; the gases in fizzy drinks expand during flights and cause stomach-ache. Think about how much mess each item will create too: chocolate, for example, is not a good idea, unless you also carry wet-wipes. Indeed wet-wipes are a boon, and good for freshening up sweaty parents too. It can be good to have a face cloth and baby lotion plus toothbrush and paste: toiletries will also improve morale in the travel-weary family. Most international aircraft have one or two toilets with a flap-down table for changing a baby and this facility is indicated on the door.

Collect together surprises and activities for the journey, wrap these up to look like birthday presents and then ration them so that one is opened every hour. You can make an event of building up to The Opening; then there is The Unwrapping, a time when children are occupied with the puzzle/book/toy; and then it is not too difficult to spin things out to the next Opening. This ploy works well for a five-hour flight, especially if there are a few other treats like a visit to the galley to see where the air-hostess works. Old-favourite story books are also invaluable. Books about air travel are useful to entertain at airports and on the plane; examples are *Harry at the Airport* and the *I-Spy* series. Sticker books and particularly for the over-fives sticker mosaics are good entertainment. Some families will enjoy board games like Cluedo, chess and draughts.

Entertaining toddlers on the plane is challenging. They are energetic and curious, but their attention span is very short indeed and they quickly bore of everything. However many toys you pack, they will only engross the toddler for a short while, so many experienced travelling parents opt to fly at night and hope the toddler sleeps. Some parents also recommend drugging children. Americans tend to use *diphenhydramine* (Benadryl), while British doctors favour *promethazine* (Phenergan); *hydroxyzine* is also effective. Medicines intended to sedate frisky children can make some hyperactive, so try it out one evening well before you fly. Physicians are increasingly familiar with melatonin, the body's own sleep-inducing chemical messenger. This is not yet widely available for children but is now being used in children in the UK with sleep disorders that have not responded to more conventional behavioural approaches. One 2mg capsule is given half an hour before bedtime. We have no personal experience of its use to manage sleep in transit but in principle it appears to be a better bet than the sedating agents previously employed.

Finally be aware that luggage goes astray from time to time; whenever ours has been lost it has always caught us up, but we have been separated from essentials for 4–7 days. Ensure you have any essential medicines with you and plenty of spare nappies: enough to cope with delays and 'technical problems' too.

Food

Special children's meals, or special diets including vegetarian food, need to be booked before you fly. Some smarter airlines will also provide some nappies, cream and certain baby and toddler foods (eg: beefburgers), although on long-haul flights these are more likely to be available outward than on the return.

GOOD LISTENING
Lindy Fleming
Essential to successful travel is the ability to pull something out of your bag to absorb children. I never leave home without Audio Books and music. I've trawled shops and libraries for years to find entertaining tapes and CDs to occupy my boys on 26-hour flights to New Zealand, and some long car journeys.

Often seen as the poor relation of a cosy reading time, the quality of audio books makes them more of a favoured friend especially to the travelling family. The extensive range caters for all ages. Their size and durability alone means a good selection can be packed to suit most tastes. As well as picking favourite authors, travelling time provides an opportunity to introduce new titles or try stories that may not have appealed in book form. Reluctant readers can be encouraged through tapes and CDs to try again. Look in libraries first if you are not away for too long. Not only will you find a wide range of titles but gems that are difficult to buy or out of print.

Some tapes are listened to once but others have a more enduring quality. For sheer performance value, readers such as Martin Jarvis, Derek Jacobi and Alan Bennett are not to be missed. Tapes read by the authors may seem flat in comparison but it can be exciting to hear the voice, delivery and accent of a well-loved writer.

Here is a short list of audio books to get you started. The most popular authors are easy to find so I've concentrated on some titles that are less obvious and those that are wonderful on tape or CD.

Those airlines which offer special children's food may serve it up and clear it away before other passengers eat, so that parents can dine in peace later. Some airlines are poor at this, even in business class. Unfortunately – and it is sad to say this – it seems that when you are travelling with children you may have to become assertive to get what you need; if you are not, your child may become so! If you have a child under two years for whom you have bought an infant ticket (usually for 10% of the adult fare) there may be no food at all offered; this is more likely on shorter flights on Third World airlines.

Ears and problems with pressure changes
For ears to be comfortable and free of pain the pressure on each side of the eardrum needs to be equal. When atmospheric pressure changes, especially during take-off and landing, the pressure in the middle ear can be slow to equalise, especially in children when the tube linking the middle ear and the throat is small and is often partially blocked with snot. Swallowing helps speed pressure equalisation so drinking, eating, sucking a sweet, yawning and/or chewing gum can relieve pain (indeed there is evidence that chewing sugar-free gum reduces ear infections in children); babies should be breast- or bottle-fed. If the child is old enough to follow instructions he can equalise the pressure more actively. During ascent the atmospheric pressure is falling so

Age five+
Winnie the Pooh, A A Milne and any other tapes read by Alan Bennett; My Year, Roald Dahl's countryside diary; Flat Stanley, Jeff Brown; Ivor the Engine, Oliver Postgate; Little Tim series by Edward Ardizzone; Clever Polly and the Stupid Wolf, Catherine Storr; Doctor Doolittle Adventures, Hugh Lofting; Silly Verse for Kids, Spike Milligan.

Age seven+
Just William series by Richmal Crompton, read by Martin Jarvis; Wilma's Wicked Revenge and Wilma's Wicked Spell, Kate Umansky, read by Sandi Toksvig; Vlad the Drac, series by Ann Jungman; Kensuke's Kingdom, Michael Morpurgo, read by Derek Jacobi; Children of the New Forest, Frederick Marryat.

Age nine+
The Demon Headmaster, Gillian Cross; Boy Overboard, Morris Gleitzman; Witch Week, Charmed Life and Howl's Moving Castle, Diana Wynne Jones; Skellig, read by author David Almond; The Wind Singer, William Nicholson; The Hitch Hiker's Guide to the Galaxy, Douglas Adams. The Curious Incident of the Dog in the Night-time, Mark Haddon; Biggles Learns to Fly, WE Johns.

For very young travellers, music is often most successful. Through the internet you can buy the wonderful Playsongs series sung by Sandra Kerr, Leon Rosselson and Janet Russell. Pete Seeger, the American singer-songwriter, has made some exceptional tapes for kids as has Raffi, a Canadian who describes himself as a 'children's troubadour'.

reduce the pressure in the middle ear by telling the child to hold her nose, close her mouth and suck in. During descent (which is the commonest time for problems) the pressure needs to be increased by holding the nose, closing the mouth and making as if to blow out or blow up a balloon. The phenomenon of unexpected vomiting on landing is probably due to pressure on the balance organs in the ear.

In children over five, pain behind the eyes or forehead implies congested sinuses and nothing much will help except decongestant medicines, menthol vapours and/or, when down on the ground again, steam inhalations (sinus pain can persist after returning to normal atmospheric pressure). Decongestant medicines take 30 minutes or so to work. As with most things, the travelling parents will know their child and those suffering a lot with pressure changes may benefit from a decongestant before flying; sinus problems respond best to nasal drops while ear problems respond best to syrups or tablets.

TRAVELLING AROUND ABROAD
A diary
Probably the most successful travelling project for any age over about three is for everyone to write a 'diary': this is a lovely habit to encourage. Towards the

ENTERTAINING THEM

The big challenge of parenting is entertaining the children and, if the journey itself does not provide enough stimulation, travelling parents need to be inventive. Pack some small not-so-precious extras that can be shared with new local friends, or simple unbreakable toys like an inflatable beach-ball or Frisbee so that your child can play with other children. Familiar story books and a soft toy make a strange environment friendlier. Pack a selection of small toys and entertainments into a zippable bag which can be kept with a child while travelling or being carried: try coloured pipe-cleaners, wipe-clean slates, Fuzzy Felt, small cars, toy camera, stickers and a few games like snap or Guess Who? Balloons are great for occupying most children anywhere. An oblong bean-bag which is attached to a tray by Velcro is useful for children to play with Duplo, Lego or other toys while riding in a car. I-Spy books or books about the area, particularly the wildlife and mythical creatures, make a trip really come alive; although some children can be alarmed at temple guard-spirits or traditional stories about destruction and mayhem, other children lap it all up. Penguin children's '60s series of tiny format books are ideal to keep to hand in case of the need for an instant story.

Projects which appeal to many children include collections from nature while walking; when our eldest was aged five, he collected tree leaves and asked the Sherpas what the Nepali names were for each species. On another trek he collected one of each kind of flower (you will have to consider whether collecting a few daisies has any conservation significance) and then when we stopped at the end of the day either pressed them or arranged them in a tin mug to decorate our dinner table. Otherwise you can make a small flower press out of two pieces of hardboard, a strap and some pieces of newspaper. A lens, magnifying bug-box, binoculars and appropriate books will help. When morale plummets on a walk divert the children by singing or telling stories, or suggest a treasure hunt of spiders' webs, coloured stones, pine cones, particular leaves, colourful insects or even bottle tops – or indulge in some chocolate. Point out the small creatures which children enjoy, such as water 'boatmen', pond skaters or tadpoles, and show them chickens or goats to pet or chase. Kids love to conquer their own little mountain peaks and boulders along the paths, and to pause by streams to cool off and play.

Making a small allowance of pocket money makes wandering in bazaars more interesting; there will be an array of cheap glitzy trinkets which will be like treasure to most small children. From the age of about six or seven some children will get a great deal out of using their own camera; there are plenty of attractive models to choose from, or take a disposable camera. And the universally popular diary idea is one of the best sources of interest and fun.

end of the day, or when you are waiting around for a bus, you can take out an exercise book and coloured pens and encourage each child to write or draw something, so that each day they put something on paper. Some may decide to draw whatever they are obsessed with at the time (like castles, aeroplanes or dinosaurs); some will draw what they can see; and some will record a highlight of the day, like mum slipping over in a puddle. Depending upon the age and motivation of the family, you can decorate this with pressed flowers or leaves, or later with photographs. Some parents act as scribes while the child dictates what is to be written in the diary. Later the children often feel really proud of the 'book' they have written about their journey.

Hiring a car

Hiring a car and driver for a day or two is good value for a family and allows you to see the new country, to stop wherever and whenever you want, and to talk to a local informant who will help you understand the local culture – or at least entertainingly misinform you. Be assertive and do not travel in a car that appears to have lacked normal maintenance; we were once invited to travel a twisty precipitous mountain road in a taxi whose steering had been 'fixed' with a coat hanger. How will you entertain the family? Looking down makes travel sickness worse so children cannot read; try I-spy, counting-the-buffaloes games, or competitions to see who is the first to spot ten windmills, traffic lights, temples or red trucks. It is safest for both parents to sit in the front of the car, but this leaves the children isolated in the back and it is harder to point out exciting things; sitting with the children will allow you to tell stories or play games. Do encourage children to be interested in the passing countryside by answering all their questions and talking about what you observe. Many parents recommend a Walkman for each child so that they can listen to stories or music while travelling; this can give a break from incessant questioning; it also seems to help distract children who are feeling a little travel sick.

Safety

Hired cars may not have seat belts and children's car seats are unlikely to be available unless pre-booked. Consider whether you want to pack one if you are on a fly-drive package. Car seats improve safety, allow the child to see out better and aid sleeping while travelling, but check that the child is not too securely strapped in: you should be able to slide two fingers under the straps. A child who is used to one at home may become frisky in a car without one and is unlikely to sit belted up for long; boredom and mischief will set in quickly especially if she cannot see out of the window.

Rules on who has to wear seat belts vary from country to country; check what the law requires locally.

Local transport
Two-wheelers, buses, trucks

Motorbikes and mopeds are the most hazardous form of transport yet families sometimes follow the local example of all piling on to a moped without helmets. Remember that driving tests and laws about wearing helmets, discouraging drunk driving and not allowing more than two people on a motorbike were instituted to save lives. **Buses and trucks** are the main means of long-distance travel for most of the world. Bus tours are an excellent way to start to find your way around a new city. In the developing world, long-distance bus rides carry some risks. Avoid night buses if possible: drivers sometimes use alcohol, or chew *qat* or coca leaves to keep awake. The back of the bus is more likely to induce travel sickness than the front where other people's vomit is also less likely to hit you.

Trains and planes

Trains are a major attraction for some people and the folding bunk beds in sleepers delight children. They can offer a perfect compromise of seeing the countryside whilst reducing hassles; levels of comfort depend upon which country you are in and how much you are prepared to pay, although sometimes you can see less from air-conditioned first class because the windows are so dirty. Second class may have no windows – although there will be bars – so watch out if your toddler likes climbing. Indian trains are usually full and booking seats ahead is the only way to guarantee a moderately comfortable journey.

Domestic flights can be relatively inexpensive, and some attractive deals can be bought before you arrive. They are the safest way of getting into difficult remote areas and the time you gain can be spent exploring distant, more traditional, areas on foot. Particularly on internal flights, there may be unscheduled delays so have extra amusements, refreshments and nappies handy. Small aircraft are fun but more likely to cause air sickness. They are usually unpressurised, and may be unheated and have no toilet: remind children to go just before boarding. However, Royal Nepal Airlines have been known to make impromptu stops in an emergency if there is a nearby airstrip!

Rules of the road and pedestrians

On the busy roads in other countries it often seems as if there aren't any rules. In fact all cultures have their own unwritten Highway Code. In most, the lowly female or child pedestrian comes right at the bottom of the hierarchy and is expected to give way to all other traffic. Pedestrian crossings are often ignored by drivers too, so you may need to keep a very close eye on children who are used to cars stopping the moment they put a toe on a zebra crossing. Chaotic and seemingly unpredictable traffic can also turn a stroll with an impatient toddler into a nightmare. Probably the easiest way of getting around busy streets is to carry your baby or toddler in a backpack, or plonk your older child on your shoulders for the most crowded streets. The child will then be able to enjoy the chaos and anarchy from a safe vantage point, rather than being intimidated by the crush or frightened by dogs.

Walking

Walking on footpaths is still the safest, healthiest and pleasantest way of getting around in rural areas. Approach all houses and villages with care since guard dogs are trained to confront and even attack unknown visitors. Remember that walking and trekking holidays with lots of scene changes do not necessarily

BICYCLING ABROAD

Hallam Murray

One of the most rewarding ways of exploring a country with a child (or at a pinch two) up to about seven years of age is by bicycle, but the destination and terrain have to be carefully chosen. No-one in his right mind would pedal the Grand Trunk Road through northern India even without children, but for rural areas almost anywhere in the world the bicycle can be a passport to freedom and a wonderful way to introduce young children to some real adventure. It is often best to hire or buy bikes locally (as some friends did in Mauritius) but it is essential to bring child seats (buy from a specialist cycle shop), helmets and panniers, including front bags and supports, from home, since they will rarely be available in the developing world or the quality may be poor which could put the expedition in jeopardy. Volume and weight of equipment are limiting factors so it is important only to carry the essentials. It is probably not worth planning a trip lasting less than two weeks unless you are cycling close to home since exotic trips take a lot of time and preparation. Before setting out for the unknown it is a good idea to make a journey in your home country to test out the child's aptitude for this form of travel and to 'shake down' on equipment. It might be best to head for a warm dryish climate since clothes can be kept to a minimum and camping is a pleasant prospect. Often children are happy day-napping in their bicycle seats – with an improvised support for the head – but a Karrimat is invaluable for horizontal sleep and to use for spreading out the lunchtime picnic. Sun protection is important as children will burn easily before becoming uncomfortably hot so a tie-on hat, long clothes and sunscreen are essential. To keep up the interest, children will need to be talked through what they are seeing and a few I-spy games might be fun; dead roadside animals can provide materials for biology and road safety lessons! And a little zippable bag of small toy-treasures can be kept to hand on the back of a bike to help amuse when whoever is pedalling is too out of breath to tell any more stories.

entrance toddlers. They don't want to be carried through intoxicating landscapes and fascinating forests hopping with birds; they'd rather be down in the dirt, throwing stones and digging with sticks; allow extra time. Some toddlers can be bribed to stay in a backpack with supplies of cheap, local biscuits; Bickiepegs teething biscuits (from British pharmacies) clipped on to clothes will also help amuse. If you are doing a fairly long walk there will be low points in the children's morale; singing or stories or a treasure hunt can cheer them up. Children will find birdwatching difficult, as so many small brown birds fly off before anyone gets a good view; although most will be impressed by a vulture with its head inside a carcass, dive-bombing ospreys, pelicans or circling raptors.

Motion sickness

Travel sickness is caused by a mismatch between what the balance organs within the ear are telling the brain, and messages arriving via the eyes. This means that lying down with the eyes shut can help. The greater the amount of movement, the more motion sickness there is likely to be, which is why sitting in the back seat of a bus so often makes people feel unwell. The position which moves least is most comfortable so in a plane between the wings is best; in ships on the middle decks amidships; and in cars and buses at the front facing forward, preferably focusing on the horizon. Although it is difficult, it is worth trying to get a car-sick child to listen to a tape or concentrate on 'what can you see on the horizon?' games. Certainly if children are looking down at books they will feel worse.

Symptoms of motion sickness are:

• Lack of appetite
• Stomach awareness

MEDICINES TO PREVENT MOTION SICKNESS

Generic Name	Common Names	Minimum age (years)
cinnarizine	Stugeron (UK, India) Vertigon (India)	5
cyclizine	Valoid (UK) Marezine (US) tablet	6
dimenhydrinate	Dramamine (UK, US) tablet	1
diphenhydramine hydrochloride	Dreemon, Medinex, Nytol (UK) Benadryl (US) tablet or syrup	2 (12 kg+)
hyoscine (scopolamine)	Joy-rides, Kwells Melt in the mouth or chewable tablets	4
hyoscine (scopolamine) patch	Scopoderm (UK) Transderm-scop (US) patch	10
meclozine	Sea-legs (UK) Antivert, Bonine (US) tablet	2 (half-tablet)
promethazine hydrochloride	Phenergan (UK, US) tablet or elixir	2
promethazine teoclate	Avomine (UK, India) Anergan, Prorex (US) tablet	5
ginger	Root ginger or ginger biscuits	Any age

* all these medicines EXCEPT *hyoscine* are antihistamines and so they are also useful

- Restlessness
- Pallor
- Yawning
- Apathy and malaise
- Cold sweating
- Increased salivation
- Nausea
- Vomiting

Motion sickness is rare below two years of age and the peak age is between three and 12 years. Females are almost twice as susceptible as males (1.7:1).

A lot of food or fluid slopping around in the stomach exacerbates motion sickness, so light, non-greasy, easily digested food is best. A marine-biologist friend recommended strawberry-jam sandwiches as a snack to take on boat trips; he said that they taste as good coming up as going down. Italian boatmen recommend a little spaghetti. If you travel a lot, make sure your

Dose	Onset of effect	Lasts	Notes
15mg tablet	4h	8h	Less sedating; not available in US
25mg	2h	12h	Less sedating
1–6 years: 12.5–25mg 7–12 years: 25–50mg	2h	8h	Very sedating
5mg per kg per day	2h	8h	Very sedating
4–10 years: 75–150mcg over 10: 150–600mcg	30min	4h	Very sedating, dry mouth; most rapidly effective
Patch releasing 1mg over 72h	6–8h	72h	Prescription only in patch UK; less sedating than tablet; expensive
12.5mg	2h	8h+	Less sedating; needs to be taken well before travel
5–10mg	2h	8–12h	Usually very sedating
12.5–37.5mg daily	2h	24h	Sedating; take the night before travel or 3–4hrs before; also used in vomiting of pregnancy
500–2,000mg	30min	4h	

for treating stings, etc.

child does not get a mental block about motion sickness; throwing up is horrible and so it is a kindness to offer medicines allowing children to avoid the unpleasantness.

Remedies

Sea Bands or Travel Bands are elasticated wrist-bands each with a button which presses on an acupuncture point. They are designed to prevent travel sickness and come in sizes for both children and adults; they are free from side effects, but do not work for everyone. One of the problems is that some travel sickness is stimulated by idea-association: 'That is the smell I noticed before I puked last time.' Some kids become nauseated within seconds of setting foot inside a stationary aircraft. Bands can be very useful in this situation and are easy to carry and store; they do not need to be put on much before travel.

If you decide to use medicines to control motion sickness your choice is between two classes of drugs: the antihistamines, and those based on *hyoscine* (*scopolamine*). The most effective and fastest-acting drug in preventing travel sickness is *hyoscine* (do not confuse British Kwells with the American Kwell which is a treatment for lice); however, if more than one dose is given it tends to cause a dry mouth and drowsiness. The skin patches which release *hyoscine* over 72 hours are not recommended for children under ten years: see table of some medicines for motion sickness on previous page. There are two reasons for listing so many. One is that people vary greatly in how well they respond to different medicines so you may need to try several before you find one that works well for your child. The second reason is that you may only realise you need such medicines when you are already abroad, and without a few generic names you will never be able to sort out what you are buying.

MEDITERRANEAN SEA-SICKNESS
Dr Mary Styles, Rome

Twelve-year-old Emma was booked for a week of sailing in Sardinia so I decided to get some travel-sick tablets and went shopping in Rome. It all proved a bit difficult. One shop could only offer 'dimenidrinato' (Dramamine) in various forms which is supposed to be effective; I bought some chewing gum. She tried it and felt sick before she got in the car. We went to a more helpful chemist who looked things up and said they didn't have *hyoscine* but managed to produce some *scopolamine* in patch form for sticking behind ears (at the time neither of us realised that *hyoscine* is the same as *scopolamine*). We didn't try it before we left but she put one on when she boarded the ship on the way there. She thought that it helped, but then was terribly nauseous on the coach once off the boat. We realised afterwards that she hadn't put the patch on early enough. Asked later, Emma reckoned that Sea Bands are the thing that work the best for her ... and also distraction!

HUNGRY BABE

We were packed into a crowded trolley-bus coming back into Kathmandu; three-month-old David, in the front-carrier, was tired, hot and unimpressed with being buffeted. Everyone stared as he howled, but I was jammed and there was nothing I could do. Women pointed at my breasts and commanded: 'Give him milk!'

I could hardly have even picked my nose let alone feed a baby.

'Feed him!' they insisted; a seat was freed for me, and everyone beamed as, slightly embarrassed, I sat down to suckle my infant.

All antihistamine-based anti-sickness preparations need to be taken well before travelling; although the manufacturer's instructions suggest as little as 30 minutes before, it is best to aim for 2–3 hours, or in excess of five hours in the case of *hyoscine* patches. For journeys starting before lunchtime, dose at bedtime the day before travel. *Hyoscine* is most likely to alleviate symptoms while travelling but no preparations help much once the child feels queasy.

Child Care from One Month to Adolescence

TOTS TO TEENS

This chapter looks at the routine care of your child, and the extra precautions which are necessary whilst travelling or living abroad.

The first six months of infancy are generally healthy, especially if the child is exclusively breast-fed; and so this is a great time to begin travelling as a family. From the age of six months, babies inevitably start to get more infections (whether they travel or not); colds, ear infections, diarrhoea and stomach upsets start to happen. And once they become independently mobile (usually when they start to crawl at eight or nine months) they are more susceptible to both infection and accidents. Toddlers are the most challenging travelling companions; travelling with a child between the ages of nine months and three years will stretch most parents. By the age of five or six children are not only open to bribery but also shake off illnesses more easily and contribute more to the family routines, but unfamiliar hazards must be highlighted.

Travelling adolescents present different challenges. This is the age when children are submerged in their own turmoil of working out who they are, and they often get into tangles as they oscillate between wanting and not wanting to separate from parents; rebellion is normal. There are hormonal surges to deal with too. Adolescents may be unwilling to take parental advice: at this age, they feel immortal. You may need to dissuade them from joining the local blokes who specialise in doing hair-raising dives into shallow rivers. You'll need to insist on helmet-wearing, on hired motor bikes especially. And are you able to discuss the need for precautions to make any sexual adventures safer?

TROPICAL HEALTH PROBLEMS

Travelling parents – particularly parents travelling with their first child – worry a great deal about infectious diseases; and some people imagine a sea of filth and infection in which travellers and expatriates are surrounded by lousy, worm-infested locals. Although childhood is hazardous for those who are born and raised in developing countries, this is not because of exotic environmental dangers. It is the result of poverty, lack of knowledge and poor access to health care and medical services. With the right preparations, your visit overseas will not expose your child to undue risk. Although there are plenty of infectious diseases looking out for someone to colonise, these are usually more troublesome than dangerous – like the common cold and sore throats. What infections should we worry about then? The answer is severe diarrhoea, pneumonia, skin infections and malaria. And accidents.

Being aware of the four problem areas (diarrhoea, pneumonia, malaria and skin problems) will reassure you whilst travelling. You will not be constantly concerned that any symptom might be the start of some awful tropical disease and you will be confident that a slight cough really is nothing to worry about. You will also realise that the occasional loose stool is only inconvenient and otherwise no problem. Rarely, children do get ill enough to need immediate medical attention; so, if you plan to travel off the beaten track with a child, you should have an escape plan just in case.

Severe diarrhoea

This may be life-threatening, especially to babies, due to the danger of dehydration; but the risks can be reduced to a minimum by following the hygiene precautions and knowing which foods are high risk – pages 72–3. Exclusively breast-fed infants are at exceedingly low risk, but grovelling toddlers catch diarrhoea easily; the risks are high up to the age of about three years. Older children are most often struck when tempted by familiar-looking Western food (especially sausages and ice-cream) in expensive international hotels and other unhygienic environments. Wise parents are familiar with the signs of dehydration and carry oral rehydration salts and thus will know enough to prevent problems before they arise. See *Part Two*: page 135 for infants and page 159 for children over one year.

Chest infections

These can become serious quickly in small children and there seems to be an increased prevalence of respiratory illness in all travellers. It is important to be able to recognise breathing difficulties in your infant; telltale signs (rapid breathing and chest in-drawing) are described in *Part Two*: see pages 138–9 for infants and page 166 for children over one year.

Skin complaints

These are common in all age-groups in hot moist climates and, although they are rarely serious, they are commonly troublesome and can be worrying. Any break in the skin should be treated carefully, whether it is a mosquito bite or a **graze**; such trivial scratches can easily become infected if they are left uncleaned. Take measures to reduce insect bites to a minimum. **Acne** tends to gets worse in strong sunlight and **cold sores** break out more often after sunbathing too; pack *aciclovir* cream if any of your children suffer. And if the children have **eczema** or sensitive skins be sure the repellents and suncreams you pack suit them; test them before travel. One final point on the subject of skin: remember that the incidence of skin cancer is rocketing in Britain. Over the last 20 years the number of new cases registered has doubled and there are now about 40,000 new cases every year. The increase has a lot to do with many of us spending more time in hot places. Children exposed to lots of strong sun, especially if allowed to burn, are particularly likely to develop **skin cancer** later, especially if they are light skinned. Protect them!

Malaria

Malaria is an immensely dangerous disease, particularly to young children, and preventive measures must be meticulously observed for all families travelling to malarious regions, especially sub-Saharan Africa. If you are considering a holiday in a region where malaria is rife, question whether you might reschedule and go to a safer country, or higher altitude! If professional commitments dictate that the family stays in a malaria zone, think carefully about **prevention** of mosquito-bites. Take expert, up-to-date advice on prophylaxis (see travel clinic addresses in *Appendix 1*, page 191).

Malaria prevention

The key to malaria prevention is three As:

- AWARENESS – of where you are at risk of malaria (check with a travel clinic before travel)
- AVOIDANCE – of mosquito bites from dusk until dawn
- ANTIMALARIAL medicines – don't forget them and continue taking them as directed after leaving the malarious region

And AWARENESS again – remind any doctor that you've been to a malarial region if ill later.

Warnings about malaria

- Malaria prophylactic medicines do not completely protect anyone and are difficult to give to babies and toddlers; palatable prophylactics don't exist for children less than 11kg in weight
- Everyone must also take meticulous precautions against being bitten
- Never sit outside unprotected watching the children play as the sun goes down
- At dusk, retire to a mosquito-screened or air-conditioned room which is sprayed daily with insecticide or use electrical mosquito mats or burn mosquito coils inside
- If you must stay outside after dusk, make sure everyone puts on long clothes and applies insect repellent to any exposed skin. Malaria mosquitoes attack most vigorously at ankle level; tucking trousers/pants into socks helps
- Malaria is not usually found at altitudes over 1,500–2,000m or 5,000–6,000ft
- On average a dozen returning travellers die in Britain each year from malaria; responsible parents protect themselves and their children
- Everyone should sleep under the protection of an insecticide-impregnated bed-net (page 21)
- Consider travelling with a curative course of malaria medicine; take expert advice before travel
- *Permethrin*-proof your children's long evening clothes
- Accoutrements to help avoid mosquito bites are described on page 19–22.

ACCIDENT PREVENTION

Parents of travelling toddlers need to be constantly alert to possible dangers: this is the age of exploration! Toddlers bore easily and go exploring in places

HAZARDOUS SHOWERS
Janet Sinclair, SRN
Check hotel showers before use and while still dry, since pieces of broken clear glass are an occasional hazard and become invisible when wet. Glass is very difficult to see in a wound partly because it causes profuse bleeding. On two occasions, when I've offered first aid to children who had trodden on glass (in a hotel shower and in a swimming pool), raising the injured leg and mopping the blood slowed the bleeding so that I could see to remove the piece of glass. I then closed the cut with Steristrips and applied a firm pad to prevent further bleeding. It was challenging getting the children to rest with their feet up for a while until the bleeding had settled.

that may not be entirely safe. Apart from keeping children entertained non-stop, safety is undoubtedly one of the biggest issues, and this includes keeping other people's medicines and noxious cleaning fluids, diesel, etc out of reach. The commonest time when toddlers accidentally swallow a dangerous substance or medicine is during a visit to a relative or friend. At home medicines and other noxious substances are locked away safely, but Granny may leave her medicines lying about, or in less developed regions dangerous substances may be stored in misleading containers like Coca-Cola bottles.

Domestic hazards
Electricity and falls are the commonest hazards. Bare wires and overloaded circuits are normal in developing countries. Often people do not bother with plugs, since it is easier simply to stick two bare wires into a socket. Therefore, when you arrive at your hotel room, do check the electric outlets and, before you relax, block off any dodgy ones with furniture.

Falls are common because of poor building standards. Marble floors and staircases look beautiful and are cool but are hazardous especially when wet, and increase the risk of injury if a child falls against a sharp corner. Check the windows are locked and balcony struts secure, and scan wherever you are staying for unusual hazards.

Dangerous toys
Not all countries have controls to ensure toys are safe so take a good look at whatever you buy to check for sharp edges. Fortunately the body is remarkably good at dealing with swallowed objects and even the most unpleasantly barbed pieces of toys will almost certainly be passed without a problem (see also page 123). The main danger is if the piece which breaks off is peanut-sized and lodges in an airway or chokes the child. Emergency action after choking is given in *Chapter 8* on page 109.

Electric shock
There are two common ways of getting an electric shock. Domestic wiring (especially in cheap hotels) often leaves a lot to be desired. Also mains

SAFE ENVIRONMENT?
A family checked into a second-floor room of an international hotel in Kathmandu; they had just made a long dusty road journey up from the eastern lowlands. Mum was having a shower while dad was relaxing, reading a newspaper. The toddler was pottering around the room and climbed on to the windowsill. Dad was aware, but the window was safely shut. Then there was a noise, the window flew open and the toddler fell out. Dad screamed, fled out of the hotel-room and down to the car park where he expected to find the body of his son. Mum burst out of the shower to see an empty room with an open window, and assumed both her husband and the child had fallen to their deaths.
In the car park a guard heard the scream, looked up, saw the child falling and caught him! The child was completely unscathed.

electricity poles and cables in streets are often incredibly precarious and may come down in tropical storms, or may have fallen down and not yet been repaired.

Swallowing something nasty
Prevention is easy in principle – do not let young children near alcohol, oil-based or corrosive products or other people's medicines. In practice this is going to require superhuman surveillance.

FEEDING THE BABY
So now you know that tropical diseases are not such an issue, and you have become more safety conscious, what other issues are important? Food is probably at the front of most children's minds.

What to give a baby?
Breast-milk
Breast-feeding is the safest and most nutritious way to feed babies and breast-milk contains natural agents which protect the infant from infections. Even in a relatively sanitary Western environment, children who are bottle-fed are seven times more likely to be admitted to hospital than breast-fed babies; and amongst travellers it dramatically reduces the chances of your baby suffering from diarrhoea or dysentery. Breast-milk protects babies from the full range of infectious diseases as well as contributing to a slightly higher IQ. Most mothers enjoy breast-feeding too, even if it is tiring and, on an exposed mountainside, chilly. In developing countries you will be spared disapproval in public places, although you may be watched with fascination; and possibly surprise that Western women are made the same as locals! This assumption that all women – even foreign women – can and do breast-feed their babies was a refreshing revelation; it is important that we travelling women do not undermine this village wisdom since, if breast-feeding is abandoned in favour of bottles, local children will be at greatly increased risk of dying of diarrhoea.

Cow's milk

Cow's milk is quite different from human milk and contains too little iron, vitamins C and D and too much unsaturated fat to be good for babies. From one year of age, though, the local equivalent of full-fat 'doorstep' milk is fine. If there is any question that the pasteurisation process might be faulty or if the milk is fresh from the cow, yak, camel, goat or buffalo, boil it first. Or use powdered milk.

Formula milk

Modified cow's milk is available as powdered baby-milk in towns throughout the world, but there are some problems with bottle-feeding while travelling. It is important to pay scrupulous attention to the cleanliness of bottles and training beakers; carefully clean and then scald all bottles and utensils with very hot water (from your Thermos flask) before use. It is also important to follow the manufacturer's instructions carefully when making up the milk since formulations vary regionally; some taste sweeter. If this bother you, carry your preferred brand with you. Soya-based milks should only be given on medical advice; they may be difficult to find in less developed countries.

Does he need water too?

Even in the hottest Sinai desert temperatures exclusively breast-fed babies do not need any extra drinks, although they may need to suckle more. Bottle-fed infants may want to drink more in hot climates, so if yours seems thirsty you can give extra formula milk, boiled and cooled water or dilute juice as you like.

ELECTROCUTION IN LOMBOK

She was in a terrible state when she phoned:

'My son's been electrocuted – is his heart all right?'

'Is he still connected to the supply? Is he conscious?' I needed some facts.

'He *seems* OK; my husband thought quickly and turned off the mains. But I'm worried about his heart. Can I come around? Can you check him out for me?'

The nine-year-old boy looked in remarkably good shape when the family scorched into my driveway in Lombok minutes later and I could reassure them that there were no long-term effects or scars on his heart or internal organs. But the boy did have an awful-looking full-thickness burn two inches across on the palm of his hand where he had grabbed a live electrical extension cable. He had lost all the skin including the nerve endings of part of the palm so that the wound was almost completely painless. The boy's mother was meticulous in keeping the burn clean and changed the dressings daily; so, despite my predictions that infection would set in and despite tropical heat and flies, the wound remained clean and healed nicely with fresh skin growing back over the next few weeks.

BREAST-FEEDING TIPS
Mel Roche, RGN, RM
Breast-feeding doesn't come naturally and usually needs to be taught. Here are some tips on how to succeed.

- Feed as soon as possible after the baby is born; feed on demand.
- Give as much as the baby wants and let him come off when he wants to.
- **Latching on** The correct position is crucial. The secret of successful breast-feeding is for the baby to get a large mouthful of breast. He may need to be teased until he gapes, then moved firmly and quickly on to the breast so that the corner of his mouth will be open more than 90°. Mum needs to be taught this.
- **Make sure that both baby and mother are comfortable** The baby's head needs to be aligned with the rest of the body.
- **No need for anything but breast-milk** Babies do not need any extras until at least four months of age. They do not require water or juice or bottled milk or vitamins. Everything is supplied by mum.
- **Carry a light shawl** You can then breast-feed the baby in public without embarrassment, even in a very orthodox community.
- **Do not leave home before breast-feeding is comfortably established** He should have regained his birth-weight and is continuing to gain weight before travel. Bad habits of feeding technique are easier to solve sooner rather than later. Get help from the Natural Childbirth Trust in the UK (tel: 0870 444 8707; www.nctpregnancyandbabycare.com), La Leche League (www.lalecheleague.org; www.laleche.org.uk) or local breast-feeding counsellors. Renfrew, Fisher & Arms' book *Bestfeeding* is excellent.

Breast-feeding problems
- **'Not enough milk'** This is a common concern of breast-feeding mothers. A baby who is allowed to feed as often as he likes will stimulate enough milk, unless mum is severely debilitated or badly anaemic. If the

Avoid **mineral water** since it is often contaminated and may contain mineral salts which are too much for a small baby's kidneys. Boiled tap water is safest (see *Chapter 6*, page 75).

Weaning
There is generally no need to start giving your baby solid foods until four months of age. If he continues to put on weight and sleep through the night after four months then don't be in any rush to start solids. They can be introduced gradually by the sixth month. A doctor may advise starting earlier if he is not gaining weight adequately. Sieved or liquidised banana, mango, avocado and/or papaya, or sweet vegetables such as carrots, pumpkins, beetroot, parsnip, peas, etc are often popular. Start to introduce new things at a time when the baby is not too hungry or he may get frantic and spluttering might put him off.

baby is not satisfied by his feeds, offer more frequently. Babies have 'growth spurts' when they want to feed hourly for 24 hours – until they have stimulated the breasts to make more milk. Once this has been done baby and mother can sleep ... until the next growth spurt. Spurts can come frequently at first, maybe every two weeks; they are not predictable or regular. Be reassured that the pace of feeding will settle into the previous routine again: don't panic!

- **Sore nipples** Any bleeding during the first week or three of breast-feeding is usually due to incorrect positioning because of friction of the baby's tongue on the sensitive nipple. If the baby takes more breast into the mouth, the nipple will be deeper in and avoids this friction. A better breast-feeding position should improve this and an expert counsellor in breast-feeding should be able to help.
- **Thrush** Thrush of the nipples is common and soreness after the first few weeks may well be this. The baby may have a sore mouth too; sometimes there will be white patches inside. *Nystatin* or some equivalent antifungal medicine is needed both on the nipples and in the baby's mouth.
- **Sore breast** If the breast itself is sore, and there is a wedge-shaped hot area, mastitis is brewing. Sometimes you can stop this by massaging with hot flannels down towards the nipple; in addition it is important that the sore breast is kept empty of milk by offering the baby the sore breast first. If mum is feverish, she has mastitis and will need a course of *flucloxacillin* or *cloxacillin* or, if mum is allergic to penicillins, *erythromycin*; *paracetamol* regularly improves life during recovery. These medicines will do the baby no harm and it is good to continue breast-feeding whilst taking them. Correct latching on and positioning will avoid this problem since with a good position all areas of the breast are equally and effectively drained. A badly fitting tight bra (especially if worn at night) can block milk ducts and predispose to mastitis.

Food and nutrition

Children taking a varied diet do not need vitamin supplements, unless the paediatrician says they are necessary because of prematurity or illness (including repeated bouts of diarrhoea). Vitamins are dangerous in overdose and should be stored out of children's reach. There is evidence that avoiding gluten (foods containing wheat, barley, oats or rye) until the age of nine months helps avoid the risk of developing coeliac disease.

Iron and fluoride

Although various minerals are important for growth, children on mixed diets will receive all they need with the possible exception of iron and fluoride. Babies' iron reserves are sufficient until at least the age of six months, when solid foods, especially those containing meat and fish, will provide adequate additional iron. Iron supplements should probably be given to vegetarian infants over six months and also to infants who were premature. Amounts depend upon the iron salt in the preparation so look at the bottle for the right dose.

Fluoride helps to prevent tooth decay but supplementation is controversial; proper twice-daily brushing is most beneficial. Fluoride in toothpaste has a relatively short shelf life so there is no point in expatriates shipping out quantities from home if fluorinated paste is not available.

In some regions, natural fluoride levels may be so high as to cause teeth to turn blotchy, yellowy-brown and pitted; after at least five years of exposure bone deformities are even possible. Town water supplies will not have such high levels but expatriates should be aware that for children who are growing up in these regions to have beautiful teeth, fluoride supplements should not be given and non-fluoride toothpaste should be used. These districts usually have hard water that has drained through evaporite rocks; local water engineers will advise on the water quality in their region. Northern Baluchistan including the city of Quetta is one such high-fluoride area and in India a belt stretches from southern Orissa, down the east of the country to Kanniyakumari and including part of Sri Lanka. There are other areas of high fluoride in East Africa, Yunan (China), Japan, the Gulf and southwest America. Water from deep tube wells is more likely to contain high fluoride than shallow tube-well water.

Not eating properly

A common worry amongst parents is that the child never seems to eat anything. If you are worried, get him weighed and compare his weight and age with the normal graphs to see if he really is wasting away. The toddler world seems to be divided into children who eat enormous quantities and those who eat little but drink gallons of milk. Parents of 'eaters' wonder whether their child is getting enough calcium; parents of milk-drinkers also worry that they aren't taking an adequate diet. Both groups get enough calories and nutrients; the only children who get into dietary trouble are those who are allowed to get most of their calories from sweet foods and 'squash'-type drinks; older kids who are allowed to snack on junk between meals may also grow skinny. Encourage your child to eat as wide a variety of foods as you do: picky kids are more of a bother to travel with. Each day, try to ensure he eats at least one piece of fresh fruit or a meal including freshly cooked vegetables. If fresh green foods are not available though, scurvy will not set in for months, so there is no rush to start vitamin supplements. Reserve sweet foods for pudding or fuel for flagging and tired children.

Toddlers very soon realise that they can use food as a weapon to manipulate parents. The secret of coping with this is to remember that a child will not allow himself to starve; and if he starts games like refusing food or throwing it on the floor, the food can be taken away and offered half an hour later. He then soon learns that such games leave him hungry. The important thing is to be consistent and try not to let him know he's upsetting you. It is difficult because as soon as parents have won the first food battle or skirmish, the intelligent toddler will start planning the next wind-up. Furthermore, toddlers usually realise that they can have even more control over parents when travelling, because sanctions are more difficult to impose. Other toddlers' wind-up games are mentioned at the end of this chapter, page 69.

BLOTCHY AND WHEEZING
James aged five felt strange 30 minutes after eating a fish dinner while on holiday at the coast. He said that he felt sick and began to look flushed. He seemed to become out of breath and a raised red rash appeared in blotches in several places on his body. His breathing became noisy and sounded like a cousin who suffered from asthma. His mother was not alarmed though and mopping him with a damp cloth made him feel better. The symptoms went away quite quickly without any other treatment. When the family was home again the parents mentioned the episode to the GP; she was reassuring and did no special tests but prescribed an EpiPen in case of the symptoms recurring. Symptoms like this that involve wheezing need to be reported to your doctor.

Toddler foods

Toddlers are hungry grazing animals who use a tremendous amount of energy and some need feeding more than the usual three meals a day (especially if they are just getting over a bout of diarrhoea or a cold). Carry a selection of 'emergency' snacks when you are travelling, and plenty to drink. Individual boxes of juice are available in many places and those that are sickly sweet are good toddler-fuel, although less good for slaking a thirst. Some children are shy of trying new exotic foods, but most like boiled rice, pasta and noodles (especially with added tomato ketchup) which are available in many countries; or carry a little Marmite or Vegemite to improve on local tastes. Uncooked instant (pot) noodles and also breakfast cereals make good snacks.

OTHER FOOD HAZARDS

Parents should be aware of a few hazardous foods. Contaminated food (rather than polluted water) is the commonest route to acquire travellers' diarrhoea. Notes about the risks of food poisoning and details of how to avoid diarrhoea are in the next chapter. Seafood and occasionally soft fruits like strawberries can cause allergic responses.

Food allergy

Food sensitivity is a general term covering all food-related reactions. Many of these reactions are due to the body's inability to handle a particular substance – most of us have struggled with a hot chilli or especially strong curry at some time on our travels. When the symptoms are due to an over-reaction of our immune system we use the term allergy. Allergic reactions vary in their severity. Some people have a mild reaction which might include an itchy rash, tingling on the lips, tongue or roof of the mouth, stomach pain, diarrhoea or sickness. However, some people have a more serious reaction (anaphylaxis) which may include facial swelling, difficulty breathing, weakness, and/or collapse. It is important to recognise that anaphylaxis can occur with collapse or drowsiness rather than a rash or difficulty breathing. Usually allergic reactions occur rapidly (within hours) of eating a particular food. Helpfully, serious reactions come on within six hours (but usually minutes) of exposure to even a small quantity of the food to which the child is sensitive so the culprit is generally obvious. In a severe reaction there can be swelling of the face and mouth which causes breathing difficulties. If your child has had this kind of anaphylactic reaction it is crucial that you carry injectable *adrenaline/epinephrine*. Your family doctor will prescribe it and explain when and how to use it. It might also be worth getting a MedicAlert bracelet (tel: 020 7833 3034 or freephone 0800 581 420). The commonest food allergy is after eating peanuts and some true nuts. There are understandable worries about exposure to nut particles in air – on board a plane for example – but this is unlikely to cause a severe reaction: some soreness of the eyes or runny nose can occur though. You may choose to ring up the airline to ask if they serve peanuts on board. If it does, contact the Anaphylaxis Campaign which is producing a list of the airlines which serve peanuts and those who do not. It might be worth getting some cards explaining your child's allergy. Those in European languages are available for £6 each or £20 for a set of cards in English, French, German, Italian and Spanish; contact www.dietarycard.com. Consider joining the Anaphylaxis Campaign who have information about flying. They are at PO Box 275, Farnborough, Hampshire GU14 6SX; tel: 01252 542029; www.anaphylaxis.org.uk. And the British Allergy Foundation; tel: 020 8303 8583; www.allergyfoundation.com also have some excellent advice. For more on nuts also try the websites www.users.globalnet.co.uk/~aair/nuts.htm and www.nut-free-zone.co.uk.

Research estimates that one in every 200 people may be allergic to nuts and the number is growing. About one in 100 people may be sensitised, which means that they produce antibodies to nuts without ever having had a reaction. However, this sensitisation may progress to a full-blown allergy. We know that about 25% of children who are allergic to peanuts grow out of their allergy, while a proportion of children have milder reactions as they get older.

If your child is especially allergic you may be offered skin or blood tests. Unfortunately these tests may be misleading. In one UK study 1% of four-year-olds were sensitive to peanuts on skin testing, 0.5% had experienced allergic reactions and 0.25% (note the difference between test and experience) had experienced more serious anaphylactic reactions. In a recent community survey 50% of skin-prick-test positive infants could eat nuts without ill effect. A history of a previous allergic reaction in real life is a far more useful indicator of what to avoid whilst away.

To conclude, British childhood allergy specialists reassure us that 'death following anaphylaxis is a very rare event, currently estimated at less than one case per year per million of the UK population'. It appears we are collectively over-reacting to the risk.

Peanuts and choking

Peanuts seem designed to fit neatly into the breathing passages of toddlers. The highest risk is when small children are running around with peanuts in their mouths, so that when they trip the peanuts are inhaled and then stick on the way to the lungs. If several peanuts get stuck this can cause dangerous choking. Inhalation of one is more likely to cause the longer-term problem of pneumonia. In either case the nuts need to be taken out under general anaesthetic with a bronchoscope; half of all foreign bodies recovered from children's chests are peanuts. Children should sit whenever eating to reduce the risk of choking. Peanut pieces, peanut biscuits and peanut butter clearly do not pose a choking threat.

Tinned food

Never eat food from a can which has become ballooned since there is a risk of botulism.

Seafood

There is a great range of exotic parasites lurking in crustaceans, especially in Southeast Asia, and it is best to avoid any uncooked seafood. Try to ensure that any seafood is **thoroughly** cooked. Steaming is usually insufficient to kill cholera which survives in seawater and can be concentrated by filter-feeding creatures so that it has been found in fish and shellfish in Peru (beware of *cerviche*) and the Gulf of Mexico.

Fish toxins can cause different problems. In warm seas certain fish can accumulate poisons in their flesh which cause an unpleasant though rarely dangerous syndrome called ciguatera. Symptoms begin generally within six hours (but can be as fast as 30 minutes or as slow as 30 hours) and are usually vomiting, watery diarrhoea and cramps which get better within 48 hours. Ciguatera causes strange sensations, including temperature reversal when hot things feel cold and cold things hot; this can last for months. There is no specific treatment. Do not eat large tropical carnivorous reef fish: avoid grouper, barracuda, snapper and sea bass. Fish caught during red tides are likely to contain ciguatera toxins and the internal organs of sea fish should not be eaten.

Scombroid poisoning comes from eating affected tuna, mackerel and jack fish but also dolphin and bluefish. Toxic fish sometimes have a sharp or peppery taste. Minutes to hours after eating the affected fish there is flushing, headache, dizziness and burning sensations in the mouth, and sometimes a sunburn-like rash; often there is nausea, diarrhoea and occasionally vomiting. Symptoms fade within 24 hours.

Paralytic shellfish poisoning is a serious problem which, like other seafood toxins, comes from poisons accumulated as the animal feeds. Avoid eating shellfish if there has been a **red tide**, when the sea literally turns red. It can also occur in normal sea conditions and in temperate waters: around Britain cases are rare, but are most often associated with eating mussels between May and August.

Dairy products

Milk products may be unsafe unless they have been pasteurised or boiled; otherwise they can be a source of TB, brucellosis and diarrhoea. Yoghurt is often safe since it is usually boiled and lactobacilli discourage colonisation with most harmful bacteria; indeed in a stomach mildly upset by antibiotics or infection yoghurt will help settle the symptoms. Ice-cream is often unsafe; it is not always made hygienically and power cuts mean it may not have been stored properly. Ice-cream is an ideal culture medium for microbes and, if I needed to transport some new and exciting bacteria back to the Hospital for Tropical Diseases for study, I would transport it in ice-cream to make sure it was alive and well by the time it got to London.

Miscellaneous

Organic produce The definition and control of which foods are described as 'organic' may vary in some countries but organic produce could be irrigated with human waste. Whatever the food is described as, wash it and peel it or forget it. Pesticides are over-used in many places and in Kathmandu they are even applied in the market place to make tomatoes and fruit look shiny!

Local pottery A family suffered from lead poisoning which was attributed to their drinking orange juice from a poorly fired pottery jug bought in Mexico. The acidity of the orange apparently leached the lead out of the glaze; blander drinks would have been safe.

Raw meat In certain countries, notably Ethiopia and Thailand, raw meat is a great delicacy. Unfortunately it carries a high risk of tapeworm infestation: so use tact, and avoid it. Undercooked meat (for example steamed) can also be hazardous.

WHAT'S IN A NAPPY?

Breast-fed babies are diverse in their nappy-filling habits; some will dirty many nappies each day while others will not poo for a week or more. Hot climates can make babies dry and constipated, but you do not need to worry about this unless your baby's faeces seem hard and he cries when he poos or there is blood on the outside of the stool. In these cases offer breast-feeds more frequently and see page 137 for advice. **Bottle-fed babies** are more predictable and regular in their toilet habits and in hot climates they need additional fluids like boiled and cooled water or dilute juices.

Once your child starts taking **solid food**, the stools change and become more formed. Occasionally there are striking changes in the appearance of the stool because of something he has eaten. Iron supplements and also beetroot, for example, turn the stool black.

Nappy (diaper) rash

Soreness in the nappy area may be due to too much contact with urine. If the bottom has become sore, change the nappy six times a day. If you are using terry nappies and nappy rash seems to be becoming a problem put a little vinegar in the final rinse water after the nappies have been washed. A greasy cream will also help protect young skin. Worsening nappy rash may be due to thrush; this is described in *Chapter 9*, page 137.

The foreskin

At birth a baby boy's foreskin is attached to the penis so if you try to pull back the foreskin it will cause pain and damage. By the age of five, 90% of boys are able to retract the foreskin since the attachments to the penis have disappeared. From this age, whenever you bath your son, gentle retraction and washing under the foreskin is a good practice. Antifungal creams can help with soreness.

Potties and toilet-training

The later you start potty training the easier it is to get children out of nappies. Make your own decisions about what suits your travelling needs best, but remember that a child in nappies is sometimes preferable to a child who is nominally toilet-trained but who has lots of accidents or cannot wait for more than a few seconds; nappies are easier to change than clothes. And children with diarrhoea, who are ill or feel insecure, may have accidents and will regress in their toilet habits. Potties are useful when the toilet is a hole in the ground or far away, smelly or dark.

TRIVIAL BUT TEDIOUS PROBLEMS
Infants
Colic and crying

Some tiny babies (from two weeks to four months of age) have crying bouts when they go red in the face and draw up their legs. In between crying bouts they are well and feed normally. This contrasts with an inconsolable irritable infant who will not feed and also the infant who has very short-lived episodes of excruciating crying separated by longer periods (20 minutes or so) of pallid inactivity (see page 131). Colic makes a baby seem as if he has stomach cramps, but not everyone is sure that the child is particularly distressed. It most often happens when the baby is tired at the end of the day so is sometimes labelled evening colic. Many wise and clever paediatricians have tried to work out the cause and best 'treatment' for colic, but the phenomenon is still not understood. However, an approach that works is given below.

Baby under the age of four months is crying a lot

Try to find out why he is crying by considering the following:

- He is hungry and wants to be fed
- He wants to suck, although he is not hungry
- He wants to be held
- He is bored and wants stimulation
- He is tired and wants to sleep

If the crying continues for more than five minutes with one response, then try another.

- Decide on your own in what order to explore the above possibilities.
- Don't be concerned about over-feeding your baby. This will not happen.
- Don't be concerned about spoiling your baby. This also will not happen.

It is possible (although again the scientific evidence is a bit thin) that breast-fed babies suffer mild indigestion after mother eats particular foods; watch whether mother's diet does upset the suckling baby. Suspect foods include cabbage, fresh orange juice, very spicy foods and red wine, but different mothers identify different foods. Colic usually goes away by the age of four

INFANT COLIC

Our first-born went abroad for the first time when he was three months. He was an easy baby. I planned that he should live in his new home in Pakistan for a month or two before I started to wean him on to solids. Our first night was in an expensive international hotel in Karachi where we were offered tasty luke-warm samosas with our 'welcome drinks'. Not long after we arrived in our new home in Khairpur eight hours' drive further north, the welcome hit me and I spent most of the next two days on the toilet, staring blankly at the resident toads.

Alexander started acting as if he was hungry; he demanded food every half-hour even during the night. I could not get him interested in a bottle. The second evening Alexander woke abruptly, let out a loud distressed cry, went red and pulled up his legs as if he'd been gripped with pain.

Fortunately he was only hungry and, as soon as Sindh's welcome stopped pouring out of my bottom and I could eat and drink again, my milk supply re-established itself and, as planned, he was weaned on to solids at five months and breast-fed until a year.

months whatever you do. 'Colic drops' are usually unhelpful, occasionally unsafe and we do not recommend them.

Teething and slobbering

Teething is blamed for all kinds of symptoms, but although it makes some babies grumpy and unsettled it never causes fever and should not be a major cause of grief. If the baby seems unwell, do not attribute the problem to teething, but seek advice. *Paracetamol* syrup and gels such as Bonjela smeared on the gum may help. Apparently clever ideas like fridge-cooled teething rings do not seem useful (even if you have access to a fridge; there are better substances to store in it). It is normal for infants to slobber and put things in their mouths; slobbering and dribbling usually stop around 13 months whether the child is teething or not.

Sleeping

Young babies need to feed every four hours so new mothers must expect disturbed nights in the first three months at least; one authority suggests that a baby will not sleep through the night until he weighs 5kg or more. Thereafter many babies will sleep through. Never reward a child for being awake at night; feeds are obviously necessary but, right from the first week, avoid the temptation to play with the child if he wakes at night. Be as boring as possible; do not turn on the light; do not speak, smile or do anything interesting. Feed, then change the nappy quickly and silently and put him back in his cot.

Swaddling Small babies like closeness and physical comfort and enjoy being carried around all day. Some parents manage to do this but others will be exhausted by this burden on top of disturbed nights. But babies will also feel secure if tightly wrapped or swaddled. Wrapping them in a small blanket or towel will make them feel snug and warm and they will happily sleep; if you are somewhere hot, you may need to unwind the wrappings a little once they are safely asleep.

Toddlers
Sleep-walking
Sleep-walking is common in normal children especially around four to five years. It often runs in families. If your family has this habit you must make doubly sure that the night-time environment is safe, with windows and doors securely fastened.

Not sleeping
Whole books are written about why some older babies do not sleep well at night; *Toddler Taming* by Dr Christopher Green (Doubleday, 1984) is excellent on all aspects of toddler rearing whilst *Solve Your Child's Sleep Problems* by Dr Richard Ferber (Dorling Kindersley, 1985) is good for advice on all manner of sleep problems. There are also a few pointers below which might help. If babies sleep a lot during the day, they will not sleep so well at night; this sounds obvious, but it can be a point you overlook if, say, you are trekking or travelling in a vehicle for most of the day and the child is lulled to sleep by the motion. When travelling with babies and toddlers, plan for some exercise time and do not expect to move at the speed of childless trekkers.

As the child approaches his first birthday think of bedtime rituals which will signal that it is time for sleep, and consider what he will sleep in. If, when you are travelling, he is put on a mattress on the floor for the first time in his life, and expected to sleep, he might instead find this an especially exciting place to romp; and a mattress on the floor might also expose him to bites of various tropical pests (see also *Chapter 7*). Travel cots are worth considering. In India, low, child-sized *charpoys* (string beds) make good baby beds, and your child will be unlikely to fall out although once he can crawl he may clamber out.

If your child is accustomed to sleeping during the day you will need to plan to accommodate the afternoon sleep. If you are in a vehicle or carrying him in a backpack, he will sleep while travelling, but a sleeping child is difficult to carry in a pack. Think through your programme to make it easy for everyone. Children often find travelling very exciting and tiring and may need more sleep. Finally, don't expect your child to sleep while being tortured by mosquitoes; does he need a cot-net?

Toddlers' games to worry parents
Head-banging can be a very effective way to infuriate and worry parents since most rational adults do not like to see their loved one harming himself; might he cause brain damage by bashing his head on the floor? The skull is well designed to withstand such treatment, and the technique to stop this behaviour is to pay no attention. Unfortunately he will move on to the next project to attempt to unsettle you. **Biting** is another popular sport; if he bites you, time out is probably the best technique to stop him. Small children enjoy being the centre of attention and do not like to be left alone, so a good,

DEVELOPMENTAL MILESTONES

Normal children should be capable of the following skills by the age given; if they have not acquired these skills it may be worth getting them checked by a paediatrician, and also get them weighed.

Age in months	Ability
2	Looks at faces and objects; some response to nearby voices and everyday sounds
3	When held upright, able to hold head up; smiles at mother
4	Hands relaxed; not held in a fist. Interested in people and playthings
5	Reaches for objects which interest him
6	Will track and watch people moving around the room and also objects moved in front of him
7	Usually able to chew lumpy foods whether or not teeth have appeared
10	Sits independently on a firm surface. Babbles tunefully. Can bear most of his weight on his legs
12	Recognises and responds to specific words like No, Dad, Baby
18	Walks alone; has stopped drooling; picks up object from floor without falling
21	Kicks a ball without over-balancing. Says single words with meaning
27	Puts 2–3 words together into a phrase
36	Able to stand on one leg for 1–2 seconds. Talks in sentences
48	Uses fully intelligible speech. Manages up and down stairs with alternating feet
54	Knows full name and sex

Once a milestone (like toilet training) has been achieved there may be some regression – if the child is ill, unsettled or finding the trip a challenge. Regression is a normal childhood response to many life challenges including the arrival of a new sibling or moving house.

effective but mild punishment whenever he bites is to put him somewhere out of sight of you and preferably somewhere boring without toys; a corridor is often good enough, or the bottom of the stairs. Separate from him for one minute for every year of his age; two-year-olds need two minutes' 'time out'. Toddlers – and older children too – are constantly experimenting with getting reactions out of their parents, and constantly checking that yesterday's rules apply today. Try to be consistent, try to give the children quality time so that they too enjoy the travelling experience, and realise that children do not harm themselves with their wind-up games.

Avoiding Diarrhoea

Diarrhoea is not one disease but a large group caused by viruses, bacteria or parasites; it is convenient to call them the diarrhoeal diseases which also include dysentery, typhoid, and all other infections of the bowel. On average an American child will have one or two episodes of diarrhoea per year in the first five years of life, whilst a Bangladeshi child will suffer four to six attacks annually. Both groups suffer similar attack-rates from droplet-spread rotaviruses, but the Bangladeshis have an additional burden of diarrhoea caused by bacterial and parasite infections which are largely avoidable with sensible precautions. The commonest diarrhoeal diseases in less hygienic environments are the filth-to-mouth pathogens, especially variants of the normal bacteria colonising everyone's bowel, called enterotoxigenic *Escherichia coli*, ETEC.

FOOD AND DRINK

It is reassuring to know that affluence and education protect, so that expatriates living in Bangladesh should have diarrhoea attack-rates closer to the American than the local pattern. But to be so protected families need to know how filth-to-mouth diseases are transmitted. Travellers, who have less control over how hygienically their food is prepared, will experience a higher diarrhoea rate, but still much less than the 'normal' Bangladeshi pattern. Expatriates and travellers alike often get ill when they eat out in restaurants.

The age of highest risk from diarrhoea is from the time of weaning on to solids to about three years. All children whether they travel or not are likely to get some bouts of diarrhoea and vomiting; if the principles of hygiene described in this chapter are understood, the risk of acquiring diarrhoea while eating and drinking at home should be limited to an attack about once a year. Watch how often the family is suffering from diarrhoea and, if it is more often than three to four times a year, consider how your food is being prepared and whether you are often eating high-risk foods. If household staff do most of your cooking do they need some hygiene education? You cannot assume even the best of cooks understands the germ theory of disease transmission.

Can we drink the water?

Most people (doctors and public-health engineers included) believe that diarrhoea gets to you by way of contaminated water. While water-borne outbreaks of diarrhoeal disease do occur, they are exceptional. Foreign water is nowhere near as hazardous as most people believe: most travellers' diarrhoea comes from dirty hands or unhygienic preparation of food.

The diarrhoeal diseases and all the other diseases which get us by way of filth (usually other people's faeces) do so by entering the mouth and being swallowed. Surveys of adults travelling to developing or tropical countries say that half are struck with travellers' diarrhoea at least once during their visit; and in very contaminated environments (typically found in the subcontinent and Peru) the risk is higher: Dr David Shlim who ran the travellers' clinic in Kathmandu found in a pre-monsoon survey at the airport that 68% of travellers leaving Nepal had been hit. It is crucial to know how to avoid travellers' diarrhoea, particularly since these same precautions will also protect you from other, more serious, filth-to-mouth diseases including typhoid, dysentery, hepatitis and cholera.

What foods are risky?

If it is not foreign water which makes travellers ill, then what does? The commonest cause is eating food prepared by someone who has not washed his hands properly after going to the toilet. The cook may have traces of faeces left on his hands after he has wiped or rinsed his bottom, or his hand may have become contaminated from touching a toilet-door handle. Such contamination is transferred to your food and thus filth (faecal bacteria) enters the mouth. It is an unpleasant disease cycle to contemplate, but understanding this does make it easier to avoid. It is also possible to ingest faeces through food contaminated while it is growing or while left on the ground. In many places, including Peru, Bolivia, Nepal and China, crops are sometimes irrigated with untreated sewage or fertilised with untreated human excreta. Fruit and vegetables which grow close to the ground or in the soil and which are consumed raw may be contaminated. Strawberries are particularly dangerous, because they grow low and are impossible to clean. Lettuce is also a disaster since all its little crevices and nooks are impossible to wash thoroughly. And soaking these high-risk foods in chemicals does not sterilise them either.

The maxim which will protect you and the children is:

PEEL IT – BOIL IT – COOK IT – OR FORGET IT!

Is the salad safe?

Carefully washed and peeled cucumber is reasonably safe. Smooth, shiny-skinned fruits and vegetables like tomatoes are pretty safe if they have been washed properly and are not punctured or scarred; damaged tomatoes should be rejected or used for cooking.

Innumerable expatriate families and many tropical hotel kitchens soak salad and fruit in chlorine, or iodine or potassium permanganate, with the intention of killing microbes. Unfortunately these chemical sterilisation processes often fail for two reasons. These disinfectants do not work well if dirt is left on the fruit or salad and they are not effective against microbes which form resistant cysts (particularly the newly discovered *Cyclospora* parasite but also *Cryptosporidium*, amoebae and *Giardia*), nor against roundworm eggs. In regions of poor hygiene, lettuce is unsafe whatever it has been soaked in.

CYCLOSPORA – THE KATHMANDU QUICKSTEP

This troublesome little beastie was only discovered in 1990 when travellers in Kathmandu acquired an unpleasantly persistent kind of diarrhoea that lasted 6–12 weeks. It usually starts with muscle aches, and adults lose several kilograms in weight. In Nepal it is only a problem between April and November with a peak in early July (monsoon). The protozoan is now turning up elsewhere in the subcontinent, in Indonesia, China, Papua New Guinea, the Middle East, North Africa, South Africa, Central America, the Caribbean, Peru (that other diarrhoea hot-spot) and Bolivia. There was even an outbreak in New York which was traced to contaminated raspberries imported from Guatemala.

Treatment with the combination antibiotic *trimethoprim-sulphamethoxazole* (sold as Bacterium or Septra or Septrin) helps most patients; and, as with all diarrhoea, oral rehydration is important.

Cooked or uncooked?

Freshly cooked, piping-hot dishes are undoubtedly the safest travellers' foods; beware of left-overs, which must be thoroughly reheated, and even fried rice which may be made from inadequately reheated left-overs, often making people ill. Cold cooked food is high-risk. Bacteria love meat (and cream) so vegetarian travellers will stay healthier in diarrhoea hot-spots. Ice-cream is amongst the highest-risk foods; some adults will consider the pleasure of eating some of these foods outweighs the risk of a couple of days' misery, but young children should surely be protected.

My hit list of high-risk foods to avoid in less hygienic places:

- Ice-cream
- Cream
- Unboiled milk
- Lettuce
- Strawberries
- Cooked food which has been allowed to go cold (eg: quiche and cold pizza)
- Cooked food that has been hanging around in hotel buffets
- Cooked food which has been inadequately reheated
- Dishes containing meat, which are more hazardous than vegetarian food
- Fried rice (gracefully called cow-pat in Thai)
- Drinks like yoghurt, ice and fruit mixtures (eg: Indian lassi) with ingredients which are likely to have been handled during preparation

Eating out

Perhaps surprisingly those rather unpleasant looking street-side snacks that are freshly fried in smelly dark-yellow oil are safe from microbes. Busy little cafés and hotels which are popular with locals often have such a rapid turnover that their food never has a chance to get stale and is far safer than international cuisine cooked in pretentious hotels. It has been said that the rats and cockroaches in one of the top international hotels in Kathmandu are the fastest and best fed in the subcontinent! I have certainly got my worst doses of gastroenteritis ever from the most expensive international hotels in Kathmandu and Antananarivo (Madagascar).

Dirty hands and sore tummies

It is important to be meticulous about hygiene while travelling; wash your hands before touching food or feeding children and make sure they wash their hands properly before eating. If children's nails are kept short, they are less likely to carry bacteria and pinworm eggs under their fingernails. Dummies or pacifiers are difficult to keep clean whilst travelling (and so are thumb-sucker's thumbs) but, if your child uses a dummy, pack several and pin the one that is in use to the clothes via a ribbon.

YUMMY TOAD TURDS

When Alexander started crawling at the age of nine months, our home in Sindh was unpretentious; we had a resident population of rather slow and portly toads which Alexander found particularly attractive: he would pursue them either until they squeezed under a door and escaped or until he got them cornered. Cornered toads would then usually relieve themselves and Alexander would be delighted at being supplied with such a fresh snack. At first this rather upset me because amphibians and reptiles theoretically carry all sorts of exotic and unpleasant diarrhoea-causing Salmonellae. But Alexander persisted with the habit and would often emerge from some corner with his mouth smeared with black, partially digested, beetle wing-cases; yet he remained very well and did not get his first dose of diarrhoea until much later when I was foolish enough to feed him improperly reheated chicken curry somewhere up the Karakoram highway. Animal faeces are theoretically somewhat hazardous: cowpats may carry *Giardia*, piggy poo carries tapeworm eggs, doggy doo may carry toxocara worms and hydatid disease; but by far the biggest hazard is food contaminated with human faeces from people not washing their hands after visiting the toilet. Similarly, piles of stinking rubbish at street corners are harmless if unaesthetic.

Water sterilisation

Although water-borne illness is uncommon, it is worth taking some precautions and some notes on water sterilisation follow. Before choosing how you will purify water consider first where you are going and what are the risks. In the Indian subcontinent, Egypt, Bolivia, Peru and Ecuador the risks are relatively high whereas in sub-Saharan Africa and Southeast Asia you can get away with taking fewer precautions. And for all practical purposes, although boiling is best, any method will do and iodine will kill most nasties.

Boiling is the most effective method of sterilising water. It does not need to be boiled for long; merely bringing it to a good rolling boil is sufficient to kill everything significant, even at extreme altitude: amoebic cysts can survive for about a minute and a half at 55°C but at 60°C survive only for a fraction of a minute. Keeping water hot in a Thermos will doubly cook any microbes.

Bottled water may be just treated tap water; tests in India, Nepal and Pakistan have found that even bottles with an intact seal sometimes contain faecal bacteria and there is no guarantee that bottled water is safe. It is expensive, causes an unacceptable waste/litter problem, and the water can taste of plastic. True mineral water of the pure spring kind that is popular in Europe often contains unsuitable levels of minerals for very young children. Boiled tap water is safest.

We travel with a **Thermos flask** and get this filled with boiling or almost boiling water. The Thermos provides a ready source of hot water for making up baby-food or milk, for washing up, and for rinsing or scalding children's utensils. Where it is difficult to be hygienic I take the additional precaution of making powdered milk drinks in very hot water, and then allow them to cool before offering them. Test that the milk is cool enough by sprinkling some on to the front of your wrist. A little immersion heater is good if you are near a reliable electricity supply.

Chemical sterilisation

This is the most convenient, but least effective, method of improving water quality; it also gives the water an unpalatable taste. Chemical sterilisation is achieved with iodine or chlorine or silver. **Iodine** is much the most effective, although even iodine does not kill all bugs; *Cyclospora* (see page 162) is resistant. **Chlorine tablets** (eg: Puritabs) and **silver-based tablets** (eg: Micropur) are less-effective treatments for they do not kill *Cyclospora*, *Cryptosporidium* or cysts of amoebae and *Giardia*. During wet-season travel (especially between May and November in the subcontinent) it may be wise to drink boiled water (boiling kills almost everything) rather than relying on chemical 'sterilisation'. Silver tablets have a shelf life of ten years so are good for people travelling infrequently.

Chemical water sterilisation is less effective if the water is very turbid or very cold (below 5°C/40°F) and sterilisation times for cold or cloudy water should be at least doubled or the water should be left to stand for as long as possible, preferably several hours; otherwise double the concentration of chemical.

Iodine comes in several forms but produces drinkable water in 20 minutes. The most convenient form of iodine is as **tablets** (eg: Potable Aqua tablets). **Tincture of iodine** is next most convenient but it is messy (iodine stains permanently) if it spills in your luggage. Add four drops of 2% tincture of iodine to a litre of water, shake and leave to stand for 20 minutes. Adding vitamin C (43mg or 50mg ascorbic acid pills are suitable) AFTER the end of the 20-minute purification time binds the iodine and reduces the unpleasant taste. The quantity of vitamin C is not crucial – it is not dangerous if you take too much! In Nepal Lugol's Iodine is readily and cheaply available although you get higher iodine intake for less sterilisation; you also need to buy some nasal drops (but throw away the medicine) in order to acquire a dropper and sealable bottle to carry the iodine in.

Iodine crystals may be better for longer-term travellers. Make a saturated solution of iodine by roughly quarter-filling a 20ml screw-topped bottle with iodine crystals (but note that this form of iodine eats through plastic). Top up with any water. Shake for a few seconds (the crystals settle and nothing appears to dissolve) and leave for at least half an hour. Shake again. Pour about 10ml of the solution (but not the crystals) into a one-litre bottle of water; shake and leave for ten minutes. Top up the 20ml bottle ready for the next time it is needed. This should make up to 1,000 litres. If you can find a 20ml bottle with volume marks on the side, it makes estimating the 10ml volume easy. Daily, long-term use of iodine is probably not a good idea for children, but intermittent use, or use for up to three months, is safe. Ideally though give a range of drinks so that not all fluids contain iodine.

Filters and water purifiers

There are innumerable water-purification devices on the market. The most effective units are expensive and rather heavy, but they are quick to use. Most rely on a combination of filtration and iodine treatment. The advantage of those containing charcoal in the filter is that they also remove chemical pollutants including pesticides. Filters with iodine matrixes do seem to produce completely safe water, but these range in price from £45 to £180 so you have to pay for truly sterile water. And the expense continues because all filters have a finite life and need to be replaced after filtering 100–2,000 litres depending upon the model and impurity of the water. Nomad, Cotswold and Field and Trek sell a good range of these devices (addresses in *Appendix 1*, page 192) and travel clinics also sell some.

In the subcontinent most kitchens and hotels are equipped with large ceramic water filters, but water which has been only filtered and not boiled will not necessarily be safe; indeed, unless the filter is cleaned every couple of weeks it could be more hazardous than unfiltered water.

Domestic water filters

Many expatriate families keep water filters in the kitchen; good locally made models are readily available in the subcontinent but not in Indonesia. Drinking-water experts say that water should be filtered then boiled so that there will be no risk of it being contaminated during the filtering process. Although this makes bacteriological sense I know no expatriates who follow this advice; we pour hot water into the filter so that it cools as it filters and thence it can be dispensed into bottles and kept in the fridge. Every two weeks or so the porcelain filter candles need to be scrubbed clean (with a brush reserved for this purpose alone), boiled for 20 minutes then cooled on a clean cloth and inspected for cracks before being reinserted with clean hands. Such candles last for several years.

From the medical point of view filtering is unnecessary in most situations, although it improves clarity and may help reduce the amount of pesticides in your water. I have been told by many people that mica particles which occur naturally in drinking-water in Nepal, for example, can cause diarrhoea; if this is true the effect must cause the mildest of symptoms. Clearly the crudest of filters will remove mica, soil and any other products of mountain erosion.

Other safe drinks

When the family tires of the taste of water purification tablets, try other safe drinks – hot lemon, chocolate, tea, camomile tea (*manzanilla* in South America) or in Indonesia *air putih*: boiled water which is often served warm (but beware of added ice). In Madagascar *ranovola* – water boiled with a little burnt rice – is safe. Otherwise ask for boiling (rather than boiled) water for your water bottle: if it is hot, it is safe. Many children will prefer cold water; ask in time for it to cool.

Bottled drinks (but often not bottled water) are also safe if the seal is intact. In many countries you can also find individual boxes of fruit juices. These are often incredibly sweet but this means that they can be good bribes for flagging children and the sugar content improves energy levels and enthusiasm.

Bathwater

There's no need to take special precautions before bathing children, unless you are in bilharzia country: see *Bathing with bilharzia* on page 78 and also 96–7. Tap water is unlikely to be badly contaminated unless you are amidst a cholera outbreak, or if war or natural disaster has led to contamination of mains water supplies, or if the water smells bad or looks dirty.

Drinking the bathwater

Generally it is not necessary to bathe the baby in boiled and filtered water, and do not be concerned if your child drinks the bathwater. Water which looks and smells clean will be clean enough, and is unlikely to contain the critical infective dose of bacteria sufficient to cause illness. Most microbes need to invade in their millions to make people ill, so usually swallowing a few drops of contaminated water will do no harm. If the idea of the baby swallowing the odd mouthful of bathwater does worry you, drop in a quarter-teaspoon of potassium permanganate. This has two additional benefits. It turns the bathwater purple (an exciting phenomenon), it changes colour again when soap is used (magic) and it helps clean scratches and abrasions. It is cheap and readily available in most parts of Asia and Africa.

FIZZING BATH-FUN

It was bath time; Dad had just dropped in a Milton tablet to sterilise the water. In went two-year-old Katharine who, delighted to find such a fascinating fizzy toy in her bath, swallowed it! The worried parents bundled their toddler into the car and whizzed down to the local clinic where the child received a dose of *ipecacuanha*, the jollop given to induce vomiting in children who have swallowed noxious substances. They waited. Nothing happened. She was given another dose. Nothing happened. Everyone waited. Everyone wanted to go home. The family climbed back into the car, where Katharine vomited extravagantly.

Bathing with bilharzia

It is possible to acquire bilharzia or schistosomiasis from showering or bathing in contaminated water in problem regions. Water stored snail-free for two days and water which has been filtered, boiled or treated with chemicals such as Dettol or cresol will be safe as will water from wells. Further information is on page 96–7.

Kitchen precautions

Some children's utensils, especially training beakers, can be difficult to clean, and deposits of old food or milk represent an infection risk which will not be removed by any amount of chemical sterilisation. If utensils look clean you can be pretty sure they are clean enough. Simply boiling utensils for five or ten minutes effectively sterilises and also tends to boil off food remains. Steam sterilisers (eg: by Avent) are also much more effective than any form of cold chemical sterilisation.

Natural and Environmental Hazards

BUGS AND BITING BEASTS
Small biters and stingers (invertebrates)

The more people travel, the more totally misleading stories they seem to collect; perhaps there is some perverse pleasure in terrifying other globetrotters with images of man-eaters, pythons swallowing people whole, highly venomous snakes killing people in seconds, crocodiles consuming people washing at the riverbank, and sharks tearing people apart while bathing in the sea? Despite the stories, the dangers of all these bad beasts are wildly exaggerated almost to the level of fiction. Those which do pose any risk to travellers are discussed rationally below; most are inconvenient or irritating rather than dangerous. Some small beasts which bite (at the front end) may transmit disease, but critters which sting (at the back end) never do. And since disease transmission is the most serious hazard of exotic wildlife, we must first highlight a real killer.

The most dangerous animal commonly encountered in warm climates are mosquitoes: these insects that feed on human blood are responsible for huge numbers of deaths. Perhaps two million people die annually from mosquito-borne malaria: most are poor local children. Compare that staggering figure with estimates of deaths due to sharks (fewer than 100), crocodiles (1,000) and venomous snakes (40,000, mostly agricultural labourers). Then compare these world figures with the risk of being murdered in Britain (746 deaths a year) and you will realise that you should fear the small biters and forget the large predators.

Protect yourselves from bites and stings of all kinds by wearing long clothes, long trousers tucked into socks, stout shoes or boots and long-sleeved shirts.

Mosquitoes

NB Drawings in this section are not to scale.

Mosquitoes – particularly those active after dark – are dangerous because they spread disease. Bites also itch, allow access to skin infections and wake sleeping children.

Most of the dangerous mosquito-borne diseases are spread by *Anopheles* mosquitoes that emerge from their slumbers at dusk and are vigorous in their assaults until dawn. *Anopheles* mosquitoes are distinguishable from less dangerous species by their resting position on walls, as illustrated. They tend to be noisy fliers; they whine. It is crucial in malarial regions to protect the family and remember the three As of malaria prevention: Awareness, Avoidance of bites and Antimalarial medicines. See page 56.

Night-biting mosquitoes can also transmit a range of other serious diseases, including elephantiasis and various forms of untreatable encephalitis. Take precautions against being bitten to protect yourselves and also to reduce the misery of itchy bites.

Aedes mosquitoes have strikingly black-and-white striped legs. They bite during the day, can spread dengue fever and, in parts of South and Central America and sub-Saharan Africa, yellow fever. The immunisation against yellow fever gives good protection, but there is not yet a vaccine for dengue. It tends to appear in massive outbreaks which are reported in the local press; it is a perennial problem in Southeast Asia and parts of South America, and most recently India has been struck; it is rare in Africa. The mosquitoes responsible are common in tropical gardens where they breed in water tanks and other collections of clean water; their bite is slightly painful and very itchy. Baggy clothing and insect repellents help prevent bites. Expatriates should keep their gardens free of standing water and should seal their domestic water tanks with a lid or mosquito gauze.

Anopheles mosquito

Aedes mosquito

Midges

Unbearable at times but not dangerous.

In midgy country (northern Eurasia and America) the avoidance measures are the same as for tropical biters – long clothes and repellents: long sleeves, long trousers and (if they are really bad) trousers tucked into socks plus a cotton kerchief to seal the neck of the shirt, and then repellent on the remaining exposed skin.

Hairy caterpillars

Hairs penetrating the skin cause itching and discomfort for a few hours to some weeks; some South American species can be dangerous and all will be nasty if caterpillar hairs enter the eye.

Certain moth caterpillars are covered in hairs so that they look soft and furry; they are common worldwide, but only the South American species are really noxious. Children may find these miniature moving teddies attractive and wish to pick them up. The 'fur' is a fierce defence weapon, though: each hair is a brittle hollow straw containing highly irritant chemicals. When a child picks up such a caterpillar, falls on one, brushes against one or one gets inside the clothing, the 'hairs' penetrate the skin and cause pain and irritation. The treatment is to calm the child down, sit down in a good light and pick the hairs out – one by one – with a pair of pointed tweezers. Do not use eyebrow tweezers since they squirt the remaining venom from the hollow hairs into the child's skin which will hurt all the more. Sellotape is no help. Be careful what you do with the hairs that you pull out; if they enter the eyes they are very dangerous, and if they fall on to your lap you too will be itching and uncomfortable. If the irritation persists,

Hairy caterpillar

paracetamol (Tylenol) syrup helps and so will antihistamine tablets or syrups, and a cool or tepid bath. Most children will be fine by the next morning.

Bees, hornets and wasps
Stings are painful, but dangerous reactions are enormously rare in children, and attacks by 'killer bees' over-emphasised. The faster you get bee-stings out the better: speed is more important than technique.

This group of thin-waisted flying stingers is well known to everyone, although exotic species come in different colours, like elegant navy. Wasps and hornets sting and leave, while plumper hairier bees leave a sting behind. Bees empty 90% of their venom within 20 seconds and the remainder within a minute, so the faster you can get the sting out the less painful it will be. Research reported in the *Lancet* proved that speed of removal is more important than technique: you can try to flick the sting away with a fingernail, but the important message is to get it off as soon as possible. After any sting apply AfterBite if you have it, and/or ice or cold compresses (apply a wet cloth); applying vinegar or baking soda has no effect. There can be quite considerable swelling after a hornet sting but this usually settles overnight. If not give an antihistamine tablet or syrup. While dangerous allergic reactions are common in adults, children who are stung are rarely affected in this way.

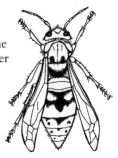

Hornet

To reduce the risk of stings clean children's faces promptly after eating sweet food and avoid flowery-patterned clothes; perfumes are also said to attract wasps. Try to be a good model for your children and if you encounter wasps or bees calmly move away. Flailing about encourages insects to sting, and once one has stung an alarm pheromone is released which summons more stingers. Children who become hysterical on seeing a bee or wasp invite further stings. Normal insect repellents do not repel wasps and other stingers, although special wasp repellents exist. Finally, be aware that skin infection can follow wasp (but not bee) stings; an area of spreading redness may need either antibiotic or antihistamine. Give both if a doctor cannot advise you.

Ants
Can be intensely irritating, but not dangerous; again, while allergic reactions occur in adults, they are most unlikely in children.

There are innumerable kinds of unpleasant ants and the closer you get to the Equator the larger they are and the bigger are their jaws. Ants like sweet things and dead animals (from caterpillars to beef); they are useful in clearing up some of nature's rubbish, but if they bother you, consider how to keep them out. If you are camping, don't eat or keep food anywhere near where you want to relax (like inside the tent), and if in a house, sweep out the kitchen area as soon as the food preparation and eating is over. In some tropical places the kitchen is in a building separate from the rest of the house to help reduce the ant problem. Ant powder is available in many countries where ants are a pest and things attractive to ants can be encircled in this chalk-like material.

There are lots of aggressive kinds of ants which inhabit tropical and subtropical forests and they attack children who kick joyfully through leaf litter or brush carelessly through scrub. Few cause much more than discomfort, but they may ruin a three-year-old's day; the red or orange ones seem the worst. Pull them off carefully, trying to detach the jaws from the child's skin without dismembering the ant; then cold compresses help.

Scorpions

Most scorpion stings are more painful than dangerous, but there are dangerous species (especially for children) in Mexico and Arizona, North Africa and the Middle East, and in south India.

Scorpions are eight-legged creatures with claws and a long sting which curves over their back when they are angry; they are usually black or dark brown and leathery-looking. They are highly dangerous in the tropical Americas, especially Mexico and Arizona and including Trinidad (but antivenom is available – in the States at least – for these species), in a geographical band from North Africa through Israel and the Middle East; South African and south Indian species are also nasty. Scorpion stings are particularly dangerous in children and, even in regions where the species are not so venomous, their stings are exceedingly unpleasant. Yet if you know a little about scorpion habits they are avoidable. Scorpions are common in hot dry places in the tropics and subtropics and are nocturnal. They emerge to hunt at night (and also come out after rain showers) and then find somewhere small and secure to hide during daylight hours. Children looking under stones for treasures often disturb and annoy a slumbering scorpion; teach children to lift stones and logs away from themselves. When camping it is wise to sleep in a tent with a sewn-in groundsheet or to sleep on a camp bed or in a hammock. Do not move rotting logs in order to pitch a tent and do not let children sit on decaying logs in forests. Discourage children from digging around in deep forest leaf litter.

Scorpion

Spiders

Dangerous spiders are very rare; a few cause a painful bite. Try to teach your children not to be frightened.

The precautions for avoiding spiders are similar to those for scorpions; many of the large tropical species are rather frightening, but very few are dangerous. Bites should be treated with cold compresses (plus antihistamines by mouth perhaps if it seems bad) and medical help sought if the wound doesn't begin to improve after a couple of days. An area of spreading redness or pus are early warning signs of complications.

Leeches

Harmless if revolting; little bite-wounds can get infected easily. Leeches do not spread disease.

These usually black, worm-like creatures dine on blood, but are otherwise harmless. Fortunately only the smaller species go for people and they only seem to be a big problem in Southeast and South Asia, Australia and Madagascar. They are a problem in rainforests and in some dry forests in the rainy season. They are a great nuisance in Nepal and the eastern Himalayas during the monsoon (mid June–mid September). Keep them off with insect repellents and long clothes, and remove them with a grain of salt, or tobacco, or chilli. Clean any wounds with a drying antiseptic (creams encourage secondary infections) and cover if possible. Leech wounds bleed for 12 hours or so after the leech has finished feeding, but blood loss is trivial; applying a poultice of leaves from plants related to woundwort (*Stachys)* or self-heal (*Prunella)* will staunch the flow. This is illustrated in *Chapter 8* on page 114.

Ticks

Tick bites occasionally spread disease, but even in a Lyme-disease region the risk of getting the disease after a bite is only around 1–2%. Inept attempts at removing ticks can leave their mouthparts behind and thus a troublesome infected wound.

Quick tick removal Get any tick off as soon as you find it. Grasp it between finger and thumb as close as possible to where it is attached and pull steadily away from the skin, at right angles to the skin. Never jerk or twist the tick; just pull steadily and it will come away in one piece. If possible then flood the bite-site with diluted iodine or alcohol (whisky, gin or local spirit). Prompt removal and sterilisation of the wound makes disease transmission less likely. Some tick-borne infections can be transmitted across the skin of the tick so if you are taking a tick off someone else put the removing hand into a plastic bag or surgical gloves if you have them.

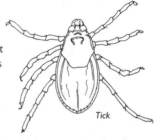

Tick

Ticks, which occur throughout the world, are most often encountered in regions where wild deer or sheep or cattle graze. Unfed ticks are flattened and measure 2–5mm across and look like slow-moving sesame seeds. They have the remarkable skill of being able to crawl about on skin unnoticed, so they climb over shoes, up a trouser leg and usually settle down to feed where the clothes become tight. Commonly you will discover one when bathing your child and by then it will look like a dark red kidney bean firmly attached to the skin, usually somewhere near the underpants. Brushing the skin with Sellotape wrapped around the finger sticky-side-out is great for getting immature 'seed' ticks off. Seek medical help if anyone is ill after a tick or mite bite, or there is an area of redness around the bite or you notice enlarged lymph glands close to the bite-site. Most tick-borne diseases start with vague flu-like symptoms: fever, headache, aches and pains. Anyone bitten by a tick in lowland forest in Austria, western Germany, the Czech and Slovak Republics and the former Yugoslavia – and particularly if a fever develops – should see a local doctor promptly.

Lost mouthparts If leeches or ticks are pulled off clumsily by a panicking victim or parent, fragments of the mouthparts may be left behind. This will make the wound slow to heal. If the wound is still active after two weeks and you suspect there is something inside apply a small blob of magnesium sulphate paste (a good pharmacy will make it up) under a waterproof Elastoplast or Band-aid; repeat this treatment whenever the dressing comes off or replace the paste every day for a few days and this will aid expulsion of the mouthparts. Dousing in plenty of a drying antiseptic will also help. Spreading redness implies an infection has got in too and antibiotics (by mouth) will probably be needed.

American chiggers and Old-World scrub mites
Bites of American species cause excruciating itching while Asian mites transmit typhus.
Chiggers and itch mites are like miniature ticks which are related to, and look like, the tiny red 'harvest spiders' which run frenetically about gardens in English summers. They are minuscule (1mm across) but, even after they have feasted and departed, their presence causes excruciating itching for ten days. They are a particular problem in tropical American jungles, where 'seed' (immature) ticks also climb on to people in enormous numbers. In a geographical region encompassing much of South Asia (including Pakistan and Sri Lanka), East Asia, the Pacific and Australia there is a similar pest: the scrub typhus mite. Their bites do not itch so they can go completely unnoticed, but they spread scrub typhus: an unpleasant but treatable disease.

Things that get under the skin
Jiggers
When these get under the skin they cause a pea-sized, boil-like swelling; they are rarely much of a problem unless there are lots of them.
Jiggers occur all over the tropics but are common only in Africa, Central America and South America. Jiggers are also sometimes called chigoes or sand-fleas. They are fleas which degenerate once inside someone's foot to become a pea-sized boil. They are completely different from chigger mites. The first thing you will notice is a slightly red lump, often close to a toenail, and possibly oozing blood or pus; here lurks the flea distended with eggs. Treatment is to pick the roof off the swelling and tease out the flea. It is best to get a local to do this operation for it is a skilled job and if the flea bursts you will have a crop of eggs (which are capable of reinfection) all over your bedroom floor. The 'surgeon' should use a needle sterilised in a flame, and if the flea does burst douse the wound and flea and floor with spirit, alcohol or paraffin (kerosene). Clean the wound with a good drying antiseptic (eg: dilute potassium permanganate solution or iodine) and dress it.

Flesh-maggots
Disgusting rather than dangerous; can leave scars.
These bizarre nightmare hitchhikers are common in parts of tropical Central and South America. Mummy **bot fly** lays her eggs on a mosquito so that they can hatch and get into a victim's skin through the mosquito-bite hole or hair follicle. The larvae feast for two or three months then a new fly emerges from a 2cm boil. If you are travelling intrepidly with your children in the American tropical forest, make sure they are covered with long clothes and insect repellent.

Central African **tumbu flies** also have a horrible lifestyle; they lay eggs in soil or drying laundry. Clothes left to dry on the ground or hung up in the shade are particularly vulnerable but ironing kills the eggs. Babies' nappies, bed-sheets and elasticated waistbands must be ironed in *tumbu* country. Clothes left out in direct sunshine until crispy dry should also be safe, or dry clothes inside a screened house. These flies are rarely encountered in southern Africa.

Flies and beetles
Blister beetles
Contact with the body fluids of these beetles, once damaged, can cause blistering.
Small long thin beetles, belonging to the Staphylinidae and Meloidae families, secrete fluids which after a delay of some hours cause inflammation, swelling and even blistering of the skin; they are particularly unpleasant if one enters the eye. Problem Staph species are found in sub-Saharan Africa, in Thailand and elsewhere; they are colourful (black and orange usually), the same kind of shape as earwigs but without the pincers, and can curl their tail-end up and over the rest of the body so that to the uninitiated they look like baby clawless scorpions.

Meloid blister beetle

Blister beetles occur in the Mediterranean area where they are metallic green and called Spanish 'flies'. In Kiribati/Gilbert Islands there is another kind of beetle (family Oedemeridae) with similar inflammatory talents. None of these beetles exudes the irritant fluids unless annoyed or damaged so try to brush them away without upsetting them.

Paederus (Staph) beetle

Horseflies
Bites are painful, but otherwise harmless.
These housefly-like insects have the most beautifully coloured iridescent eyes. Their bites are immediately painful and they can bite through thin cloth but they do not spread disease. They are commonest around cattle and horses and will persist in biting you unless you kill them, so if they are troubling you, find somewhere else to stay; repellents don't work. Horseflies sleep at night.

Tsetse flies
African tsetse flies have a painful bite and transmit sleeping sickness.
Tsetse flies are found only in tropical Africa and transmit sleeping sickness (African trypanosomiasis), mostly in game parks; they like leafy edge habitats so occur at forested lake shores, riverbanks and in forest-savannah mosaic; one variety has been able to extend its range almost into the Sahara desert. Locals know

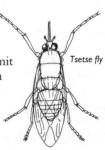

Tsetse fly

where tsetse is a problem for those venturing into the bush. Tsetse flies are twice the size of a housefly, are active during the day, their bite is painful and they are attracted to blue.

Sandflies

Transmit leishmania in tropical America, the Middle East, Bihar and Sudan and sandfly fever elsewhere.

These tiny hairy flies are most active at twilight but bite throughout the night; they are so small that they can get through mosquito netting but will not penetrate insecticide-treated nets. Families who are out in tropical forests in Central or South America after twilight must protect themselves with long clothes and repellents and sleep under *permethrin*-treated bed-nets.

Sandfly

Leishmania is called Kala Azar in the Old World, and in Central and South America the nastiest form is called *espundia*, a condition rather like leprosy but not so easy to cure. The highland Peruvian form, *uta*, heals by itself.

Squirters

Beware of anything which squirts near the eyes; assume the fluid is corrosive and wash it out with lots of water from your water bottle as soon as possible. Lie the child on his back and pour water from close up while encouraging him to blink.

Treat exotic animals (even the smallest creatures) with profound respect; beasts continue to take us by surprise even though – or perhaps because – we are interested in natural history. **Cicadas** squirt fluid in defence. This does not irritate the skin, but

Tail-less whip scorpion

Cicada

it would be wise to assume anything squirted in aggression would harm the eyes. Other animals which can harm with specially toxic squirt-fluids include **tail-less whip-scorpions**; American whip-scorpions are known as vinegarroons because of their ability to squirt 84% acetic acid; whip-scorpions are also found in the Old World tropics including Australia. In North America there are insects known as **walking sticks** or musk phasmids which exude white liquid with a pleasant musky smell. One species, a 7–12-cm-long yellow-and-brown-striped **stick insect**, *Anisomorpha buprestoides*, can spray its musk a distance of 40cm; if inhaled the musk causes pain and if it gets into the eyes the burning sensation can take 36 hours to go. **Snail and slug** slime is irritant if rubbed into the eye. Try to educate the children to be cautious and gentle when playing with small animals.

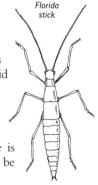

Florida stick

Centipedes and millipedes

Millipedes are rounded with their many legs tucked beneath their bodies which can give them an almost snake-like appearance. Only a few tropical species can harm if irritant secretions get on to the skin or into the eyes. They are fascinating placid ponderous herbivores and if handled respectfully will not exude their child-repellent. In contrast centipedes are ferocious be-weaponed predators which have a venomous bite. They are flattened with obvious legs which stick out to the sides allowing them to move extremely fast.

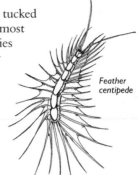

Feather centipede

Flightless biters
Head lice

Bites cause some itching of the scalp, but are not dangerous. Bad infestations may cause secondary skin infections and may make children irritable.

Lice and nits (the eggs) are common in children's hair all over the world and are a problem in schoolchildren everywhere. They are small, usually dark, slim creatures about 1mm broad and 2–3mm long and they feed on blood. Lotions which can be left on overnight are far more effective than shampoos. This is not as messy and unpleasant as it sounds; lotion is applied in a well-ventilated place and allowed to dry. It can then be shampooed out the next morning. Alternatively applying conditioner and combing carefully (preferably with a fine-toothed comb) every few days for three weeks should get rid of them. Nits are white and firmly cemented to the hair; they do not come off when dead, so persistence of the nits does not mean that treatment has failed.

Head louse

Fine-toothed diagnostic metal combs work best when the hair is wet with conditioner, oil or other lubricant. If you haven't packed one, use an ordinary comb with the teeth pushed through a scrap of gauze to snag the beasts. Otherwise employ a local skilled in removing lice. Lice transfer readily between people; they do not like smelly cosmetics so hair lotions and mousses help keep them at bay. Adult lice can survive without feeding for five days and exchanging hats, headscarves and hair-ties are efficient ways for children to share them; put hairbrushes etc out in direct sunshine or wash in vinegar water. Louse infestation can cause swelling of the nearest lymph glands in the neck.

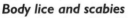

Nit on hair

Body lice and scabies

Bites cause itching, but are not dangerous.

Body lice are sluggish, translucent and difficult to see; scabies mites are tiny and hardly visible. These two infestations – which cause a great deal of itching – are best treated with *malathion* or *permethrin*. Preparations containing alcohol sting so are best avoided; *benzyl benzoate* is sometimes all you will be able to buy in some countries and the big disadvantage of this is that it further irritates broken skin and so is unpleasant for children – but so are parasites.

Fleas

Leave raised itchy bumps; not dangerous, but a hazard of cheap Third World hotels.
Fleas are very fast-moving jumpers which attack at night in budget accommodation; they usually leave a line of a few (say six) bites showing where they have eaten. The bites sometimes have a pus-filled centre and itch a bit; there is no need to treat the bites or worry about them. Evict fleas by spreading clothing or sleeping bags out in the sun.

Bedbugs

These bite at night; the bite is painful and disturbs sleep, but they spread no disease.
Bedbugs live in badly maintained hotels and are about 5mm long. Avoid rooms with pieces of wall plaster missing and streaks of blood where previous victims have splattered the insects against the wall. If you discover bedbugs after you have settled for the night pull the beds away from the wall and leave the light on – if there is electricity. Lately there have been infestations in First World student accommodation.

Bedbug

Assassin bugs or vinchuca

Cone-nosed bugs from parts of tropical South America emerge to bite at night; there is a small risk of transmitting Chagas disease. The disease is extremely rare in travellers and is avoided by sleeping under impregnated bednets or in a hammock with inherent net.
These large (2–2.5cm-long) biting bugs skulk in poor adobe huts and bite at night. The disease is known from all Central and South American countries but the risk to travellers is tiny; see also page 189.

Assassin bug

Dangers of sleeping on the floor

In some parts of the tropics and subtropics sleeping on the floor or on a mattress on the floor carries a few risks, unless you are in a second-floor hotel room or in a tent with a sewn-in groundsheet. Troublesome, night-active, ground-level creepies include centipedes, scorpions, snakes, blister beetles, assassin bugs and, in Central Africa, Congo floor maggots which draw blood when they bite. Children sleeping on the ground or floor might also roll on to a hairy caterpillar (see above). Hammocks are an enjoyable alternative.

Worms that hide in the sand

There are two worms which children may pick up while playing in sand; neither is dangerous. The commonest is **hookworm** which lurks in soil contaminated with faeces; pollution need not be obvious for the ground to be hookwormy. Larval worms digest their way in through the skin where the entry point itches for a while. They then ride in the bloodstream and settle on the gut wall where they browse and cause slight bleeding at a microscopic level. They are unlikely to cause problems unless there are huge numbers, and the infestation will die out naturally, untreated, once the family has returned to a temperate climate. Travelling children are unlikely to collect enough to be harmful, and long-term expatriate children will largely avoid them if they wear shoes whenever playing outside. Expatriates should sun-dry (for at least a week) any sand to be used for a sandpit.

The second skin invader is the **geography worm**. This is a dog (or cat) hookworm which is acquired when people sit or walk on a beach, or play in a sandpit polluted with doggy doo. Its name comes from the profoundly irritating map-like patterns the worm leaves as it wanders beneath the skin. The 'head' of the worm advances a few millimetres each day. Treatment is to 'freeze' the head end with carbon dioxide 'snow' (used to treat warts) or ethyl chloride spray. Otherwise try the method recommended in medical texts which seems messy and doomed to failure: crush up some *thiabendazole/tiabendazole* tablets, mix them with some bland cream and apply the mixture to the area, keeping it in place with a waterproof dressing. No harm will be done if no treatment is given: the worm will die after some weeks, but it will cause a great deal of itching during that time.

REPTILES
Dangerous lizards
There are no records of deaths or serious problems after bites from the world's only two kinds of venomous lizards, but Komodo dragons can kill; Nile crocodiles in Africa and estuarine crocs or 'salties' in Asia/Australia are also highly dangerous.

Lizards are all essentially harmless (despite what locals will have you believe). There are just two kinds of venomous lizard, the gila monster and the beaded lizard; both are.large (45–80cm) and both live in the southwest US and in Mexico. They rarely bite people and there are no reliable reports of deaths due to their bites. The carnivorous Komodo dragons of Indonesia which have become accustomed to being fed by tourists have killed adults; approach with caution.

Nile crocodiles in Africa and Madagascar and estuarine crocodiles or 'salties' around Australia and into Asia as far as India and Sri Lanka are dangerous. Locals will advise on safe places to bathe.

Snakes
Snakes engender a disproportionate amount of fear; deaths from snakebite are extremely rare in travellers and expatriates.

Most snakes are harmless; of about 3,000 or so species of snake in the world fewer than 200 are capable of killing or causing permanent disability. Even if a snake is dangerous there is only a 50:50 chance that any significant quantity of venom will be dispensed after a bite. Farmers (especially in Myanmar) and people who keep snakes as pets are most often bitten; it is very rare for tourists and expatriates to be attacked – snakes are shy and don't like people. Snakes are active from late afternoon and at night; so ensure that, if the children are out in jungly areas at or after dusk, they are wearing substantial shoes or boots with trousers tucked into socks. If you are camping or needing to push through scrubby vegetation to reach the toilet area, try to cut back the vegetation; anyone

EUROPEAN SNAKES

The snakes most commonly seen in Europe are non-venomous grass snakes, although even a grass snake bite needs proper medical attention – infection is common. Venomous vipers are quite frequently seen in southern Europe; they are good swimmers. They are recognised by their striking dark zigzag markings and also by the fact that they have a neck – a clear difference between the head and the rest of the animal. Tourniquets applied after a viper bite INCREASE tissue damage so should never be used in Europe. Firmly bandaging a wad of cloth directly on top of the bite wound will help slow the spread of the venom. Viper bites happen in Britain but it may be reassuring to know that there were just 14 deaths to viper bites in the 100 years between 1900 and 2000, with an average of 200 bites a year.

relieving himself outside after dark should carry a torch/flashlight. Snakes do not want to pick a fight and will get out of the way if warned of your approach.

Expatriates living in snaky country should keep the area immediately around the house and the route to the outside toilet free from vegetation; scrub hides snakes and is also a good daytime resting-place for mosquitoes. Keeping chickens attracts mice and mice attract snakes; if you are worried about snakes either don't keep chickens or other grain-eaters, or make sure any animals are kept well away from the house. Geese kick up a tremendous fuss if a snake is around and are good snake-repellents.

Snakebite: what to do

Encourage the victim to keep still, and as calm as possible. The bitten part should be washed with water and soap (unless you are in Australia, see box below) and wiped gently with a clean cloth; this removes any venom from the skin surface. If venom has entered the body, there may be swelling; so remove any rings, watches and jewellery. Even in expert hands tourniquets are dangerous. There are many limbs lost to tourniquets applied after a harmless bite, and if the snake was venomous a home-made tourniquet will not help. Splinting the bitten limb slows venom and reduces pain. Applying a firm crêpe bandage also slows the effects of any venom, but it must be released every 30 minutes to allow blood to reach the tissues.

SPECIAL ADVICE FOR SNAKEBITE IN AUSTRALIA

The Australian medical services are fantastically well geared up to treating snakebites; and the snake – and thus the antivenom to be given – can be identified from venom left on the skin surface. Therefore do not wash the bite area, but apply a clean cloth and then a firm crêpe bandage; otherwise grasp the child's bitten limb firmly and hold on until you are in a hospital with the antivenom ready!

Next evacuate the casualty to a doctor or hospital. If he begins to show signs suggestive of venom circulating in the body, antivenom will be administered in the safe environment of the clinic or hospital. The symptoms caused by venom are rather similar to those of terror (rapid heartbeat, sweating) so it is important that experts assess the bitten person. Administration of antivenom carries its own risks and should not be done by amateurs, and it is pointless giving potentially dangerous antivenom if no venom has been absorbed. Some people suggest capturing the offending snake, but do this only if there is absolutely no risk of anyone else being bitten, and beware since even a decapitated head is able to bite in a reflex spasm after death.

Many 'first-aid' measures will actually make things much worse; so, if in doubt, do nothing! While evacuation is being organised, the following rules will help protect the victim:

- DON'T panic – it is likely that no venom has been dispensed
- DISCOURAGE movement of the bitten limb by applying a splint
- KEEP the bitten limb BELOW heart height to slow spread of the venom
- GIVE *paracetamol* or Tylenol
- DO NOT incise or suck the wound
- DO NOT apply a tourniquet
- DO NOT apply ice packs
- DO NOT apply potassium permanganate

Electric shocks or stun guns do not inactivate venom but they may be useful in giving the impression of action and thus help keep everyone calm. Suction or cutting devices are harmful and must never be used.

MAMMALS
Bears
Bears are not nice furry teddies but powerful killers; never approach a bear on foot.
Bears are responsible for a few deaths a year in wild mountainous parts of the world, although most attacks are on adults. On walking safaris in bear country make sure you can see far enough ahead so as not to surprise a bear: don't push through dense forest. When camping take some special precautions. First, carry a rope and use it to hang your food (including tinned food, foody rubbish and even toothpaste) up in a tree away from where you are sleeping. Bears have been known to claw into tents after smelling food inside. If you hear a bear sniffing around your tent, as Matthew once did in the Adirondacks, stay calm (absolutely impossible he assures us) and channel your nervous energy into banging pots and pans.

Monkeys
Monkeys in Asian temples and African national parks often bite provocative children; bites get infected and carry a risk of rabies and tetanus.
Monkeys are quick to learn on which side their bread is buttered; primates spoiled by tourists in game parks or used to taking offerings left at Hindu temples can be very troublesome. Do not eat in front of them, or they may bite in an effort to steal the food; it is even unwise to carry plastic shopping bags (they assume something edible is inside) or anything that looks remotely

edible including some toys. Rhesus monkeys living around temples in Kathmandu are becoming an increasing nuisance and are more likely to bite children than adults, since children are more likely to tease or go too close and are less threatening. Picnic elsewhere.

Domestic dogs

Dogs are, statistically, the most dangerous of animals (after mosquitoes!); they do inflict horrible injuries and can transmit rabies. In the developing world, dogs are trained to be fierce; they are the village police force.

Most dogs in the developing world are used to being kicked and have had to fight to survive; they often bite children. Dogs spread rabies and toddlers can sustain horrific bites to the face. If approached or threatened by a dog, stoop down as if to pick up a stone (even if there are none) and then raise your arm as if to throw the stone. Dogs will invariably cower and are then less likely to attack. Encourage children to mistrust dogs (or other animals they do not know), never allow your child to tease a dog when you are travelling, and ensure you are all immunised against rabies. Immunise any mammal you keep uncaged as a pet too.

If anyone is bitten by a dog (or other mammal) good first aid is essential whatever immunisations the victim has had. Clean the wound by scrubbing with soap under running water for five minutes (time it with a watch). The purity of the water does not matter: run the wound under a tap or trickle water from your water bottle. Then pour on diluted iodine or local alcohol, or whisky, gin or rum, to sterilise the wound. Cover the wound with a clean dry dressing and change the dressing daily. Do not apply ointments or creams and do not let anyone stitch or suture the wound. Two further anti-rabies injections are needed after any suspect bite; go to a capital city or big medical centre for these. A crude emulsion of sheep or goat brain known as Semple vaccine is sometimes offered as treatment in some rural clinics, eg: in Nepal and Madagascar. This is best avoided and more effective treatment sought in the capital.

Vampire bats

Like any infected mammal, bats can transmit rabies through a bite.

Vampires only occur in the New World (despite the Transylvanian legends) and are small animals. Matthew slept through a visit in the Peruvian rainforest and discovered the next morning two deep teeth-marks in his big toe from whence a puddle of blood was still oozing: vampires (like leeches) secrete a local anaesthetic as well as a substance which stops the blood clotting before the bat has finished dining. In South America, the family would be safest sleeping in a zippable tent or indoors under impregnated mosquito nets. Do not let children pick up any bat or other small wild animal that they find. Sick or abnormally tame animals may well be dying of rabies; half of the confirmed rabies deaths in the United States since 1980 have been linked to bats.

PLANTS WHICH STING OR IRRITATE

Stinging nettles grow in many regions but the antidotes vary from continent to continent; their sting is immediately apparent. Any plant or part of a plant which is covered in hair is a guaranteed irritator; warn children that furry pods are not soft but are unpleasant to play with.

Poison ivy and poison oak are a problem in North America; if you are camping or walking in the forest get a local to show you what they look like. Red streaks or patches are the beginning of the problem and these break down into blisters that ooze then crust over. The irritation starts several days to a week after contact with the plant and, if a victim uses a towel, the irritating oil can affect someone else and the whole family can suffer. There is no particularly good treatment, although cold compresses help and the symptoms will settle in four to seven days. Cashews and mangoes are related trees and can cause a lesser allergic dermatitis. European **primroses** can also cause blistering rather like the poison ivy rash in some allergic people.

Wearing long clothing whenever heading into jungly or scrubby areas should protect you from these and other noxious plants and animals. For more on poisonous plants, see page 121.

BEACH AND SEASIDE HAZARDS

It is easy to sun-burn whilst swimming: insist children wear shirts when playing on the beach and in the sea. This is even more important when snorkelling because the back, back of the thighs and even the calves get burnt. Long Bermuda shorts and waterproof suncream are recommended.

Drowning

Risks of drowning are greater amongst travellers since dangerous places may not be labelled, rescue services may be absent, and there may be no secure railings to stop children falling off a cliff and no sign to warn of undertows or rip-tides. Dangerous tides or currents can take even strong swimmers out to sea. Get local advice; sometimes you can actually see tidal rips from the beach. People caught in rips tend to panic yet it is reasonably easy to swim out of them **across** the tide. Predictably dangerous bathing spots are where rivers enter the sea and also between islands where currents can sweep an inexperienced little snorkeller or swimmer out to sea. Make sure someone is supervising the children and beware of letting them drift out to sea on an inflatable boat: tie it to something on land. Discourage children from swimming out to sea but tell them to swim parallel to the shore. If someone appears to be drowning do not immediately plunge in after them; the maxim to maximise survival is to try the following actions in this order: Shout, Signal, Reach; Throw (a rope or something that floats); Wade, Row, Swim with an aid; Swim and Tow them.

Spines, stings and scratches

There is a whole array of stinging and venomous sea creatures: it is best not to touch anything unless wearing thick rubber gloves. Never collect live cone shells since they are highly venomous. Live coral, which looks so very beautiful, secretes substances which make any graze very slow to heal; avoid brushing against coral. It is important to wear shoes on tropical beaches, even when swimming. Old plimsolls, 'jellies' or sandals will reduce the chances of

Weever fish

treading on the venomous dorsal fins of half-buried **weever fish**; shoes also protect children from geography worm (see page 89) and from getting pieces of coral and sea-urchin spines in the soles of their feet.

Treatment for spiny injuries

Treading on something spiny can cause two problems. Firstly, there may be intense pain if there is fish or sting-ray venom in the wound. In this case the treatment is immersion in water as hot as can be tolerated; but beware, since the stung limb is so painful that the sufferer cannot judge what is scalding. Continue immersion (remove the limb from the bucket and top up with hot water from time to time) for at least half an hour and repeat if the pain returns. Hot-water treatment works for all fish venoms and stingrays but not jellyfish or 'lower' animals.

Secondly, something may remain under the skin. Even the smallest piece of coral or sea-urchin spine in the sole of a foot makes walking uncomfortable. It will need teasing out with some pointed tweezers. If you can't find it, apply magnesium sulphate paste (old-fashioned pharmacies can usually make this up) under a waterproof dressing/ sticking-plaster/Band-aid and this will speed up the body's normal 'foreign body' expulsion process. The paste will need to be replenished under a new dressing daily. Peeing on sea-urchin spines which are embedded under the skin does nothing to aid healing, but it does no harm either. Should a piece of sea-urchin spine stay embedded beneath the skin, the body will deal with it by slowly reabsorbing it – it is a source of extra calcium.

Stingray

Jellyfish

Jellyfish are most likely to be encountered on bathing beaches after storms, and often if there is a lot of seaweed in the water it will be mixed with broken tentacles which can still sting. Occasionally stings will cause collapse and the victim will stop breathing; the effect is transitory however, so giving mouth-to-mouth resuscitation and cardiac massage if necessary is life-saving (see pages 108–9). Any tentacles which are still stuck to the skin will discharge further venom if disturbed so it is best to inactivate the stingers before removal; if the attack has been by box jellyfish in the Indo-Pacific-Australasian region pour on vinegar, 4–6% acetic acid. If the attack is by Atlantic *Crysaora* apply a 50:50 solution of baking soda in water.

'**Sea lice**', sea-bathers' eruption, ocean itch, caribe or sea poisoning is a problem that had been recognised recently amongst swimmers in tropical seas and there have been numerous cases in Florida. Swimmers notice raised red weals a few hours after bathing which last several days. The rash is mostly on skin that has been covered by bathing suits or in places where the skin is rubbed, such as armpits, the backs of the knees and where there has been contact with a surf board. It seems to be caused by larvae of the thimble jellyfish, *Linuche unguiculata;* these are half-millimetre long, near-invisible creatures that get caught between swimsuits and the skin.

Not everyone is affected the same way; people who have never met the larvae before will have no rash, and those who have encountered the larvae several times notice a mild stinging sensation as they swim. The thimble jellyfish is a widespread species, occurring off Central and South America as well as in the Indo-Pacific, including the Philippines. Other jellyfish larvae are probably capable of causing similar problems anywhere in warm seas. On the Florida coast 'sea lice' only occur in some years, usually, as with other jellyfish stings, when there are onshore winds and only between April and July (inclusive). Treatment is to remove bathing suits and shower (preferably initially in salt water) after swimming. Contact with fresh water with the swimsuit on will make the venomous cysts of the larvae discharge which makes things worse. Anyone who has an attack of 'sea lice' will probably experience another when they wear the same swimsuit again so either throw it away or machine-wash it with detergent and tumble-dry it. 'Sea lice' inject venom under the skin, so nothing you put on the skin will help.

Colds and blocked ears

Children suffer lots of colds (equivalent to 50 days a year) and colds reduce the capacity to equalise pressure in the ears when snorkelling or diving deep in swimming pools; if a child complains of headache or **face pain** after a lot of snorkelling or diving the treatment is to not go so deep. A decongestant such as *pseudoephedrine* (Sudafed) may also help, particularly if the discomfort is around bedtime since the medicine is slightly sedating. Steam inhalations are also helpful if the child is old enough to co-operate; this means inhaling steam by leaning over a basin of hot water with a towel over the head. Children who have had **grommets** put into their ears may swim although they probably should not dive down too deep. Trips involving lots of time in the water can predispose children to **swimmer's ear** – an infection of the ear canal. Aluminium acetate (as 8% drops) will help prevent recurrences. Very sore swollen ears will need antibiotic drops from the doctor or pharmacy; a five-day course should be enough.

Red tides

These occur at unpredictable times in warm seas and the phenomenon turns the ocean red. During a red tide, the toxins produced by the over-abundant dinoflagellates can become airborne by the action of the surf. These aerosol toxins can then cause slight irritation of the airways, a cough, runny nose and sore eyes. There is no treatment except to stay away from the surf during red tides. Eating seafood during red tides is unwise (see page 65).

Boats

Speedboats and now jet skis are a hazard to anyone who is swimming or snorkelling. Safety is rarely a high priority in countries not controlled by European, Australian or North American safety regulations, so be careful on water. Life jackets may be provided for a boat trip, but if a child is put in an adult's life jacket it may be more of a hazard than a life-saver. Beware of your child falling overboard.

RIVER AND FRESHWATER HAZARDS

The greatest hazard from river bathing is probably stubbed toes or lacerated feet. Get the children to wear rubber-soled shoes to protect them from glass, thorns, rocks and slipping. Rivers cutting through limestone, or where there are waterfalls and lots of eddies, can make swimming hazardous, and in South America there are freshwater sting-rays to look out for. Piranhas are not the hazard they are made out to be. As your brood grow older, you may need to distract them from emulating local youths in doing hair-raising dives off cliffs and bridges. Discourage diving into unknown waters since a broken neck spells the end of carefree childhood. Enter any unknown water feet first.

Rafts

White-water rafting trips are exciting but are generally unsuitable for children. Grade 1–2 may be all right for adventurous children over about five years of age, as long as they are fairly confident in water. On real white water, grade 3 and over, children should be confident swimmers over the age of 12. Rafts sometimes capsize and tip everyone out; even if they don't turn over everyone gets very wet and cold. It is really only a sport for big kids and adults. That said, we have had some wonderfully tranquil trips with babies on gentle waters watching birds, otters and river dolphins: here the main hazard was being frazzled by the sun.

Biting blackflies

Pestilential; bites are very itchy; can spread river blindness in parts of Africa and South and Central America. They are smaller than, and unrelated to, garden aphids.

Blackfly

Blackflies live close to river rapids. The minute, black worm-like larvae cling on in rapids making rocks look as if they are covered in designer stubble. The adults bite during the day and are a nuisance even outside river-blindness country (eg: in Asia); their bites are itchy for days and there is often a little bloody spot in the centre of the bite. Long trousers, socks and repellents protect the skin from bites in Africa, but in the Americas the arms also need to be covered with long-sleeved garments. Citronella-based natural repellents, eg: Mosiguard, do not repel them.

River blindness (onchocerciasis) is a risk close to fast-flowing rivers (where blackflies breed) in much of tropical sub-Saharan Africa between 19°N and 17°S and also in central and tropical South America. The disease most commonly makes the skin of one or two limbs incredibly itchy. The eyes are only threatened after extremely heavy infestations for many years. If you suspect this disease, get the problem properly diagnosed and treated.

Bilharzia

This curable parasitic disease is most commonly encountered in the lakes of the African Rift Valley, especially Lake Malawi; the tiny fluke worm penetrates the skin then sets up home.

Bilharzia or schistosomiasis is a parasite which spends its early life in freshwater snails then swims free in search of a person to inhabit. The worm gets in by digesting through the skin of someone wading, bathing or showering in contaminated water. Bilharzia is a problem in freshwater bodies in much of Africa including Egypt and Madagascar. It also occurs in the Middle East, Brazil, Venezuela, Guyana and Surinam plus some Caribbean islands including the Dominican Republic and Puerto Rico. The Indian subcontinent is clear except for a tiny area in Maharashtra State. In any of these areas it may be unsafe to swim for more than ten minutes. After a quick dip in suspect water, vigorously towel dry. Applying DEET insect repellent probably kills parasites on the skin after bathing. It is possible to catch schistosomiasis from bathwater or from showering or from a swimming pool, so take up-to-date advice on whether your destination carries a bilharzia risk (ask at a travel clinic – addresses on page 191 or check www.fitfortravel.scot.nhs.uk.). Water stored snail-free for two days, or treated with chemicals, or filtered or boiled is safe. Water collected from a well should be bilharzia-free since the flukes are sun-loving, but any water abstracted from a lake in an endemic area is suspect.

Schistosomiasis is also a risk in parts of Southeast Asia: it occurs in parts of China, Taiwan, Vietnam and the Philippines. Indonesia is free except for two remote valleys in central Sulawesi. Penetration of this oriental form of the parasite is much faster and any bathing is risky.

Some people get quite ill with a fever after catching bilharzia, and some have no symptoms so it is important to see your doctor for a blood test if you think that the family has been exposed.

SUNBURN, PRICKLY HEAT AND HEATSTROKE

The fastest way to cool a hot child is to pour a cup of water over her head and pat it in to wet her hair thoroughly; alternatively soak a light-coloured cotton hat in plenty of water, whack it back on the hot head and allow it to slowly drip dry. If there is any sign of the skin reddening get out of the sun: applying more cream will not now prevent sunburn.

Sunburn

Children burn easily in the sun; try to keep all babies and small children out of the direct sunshine especially between 11.00 and 15.00, and particularly during the first weeks of summer or on first arriving in a hot place. Children are susceptible to heatstroke when they first arrive in a hot climate. Infants in particular must avoid all direct sunlight in the heat of the day. If children have to be out in direct sunshine, build up any exposure very gradually from 20 minutes a day. Try to distract your child from exercising hard in the middle of the day, in direct sunshine. Dress them in long loose 100%-cotton clothes and a hat, and remind them to drink plenty. Wear some clothes even when swimming (a shirt keeps the sun off the back). Replenish the suncream at least once halfway through the day, and also after drying with a towel. Remember too that strong tropical sunlight reflected up off water can burn, even up inside the nose. Notes on suncreams are given on pages 22–4.

Suncream alone isn't good enough protection so also make use of the shade beside or inside buildings, umbrellas, a wide-brimmed floppy cotton sunhat and a midday siesta. Even if you are sensible and stay in the shade, there will still be some sun exposure from reflected sunlight and you can also burn from radiation coming through clouds. Sunscreens are useful whenever you are outdoors in hot climates or at home during the summer. Whilst darker-skinned peoples are at lesser risk from skin cancer, the incidence of 'prickly heat' and ageing changes due to too much sun is similar in light- and dark-skinned people. And sunscreens do not protect against the risk of skin cancer when used to extend the time spent in the sun where, without a sunscreen, there would be sunburn. Sunscreens should be seen as adjuncts to other sensible precautions providing protection during periods of unavoidable exposure like when swimming or playing sports. Those most likely to get burned and thus later at risk of skin cancer are those with red hair and freckles, and also blondes with pale skin.

Prickly heat

In hot humid climates children (and adults too) may be afflicted by a fine raised pimply and itchy rash which also produces a distressing prickling sensation. It looks like red millet seeds under the skin. It is caused by the sweat glands getting congested as the skin sweats more in an attempt to get cool. It is most often on the neck, back and chest. Treatment is to splash lots of cool water on the affected area, pat dry (without rubbing – friction makes it worse) and powder with talc or dab with *calamine*. When indoors strip the child to the nappy or underpants; when outdoors dress the child in loose 100%-cotton clothes and keep him in the shade as much as possible. If it gets really bad you may need to check into an air-conditioned hotel for a while to let it settle down.

Heatstroke

Anyone who has just arrived in a hot climate is at risk of heat exhaustion and heatstroke especially from vigorous exercise, but because children lose heat efficiently they rarely suffer; it occurs almost exclusively in unacclimatised infants or adolescents who are pushing themselves to the limits of endurance during sport or play. Collapse is usually caused by a combination of dehydration and over-heating. In any age the first symptoms are exhaustion and profuse sweating, and babies become very irritable. Sweating then stops as they become dehydrated and lose consciousness. Treatment is to cool the body and give drinks; if the victim is unconscious a drip will be necessary in hospital.

The younger the infant, the higher his risk of over-heating in extremely hot places. When inside the house small children need wear nothing but a nappy/diaper or underpants. And splashing in tepid water will cool a hot fractious child. Outside put on loose-fitting, 100%-cotton clothes; T-shirts are hotter than floppy thin cottons; and be careful of direct sunlight, even inside vehicles. Heat exhaustion is common in people stuck in traffic jams in tropical cities. If you are driving, arrange some sort of window shade; a white cloth over the restraining strap of the car's child-seat will do; or buy one from Boots. Never leave your infant unattended in a car; cars can act like a garden glasshouse slowly cooking anyone inside!

A child who, after being energetic in the heat, becomes lethargic, flushed and very sweaty is probably over-heated and needs to sit in a shady place, drink and cool off. If the child is nauseated heatstroke may be setting in and active steps need to be taken to cool him: remove clothes, and fan and sponge with a wet cloth. Heatstroke is sometimes erroneously called sunstroke; but it is caused by the heat rather than by exposure to sun.

MOUNTAINS, THE COLD AND ALTITUDE SICKNESS

Two hazards may not spring to mind when planning a mountain journey. The first is that sun at altitude, especially if reflected off snow, is very strong and sizzles skin; it is possible to get sunburned inside the nose, so don't forget to anoint under it and inside. Secondly, the Himalayan region and central Andes are also hot-spots for filth-to-mouth diseases: even on a trek there is a significant risk of severe diarrhoea.

The cold and preventing hypothermia

Children who are not old enough to walk are at particular risk of getting cold in the mountains or in cold windy conditions. You will be sweating up some steep path with the child on your back and it is easy to overlook that she is getting cold. Padded sleep-suits are perfect for trekking infants, for if the weather warms up you can free their top half but keep the legs warm. Once children are toddling they become more difficult both to entertain and to keep warm. They want to be down playing in muddy puddles and are frustrated by being carried for long periods. Keep at least one change of clothing readily available. It can be difficult keeping them warm at night too. Some kind of suit or bag which is designed to stop them wriggling out is what you need, but what you take depends on the temperament of the toddler. Some like being bundled up in bags and jackets; while others will be furious and will be hard to settle for the night. Experiment at home first. Older children usually enjoy the adventure of sleeping in a bag.

Babies and small children lose a lot of heat from their disproportionately large heads and so in cold – as well as sunny – climates they need hats. Remember that when you go out in the cold, you keep warm by moving while your child may be lying still. Wind-chill is something else to consider if you are carrying the child in a pack. Wrap him up carefully and frequently check that he feels warm. If you are using a backpack, you can feel his feet without breaking stride! For mountain treks or cold sea voyages, a mini sleeping-bag can be extremely valuable; often you can get a local tailor to make what you need.

If your child may be put at risk of hypothermia (you are planning a trek in high mountains for instance), then you may wish to pack a low-reading mercury thermometer since standard clinical thermometers do not read below 35°C. Any child with a temperature below **36°C** is getting dangerously cold and you need to find shelter and get him warm. You can assess the temperature of your child without a low-reading thermometer. Compare the temperature of his abdomen and his legs; these will feel equally warm if he is warm, whereas if he is struggling to maintain his temperature he will have cool legs and a warm abdomen. A child who is losing the battle to maintain his body heat will feel equally cold on the abdomen and the legs. Traditional birth attendants use this scheme to recognise hypothermia in babies in Indian villages.

Altitude

'How soon can I take my baby to altitude, and how high can we go?' 'At what age is a trip to high altitude safe?' The difficulty about mountain sickness is that it is unpredictable so it is difficult to give absolute guidelines. Children are probably no more likely to suffer from mountain sickness than adults but it can be very difficult to diagnose warning symptoms in children under two years of age. Children, like adults, must simply be allowed time to acclimatise to altitude while parents stay alert to danger signs. Diamox (*acetazolamide*), the medicine used to speed up acclimatisation, is occasionally used for children. Anyone ascending to 2,500m/8,000ft with children must be aware of the dangers and know the kinds of symptoms which might indicate that the child is developing mountain sickness. Dangerous altitude sickness is rare (even in adults) below an altitude of 2,500m/8,000ft. Sleeping high is riskier than walking over a pass. The only treatment is descent; so plan any trek to above 2,500m in such a way that a rapid descent of at least 500m/1,500ft is always possible. It would probably be unwise to venture much above 3,000m/10,000ft on a first trek with children and few would risk going above 4,500m/15,000ft. Children do survive higher altitudes; indeed in spring 1996 a Japanese father climbed Island Peak near Everest with his one-year-old on his back and the child survived the ascent to over 20,000ft (6,189m). The higher you go and the faster you ascend, the greater is the risk. It is dangerous to venture high for a child with **sickle cell** trait or disease and for some children with **cystic fibrosis**; **asthmatics** should be at no increased risk although the cold and new trigger factors may precipitate an attack. There may be an increased risk of altitude sickness if the child has a cold when heading up into the mountains; watch for any deterioration and descend if in doubt.

The most strenuous ages to travel with a child are between the beginning-to-crawl stage and about two to three years when they start to become reasonable and controllable (everything is relative, though). Jane has enjoyed a dozen treks in Nepal with young children from the age of three months, but has not felt the need to venture above 3,500m/12,500ft; it is not necessary to ascend to extreme altitudes to enjoy breathtaking scenery. Travel to Tibet is probably unwise: whether you fly or drive in, it is not possible to acclimatise and a few children have died from mountain sickness there. Similarly rapid ascents by road (eg: in Colorado) or rail (eg: in Peru) or aeroplane (eg: to La Paz, Mexico City or Ladakh) may be risky. Even the most experienced mountain doctors will find it tricky to identify early mountain sickness in children under the age of two; they become whingy, but I can't reliably distinguish between unhappiness because of a cold, *the* cold, wind in the face, sheer boredom or fluid accumulating in the brain. Anyone (and especially a child) who is off colour at an altitude of 2,500m/8,000ft or above should be assumed to have mountain sickness and the treatment is to descend. Going down 500–1,000m or 2,000–3,000ft should bring about an improvement.

Falls

Toddlers may find precipitous drops off mountain paths fascinating. And they may be attracted to fierce Tibetan guard dogs. Any large domestic animals that you encounter on a mountain path should be respected for their ability to push people off. Male animals are worst and even a medium-sized ram could unbalance an adult enough for him to topple over. Stand to the uphill side of the path. Mules and yaks push many unwary adult trekkers off paths in Nepal each year.

HAZARDS: A SUMMARY

This chapter has dwelt on a selection of exotic and rare environmental hazards, but it is important to keep in mind that the biggest hazard to the whole family is an accident. Third World cars are seldom properly maintained, functional seat belts are often not in place and child-seats are unheard of; hotels and other institutions are not set up as child-safe environments and you must assume nothing is safe.

- Don't worry about snakes, but insist your child wears shoes on the beach.
- Avoid mosquito bites between dusk and dawn. In malarious areas travel with impregnated bed-nets for each member of the family.
- Become safety conscious when travelling.
- Anticipate dangers and supervise the children carefully.

Part Two

Accidents and Illnesses

INTRODUCTION TO PART TWO

This part of the book deals with the treatment of illness and accidents in travelling children. Most apparent disasters are not disasters at all; and illnesses rarely cause more than a hiccup in your travel plans or a bit of mess. We have described the full range of possible illnesses, from trivial to serious, not to alarm you but so that you can assess the situation rationally if your child is ill. The text is designed to be used in isolation, but always seek competent medical advice if you can.

Tackling problems

Accidents are the number-one cause of health problems and deaths amongst travellers of all ages. *Chapter 8* covers emergencies and first aid. Major as well as common minor injuries are described and correct treatments explained.

Exotic tropical diseases and horrendous infections are uncommon amongst travellers although everyone worries about them. The commonest illnesses affecting travelling families are diarrhoea and then skin infections. Next come the mundane infections we get at home: coughs, colds, tonsillitis, etc. They occur in hot climates too. The following chapters list the illnesses most likely to assail travelling children, with the information divided into two age-groups: infants up to one year of age (*Chapter 9*) and children over one year up to adolescents (*Chapter 10*).

We begin by highlighting danger signs of serious illness; these mean you must act quickly and take the relevant action described which usually involves getting to hospital fast. We have clearly indicated the degree of urgency involved in different situations. If there is no danger sign then you have time to browse the relevant text.

MAIN DANGER SIGNS
- Stops breathing
- Has a convulsion
- Is unconscious
- Is uncharacteristically drowsy
- Is inconsolable
- Eyes are glazed
- Is unable to feed, drink or speak
- Has a non-blanching rash
- Has chest indrawing or fast laboured or noisy breathing
- Is vomiting everything
- Mouth looks dry inside

In these cases see page 129 for an infant or page 148 for a child over one year of age.

After danger signs we focus on specific signs and symptoms. Each problem is described, tips are offered for gauging the severity and advice is given on how quickly (if at all) you need to seek medical help. Fever is often a sign of a treatable illness and some notes are given (page 130) on how to measure a child's temperature.

We also cover the proper management of the common and trivial diseases that assault children anywhere. Do-it-yourself treatment guidelines are given, but we suggest that you use these to compare notes with a local doctor: see if you agree with his diagnosis. Quality of medical care is never predictable or uniform so you may want to check whether the local medic has recommended an appropriate treatment. If you are concerned the treatment does not seem right ask about it. Most doctors will discuss the situation with foreign parents, although some may be bewildered by lay-people who are well informed about health. If you are still not satisfied, seek a second opinion from another doctor.

HOW TO SEEK HELP

We encourage you to seek medical advice wherever possible. However, when things go wrong you may not know where to turn and it can be difficult to find competent medical help. In the West the local hospital emergency department provides the easiest access to a medical opinion, but in the developing world hospitals can be very crowded and not easy places to find your way around, especially if you are panicking about your child. It will often be easier to see one of the paediatricians privately (a telephone directory will list the top consultants' private clinics). If you are in a capital city your embassy will probably know how to locate a competent doctor. In a reasonably large hotel, the staff should be able to suggest some reliable practitioners; otherwise expatriates may be able to help.

HOSPITAL CARE

If you find yourself in a hospital with your child always insist on staying with him. You should always be allowed to do so, even if this means a rough night for you on the floor. The commonest cause of disaster in paediatrics is a failure to recognise a **change** in the child's condition. If you feel he is deteriorating and the hospital staff don't notice, be assertive and draw it to their attention. In serious situations you should make contingency plans for medical evacuation but you will not be able to travel until the child is stable. Embassy staff are usually brilliant in this situation, and should be able to advise on where to evacuate to. In Asia, Bangkok offers good clinical facilities, and so does Singapore but care is more expensive. In Africa, Nairobi and South Africa have good centres for sophisticated medical treatment. In Central and South America head for a capital city, or Miami.

Trust your instincts. Only you really know your child. If you think something is wrong, even if all the experts disagree you are probably right! No single handbook can deal with every situation you may face whilst travelling. If you cannot find advice which fits your particular problem and you are worried, seek help from a doctor, but also let us know so that we can improve future editions of the book.

Accidents, Emergencies and Minor Injuries

This chapter covers (in this order): resuscitation; choking; unconsciousness; drowning; electrocutions; something stuck in the throat; fits; severe bleeding; blood transfusions; cuts and grazes; burns and scalds; sunburn; bruises; sprains and strains; broken bones; pulled elbow; head injury; swallowing noxious things; eye problems; ear problems; nose problems; bleeding under a nail; toothache; knocked-out teeth.

If you can't locate what you need, try the *Index*.

TREATMENT AFTER AN ACCIDENT OR EMERGENCY
Resuscitation
The big difficulty about emergency situations is that you need to assess calmly what has happened and decide on priorities at a time when it is difficult to be calm; if the casualty is your own child it is impossible. In the case of an apparently severe injury, take things strictly in sequence. Assess the situation. And keep your own safety in mind too. The letters of the word **SAFE** will remind you of the recommended sequence of actions when faced with an emergency:

Shout for help

Approach with care

Free from danger

Evaluate

- Ask 'Are you all right?' whilst gently stroking the child.
- If she responds, stay with her until help arrives, remaining alert to any change in her condition.
- If the child does not respond, **Look** for chest movements, **Listen** for breath sounds and **Feel** for breath.
- If the child is not breathing move on to the **ABC** priorities:
  AIRWAY, **BREATHING**, **CIRCULATION**.

The ABC of resuscitation
A is for airway The breathing tubes must be open and clear to allow air to reach the lungs. The airway should be opened using the head-tilt/chin-lift manoeuvre. The rescuer places the hand nearest to the child's head on the forehead and applies pressure to tilt the head gently back, whilst gently lifting

the chin with the forefingers of the other hand. Attempt to remove any visible object in the mouth only if it is obvious. If there has been a car accident and you suspect that a badly smashed face is the reason she can't breathe, pull her jaw forward and slightly upwards to help free the windpipe. If removing the blockage allows breathing to restart, put her into the unconscious position until she wakes up (see *Unconsciousness,* page 110).

B is for breathing If the child is not breathing you must breathe for her by mouth-to-mouth resuscitation. Lie her on her back and clear any muck or objects from her mouth and nose. Tip her head back so that the front of the neck looks long. Then get into a position to blow some air into her lungs. With a small child you can seal both the nose and around the mouth with your mouth; with someone larger pinch the soft part of the nose closed with your index finger and thumb and rest the side of that same hand on her forehead. Open her mouth a little but keep her chin up. Take a breath and place your lips around her mouth making sure you have a good seal. Give five rescue breaths, each of which should make her chest rise and fall. If the child's cheeks inflate, the airway to the lungs is not clear and you probably need to tip her head back further. Blow steadily into her mouth over one to one-and-a-half seconds watching for her chest to rise. Maintaining the victim's head tilt, remove your mouth and watch for her chest to fall as the air comes out. Take another breath and repeat this sequence two to five times. Two effective breaths is the minimum per attempt. If you are having difficulty achieving an effective breath, the airway must be obstructed. Recheck her mouth for any obstruction and check that the head is properly tilted back. If this still does not help, move on to the routine for choking described opposite.

If the child vomits during resuscitation turn her on her side; wait for the vomiting to subside and then clear her mouth again and continue mouth-to-mouth resuscitation. Continue doing this until the child starts to breathe or medical help arrives.

C is for circulation Check for a pulse in the neck or groin, or listen for the heart-beat with your ear against her chest. If you can feel any pulses then the circulation is adequate. If there is no pulse then you must pump the heart artificially. By pushing down on the ribcage, in the middle of the breastbone (sternum), you can help pump blood around the body. This is called EXTERNAL CARDIAC MASSAGE and it is taught on first-aid courses. Do three quick short and sharp pumps to start with and then try to adopt a rhythm of five heart pumps to one artificial breath. The amount of pressure you apply depends upon the size of the child, and novices are more likely to be too gentle than too rough. Aim to compress the chest by about a third of the depth of the chest.

In a **CHILD**, apply the heel of one hand to the lower end of the breastbone (with the fingers raised) and apply the weight of your body by rocking forward with your arms straight. The breastbone should be compressed about one third of the depth of the child's chest. Release the pressure and repeat at the rate of about 100 times a minute (a little less than two compressions a second). In a big child (over about eight) you may need to use two hands placed on top of each other. Give cardiac compressions and breaths in the ratio of 5:1.

For a **BABY**, apply two fingertips and press the middle of the breastbone just below an imaginary line connecting the nipples. Aim to compress the chest by one-third of its depth. After five compressions tilt the head back and give one effective breath. Continue at the rate of five cardiac compressions to one breath.

Continue until:

- the child shows signs of life or
- qualified help arrives or
- you become exhausted.

Successful resuscitation is unlikely after an hour unless the victim was extremely cold. Even if the child is extremely cold, you cannot be sure she is dead (even if there are no signs of life) until she is rewarmed, so keep up resuscitation if you can (you will need a team) until the victim is warm. There was a case of a fisherman who fell overboard beneath the ice in the Arctic and was underwater for 40 minutes. He should have drowned but the cold saved him. He was revived and suffered no ill effects.

Note You cannot learn effective resuscitation from a book – anyone travelling to a remote place should go on a first-aid course or learn resuscitation at life-saving (swimming) or scuba-diving training. Effective resuscitation is very difficult single-handed; at the outset of an emergency, call or send for help. Once you have begun **ABC** show someone else what to do for either breathing or circulation and work together as a team until more help arrives.

Choking

If a child chokes, or collapses and goes blue, it is likely that she has inhaled an object, piece of toy or food. Five sharp blows on the back between the shoulder blades may dislodge the object; this can be done with the child standing or lying on her front. A baby can be held upside-down and smartly slapped on the back five times. If this does not work, the offending object can be forced out by applying pressure sharply to the lungs or to the abdomen as described next; the technique depends upon the size of the child.

Child

An unconscious child should be laid on her back, face up. Sit astride her hips and, placing one hand on top of the other, thrust down on to the abdomen between the belly button and the bottom of the ribcage; the three or four thrusts should be at an angle downwards and towards the victim's head. Remove the expelled object from her mouth and place the child in the unconscious position. The chest thrust, applying force to the bottom of the ribcage, can also be used successfully in this situation. The technique for chest thrusts is similar to that for chest compressions to aid circulation, but thrusts should be sharper and more vigorous and at the rate of about 20 per minute.

Baby

Lay the baby face up on your lap with her head on your knees; put the tips of two fingers of each hand side by side on the lower ribcage. Press gently but firmly upwards five times. Remove the object from her mouth. The object does not always appear. Whatever it was may be coughed up and then swallowed and you may never know what caused the panic. Abdominal thrusts are not recommended for babies because of the risk of damaging internal organs.

If, after three or four cycles of attempts, things don't seem to be improving and you are close to a clinic or hospital, let the child adopt whatever position is most comfortable to her and get her to the clinic for urgent attention.

Unconsciousness

Any period of unconsciousness after an accident implies a serious problem. Try to arrange medical assistance immediately. Check your **ABC** as above, meanwhile keep the child in the unconscious position which ensures that any vomit will harmlessly dribble out of the mouth rather than into the lungs. To put someone who is lying on her back into the **unconscious** or **recovery position**, start by kneeling beside her. Then tilt her head and lift her chin to open the airway. Straighten both legs. Place the arm nearer to you out at a right angle but bent at the elbow and with her palm resting upwards, like a policeman stopping traffic. Bring the far arm across her chest and hold her hand, palm outwards, against her near cheek. With your other hand grasp the further thigh and pull the upper leg up so that it is bent at the knee while the foot remains on the ground. Keeping her hand pressed against her cheek, pull her towards you so that she rolls on to her side. Tilt her head back so that the neck is long. If necessary, adjust the hand so that the head is well supported. And adjust the uppermost (bent) leg so that both the knee and hip on that side are flexed to a right angle. Check breathing and pulse often. It's less complicated than it sounds.

If this is too much to work out in the heat of the moment, then lying the victim on her front with her face turned to one side is safe. The important thing is to have the mouth lower than the chest so that any vomit trickles out harmlessly. Do not put a pillow under the head of an unconscious person.

Unconscious and not breathing

Give mouth-to-mouth artificial respiration, and consider whether external cardiac massage is necessary. Check for a pulse in the neck or groin, or listen for the heart-beat with your ear against her chest.

Unconscious but breathing

Put into the unconscious position (see above) and call for medical help. Never leave an unconscious person alone in case she stops breathing.

Drowning

Treatment after near drowning is similar to that in other causes of unconsciousness. Start with ABC – is there a pulse and breathing? If not, start artificial respiration, and consider whether external cardiac massage is needed.

Victims of drowning have often swallowed a lot of water so usually vomit profusely, many times. It is especially important, therefore, to put them into the unconscious position if they are breathing but unconscious. Once they have woken up they should be fine but admission to hospital for observation is sensible. If the child did not lose consciousness there is no need for any special action.

As long as good resuscitation is given promptly, near-drowned children can recover after remarkably long periods of not breathing for themselves; so do not abandon resuscitation attempts unless you have been trying for an hour. It may be rewarding to continue even longer if the child is cold; you can only be sure she is dead once she is thoroughly rewarmed.

Electrocutions and electric shock

A **high-voltage** electric shock (for example from a railway line or the big power cables carried on pylons which supply whole areas with electricity) causes two types of damage. First, the wave of electricity can cause the heart to short-circuit and stop. Do not approach the victim until officially informed that the current has been disconnected centrally. Until then, the victim will remain 'live', putting the rescuer at risk of electrocution within a metre or so. Then check the pulse. If there is no pulse start external cardiac massage (see pages 108–9).

The second and commoner problem is burns. There may be extensive burn damage near the site of electrical contact, although the outer skin surface may look perfectly normal because the current will damage the body along a line between the point of contact and the part of the body in touch with the ground. Children who have experienced a high-voltage shock must be observed in hospital.

Shocks more commonly come from badly insulated domestic supplies or from a child biting into a live lead. These are relatively **low-voltage** and cause only burns. First turn off the electricity supply or push or pull the child off the live wire using a wooden broom, wooden chair-leg or some other non-metallic object. Sometimes you can kick the casualty off the wire or pull the wire away from the child by holding on to an insulated part. Once you are happy the child is all right (ie: breathing and crying), examine the area of electrical contact for burns and get her seen in a hospital if the burns are bad. If the child did not become unconscious there will have been no damage to the heart; and burns (and subsequent skin infections) are your only worry.

Something stuck in the throat

Sometimes after eating fish or chicken it may feel as if a bone has stuck in the throat, but this is rare: more often the throat has only been scratched in which case no treatment is necessary. If a foreign body has stuck in the throat it will be very painful or even impossible to swallow saliva, and the large quantities of additional saliva that are secreted in this case will be spat out. The neck will often also feel very tender on prodding from the outside. The definitive test of whether it is a scratch or whether there is something stuck is to wait for 12–24 hours while taking a cool soft diet (like yoghurt, but not ice-cream unless you are somewhere hygienic please!). People with a scratch will improve whilst those with something stuck will feel worse. While you are waiting offer *paracetamol* syrup. The treatment of something stuck in the throat is its removal in hospital under general anaesthetic.

A fit, convulsion, seizure or funny turn

Most fits, although terrifying to witness, are benign. Do not force anything between the teeth. Clear furniture away. Check the child cannot injure herself – the safest place is on a carpet on the floor. When the fit has subsided roll her on to her side. Check the temperature of her forehead with your hand and if she feels hot cool her down by opening her clothes, rubbing her with a wet cloth and turning a fan on her. Give rectal *diazepam* if you have it with you. If the fit continues beyond five minutes consider heading for a hospital if you can. You may repeat the *diazepam* dose once after a five-minute interval. If the fit is still going after ten minutes and you have no hospital option, it is time to send for any paramedic available.

Otherwise wait for the fit to subside and, as the child relaxes, check there is no debris or vomit in her mouth and that she is still breathing. Place her in the unconscious position and then organise somewhere for her to sleep it off. If this is the first time she has had a fit seek a medical consultation; if the child is unwell with a fever seek medical help urgently since it is important to be sure that the fit has not been caused by a dangerous infection like meningitis or cerebral malaria. Fits are also discussed on pages 153–4.

Severe external bleeding

Press where the blood is coming from and raise the bleeding part above the height of the heart; do not use a tourniquet. Larger cuts may bleed excessively but most bleeding will stop with firm pressure for five minutes. Ideally you should press on the bleeding-site with a clean handkerchief or similar cloth, but usually you will have none and it is all right to grab the wound with your hand and hold it firmly. Don't worry about sterility; stopping the bleeding is the priority. Bleeding is cleansing and you will be able to clean the wound later. If you can, strap the wound with a firm bandage or a strip of cloth; don't worry if it is grubby. Wrap up the wound with whatever is available; if the bleeding seems to be continuing wrap more layers on and do not be tempted to check whether the bleeding has stopped; removing any bandage or compress from a big wound before a few hours have elapsed is bound to start it bleeding again.

If, despite all this, the bleeding continues, the child needs stitches. This is only likely if a major artery has been cut; which is possible if there is a deep wound at the wrist, elbow, neck or in the groin when bright-red blood will spurt at the rate of the pulse from the cut artery. Transport the casualty to an emergency centre whilst maintaining firm pressure over the site of the bleeding at all times.

When does a cut need stitches?

Stitches (or sutures) are used to pull the wound edges together. Competent doctors who have worked in the tropics long-term discourage immediate stitching of most wounds. Stitching can seal foreign bodies and dirt into an

ABOUT BLOOD TRANSFUSIONS

It is possible that your child may lose so much blood after an accident that a blood transfusion is required; but this is risky since HIV (AIDS) and several other unpleasant infections are common and testing blood is still patchy, although the Red Cross are working hard to help introduce screening worldwide.

Within the first hours of an injury lost blood can be replaced with artificial solutions, which are free of the risk of infection as long as the needles and equipment are clean. If doctors want to transfuse your child with blood you should check with the most senior doctor available that this cannot await emergency evacuation. If blood transfusion is urgently necessary, offer yourself as a donor. The Blood Care Foundation will courier 'fully screened and tested blood' to its members anywhere in the world in an emergency (address page 191). Even better would be for all members of the family to have their blood group established to see who could donate to whom.

inadequately cleaned wound and is inadvisable after animal bites or deep penetrating wounds since neither can be cleaned properly. There is no harm in waiting a week or ten days before stitching, as long as the wound is kept clean and covered. Cleaning the wound after any injury is crucial; dressings can then be applied (and changed daily) and later you can attend a clinic where you feel confident in the competence of the medical attendant, where new or sterilised equipment is used and where there will be a good cosmetic result. In many places you may have to go shopping for the syringe and needles from a stall outside the hospital, or offer to pay extra.

Lacerations or cuts or bites on the face or scalp bleed profusely and usually look horrendous. These may require stitching for cosmetic reasons. If the wound is somewhere under the hair you can often pull the edges of it together (thus reducing the bleeding) by tying together strands of hair from each side of the wound; this works best on children with thick curly hair and less well on those with straight fine blonde hair. Before pulling the edges together, clean up and also try to tease out any hair that is inside the wound; it will delay healing. After a day or two when the cut is healing, the hair-knot can be cut out and the head gently washed.

Alternatives to stitches

Steristrips are miniature sticky tapes which serve as an alternative to stitches in some situations. Their main disadvantage is that they do not stick well if the skin surface is wet with blood or water, so are not much use if the wound is bleeding a great deal. However, most wounds will stop bleeding in time. Clean up the wound. Flood with antiseptic such as dilute iodine or potassium permanganate solution. Dab it dry with a clean cloth. If the bleeding continues, elevate the bleeding part and press with a clean cloth. Try pulling the wound edges together with the Steristrips after ten minutes or so.

Butterfly closures are another useful alternative. You can either buy them, or make them by snipping two triangles out of each side of the central part of an oblong sticking-plaster or Band-aid; giving the Elastoplast a 'waist' means it works better at pulling wound edges together. Use several along the wound.

Cuts and grazes

If your child is going through a phase of falling over all the time, consider clothes that will help protect the knees and elbows. Children are always grazing their knees and elbows but in hot steamy climates you must take special care to stop wounds getting infected. Any wound or break in the skin surface needs to be cleaned and then kept clean and dry. First wash with soap and plenty of tap or hand-pump water; such water need not be sterile, just use lots. If water is at a premium, dribble it from your water bottle on to the wound while doing the cleaning. During this process, check and remove any muck or gravel. A clean cotton gauze or handkerchief will help you tease out such foreign bodies, and can be dabbed on the surrounding skin afterwards to dry the area. If there is a lot of bleeding you can use a poultice made by scrunching up whole woundwort (*Stachys*); this will help to stem the flow.

Woundwort

These herbs, which often have blue flowers, belong in the thyme family and are common in Europe and many temperate parts of Asia. If you have antiseptic (dilute iodine or potassium permanganate solution are best), drip this on next. If you are in an area with lots of flies or if the child is likely to investigate the wound with his fingers, cover it with a sticking-plaster/Band-aid. Plasters and dressings are not necessary in the vast majority of cases; sometimes, of course, they help the child feel brave, although removal can be uncomfortable too. If the child has not received the course of three DPT injections (which are usually given in the first six months of life) tetanus is a risk. An unimmunised child with a deep dirty wound should have an injection of tetanus *immunoglobulin* as soon as possible, but anyway within four days of the injury. Tetanus *immunoglobulin* is different from the childhood tetanus immunisation.

Spreading redness

If the wound becomes infected it will look red and angry, and will throb and become more uncomfortable. Scrupulous cleaning followed by dabbing with a drying antiseptic solution (dilute iodine or potassium permanganate solution) each time you change the plaster or dressing will stop the infection before it gets a hold. These measures work best if the graze is small and the infection limited to a minor area of redness around the actual wound. If infection has penetrated a little deeper, the area of redness will extend a centimetre (half an inch) or more from the wound site or there may be red tracks spreading away from the wound towards the heart. There may be gunk oozing from the wound site, and/or swelling and/or fever. In this case the wound needs to be thoroughly cleaned again, rubbing rather than dabbing with cotton wool or a scrap of clean cloth dipped in antiseptic; and check again for foreign bodies under a good light since any little pieces of grit, wood or glass will act as a focus for the infection. An infected wound will probably require a course of antibiotics by mouth so you should consult a doctor unless you feel confident you can deal with the situation yourself. A good antibiotic to choose for infected wounds is a combination of *flucloxacillin* (or *cloxacillin*) and *penicillin*. Infected animal bites are best treated with *co-amoxiclav* (Augmentin) if possible; all these antibiotics are *penicillins* so in *penicillin*-allergic people use *erythromycin* alone (doses are given in *Chapter 3, page 36*). If the infection does not start to improve dramatically within 36 hours the wound needs to be reassessed by a doctor.

Wound care

In hot moist climates, any wound or break in the skin is likely to let in infection. Animal and especially human (!) bites are particularly prone to becoming infected. Clean and sterilise any breaks in the skin. You may need to be rather brutal to get the wound clean enough. Promptly treat any areas of spreading redness (see above). Change any dressings daily; particularly in the

HOT BUFFALO MILK

We were on a luxurious trek beneath Dhaulagiri himal in western Nepal and had stopped while the Sherpas cooked lunch. They had spread out a huge tarpaulin for us on a fallow rice terrace and ten-month-old Sebastian crawled around excitedly chasing grasshoppers, ants and flies. I did not notice the Sherpa cook putting a shiny steel jug full of freshly boiled buffalo milk down on the tarpaulin; this attracted Sebastian's attention and he crawled over to it and tipped it over his hands. Hearing the shriek I looked around to see that both his hands and knees were still in a puddle of boiling milk. I snatched him up and ran with him to a nearby irrigation stream and thrust him in. The scalds did not seem too bad, but whenever I removed Sebastian's hands from the water he started crying again, so he sat on my lap with his hands in a bowl of cold water until after about 20 minutes he was happy. He got only a couple of small blisters on one wrist where his clothes had kept the water from his skin, and his crawling-hardened knees were only a little red. The wrist blisters remained intact for a day then burst and dried out without needing any special dressing, despite the wrist being a difficult area to keep clean in a crawling child.

When Alexander was six months we were in Swat, Pakistan. He was sitting happily burbling on my lap while I supped some after-dinner coffee. Suddenly he plunged his hand into my cup. I should have poured the jug of drinking water over his hand but did not think of that and took him off for a soak in the en-suite bathroom in our room. He suffered quite a nasty little scald where the hot-coffee-soaked sleeve was against his skin. Speed is crucial in getting the scalded part cool.

first days after injury, bathe in dilute potassium permanganate solution, dilute iodine or another drying antiseptic three times a day.

Burns and scalds
First aid
If your child is burned or scalded, immediately plunge the burnt or scalded part into cold water and keep it in cold water until it stops feeling hot and uncomfortable – for up to an hour. This not only soothes the burning sensation but also helps to limit damage. A delicate burn blister will form after some hours. This is a good natural dressing; it will almost always burst.

Severe burns
Extensive burns and scalds are a reason for evacuation to somewhere where they can be meticulously dressed and affected limbs elevated in slings to minimise swelling. Any burn or scald larger than the child's hand needs to be assessed at a hospital or clinic. Wrap the burnt or scalded surfaces in a clean damp cloth before heading for hospital. In a very extensive burn, body fluids leak out under the damaged skin as a huge blister or directly from the raw skin surface and this can cause dehydration; the child will then need intravenous fluids in hospital. Burns become infected very easily. You are unlikely to manage to keep bad burns adequately clean if you are somewhere remote.

Treatment of minor burns and scalds
Burns and scalds need to be kept covered and dry; it is best to use a dressing with a plasticised, non-stick, non-fibre surface (eg: Melolin) which can be kept in place with tape such as Micropore. Burns and scalds easily become infected because they ooze; watch closely for spreading redness and other signs of infection (see pages 114–15). Do not prick blisters. Do not apply any creams or potions. For those burns bad enough to need any treatment *silver sulphadiazine* (Flamazine) is often applied in clinics and hospital and is safe, but if the burn is bad you should be seeking medical help.

Smoke inhalation
If a child has been caught inside a burning building and has breathed in hot smoke or steam there is a danger of the airways becoming swollen over the next few hours, causing breathing difficulty. Such a child should be observed in hospital for 24 hours.

Sunburn
Bathe with cool water or cold compresses if it is uncomfortable; *calamine* lotion (which is rarely available abroad) and *paracetamol* syrup will also help. Never deliberately puncture blisters. Oily preparations keep in the heat and make sunburn feel worse. *Silver sulphadiazine* (Flamazine) should also help if the sunburn is severe. If the sunburn is extensive the child can be at risk of losing a lot of body heat and can become hypothermic. Give her plenty to drink. Like any other wounds, sunburn leaves the skin open to infection so take note of the advice above on wound care and treatment after minor burns.

CHINESE NOODLES

Iris Gowen, Beijing

We had secured two adjoining soft-berth compartments on the overnight train from Beijing to Xian. For simplicity's sake, I'd decided to prepare bowls of instant noodles for our dinner. Since the train was moving rapidly, I put the bowls on the floor to 'cook'. Suddenly – in the excitement of travelling with four other children – nine-year-old Madeleine jumped across the compartment, stepped right into a bowl, and began to scream. I pulled off her sock, and ran with her to the wash room at the far end of the car, stuck her foot in the sink and ran cold water over it. Part of her foot had gone white, with the top layers of skin flapping loosely. We were quickly surrounded by a circle of Chinese trying to offer sympathy and advice.

I called a paediatrician colleague of my husband's in Beijing on my cell phone. He told us that alternating *ibuprofen* with *paracetamol* (Tylenol) would control the pain, and advised keeping her foot in a basin of water for as long as possible, changing the water throughout the night to keep it cool. Even more important, he was able to give these directions and persuade the train personnel NOT to stop the train and have us deposited in rural China in the middle of the night. I was grateful to understand enough Chinese to have been able to hear and politely disagree with this plan, but I needed his intervention and expert Chinese to convince them.

We wrapped her foot to keep it clean when we carried her through the chaos of the Xian train station at dawn. A physician in Xian confirmed that Madeleine had second-degree burns, and taught me how to clean and change her dressings until we flew back to Beijing next day.

Bruises

Bruising is bleeding under the skin and, since blood in the wrong place is a highly irritant substance, bruises hurt. Cold compresses help a little and elevating the injured part (eg: propping an arm up on pillows after the child has gone to sleep) will reduce the extent of bruising. Once the bruise starts to disperse, it will dribble down under gravity going through an attractive range of colours as it fades. Exercising the affected part aids healing.

Sprains and strains

The treatment of a strained or pulled muscle is rest if it hurts a lot and exercise as the pain fades; children are perhaps better than adults in realising when to and when not to use an injured part. If the child does not want to rest he does not need to!

A lot of swelling implies a more severe injury – a sprain or break. A sprain occurs when a joint is forced past its normal limit of movement and the soft tissue around it is damaged and becomes swollen and painful. In a bad sprain the child will not wish to put any weight on the affected part because it hurts so much; then it can be difficult to distinguish from a fracture. As a rule any sprain that is severe enough to prevent the child using the affected part should be checked out by a doctor to make sure nothing is broken.

If the injured part is very painful, rest and elevation of the swollen part (eg: propping it up on pillows in bed) will help and so will *paracetamol* and/or *ibuprofen* plus cold compresses. It may be possible to improvise an ice pack by putting ice cubes (in a plastic bag or condom) wrapped in a cloth, otherwise a cloth soaked in cool water is almost as good. A crêpe bandage may be helpful to limit movement of the affected joint as the patient starts to want to get up. As soon as the pain eases the child should be encouraged to start gently moving the affected joint and then build up to using it more normally. Generally exercising a sprain aids healing and no harm will be done by a child walking on a sprained ankle 'too soon'; there is no need to try to restrict the child's activities (you won't succeed anyway).

Broken bones

Broken bones (fractures) are unusual in the infant and toddler but become increasingly common as children grow older. A broken limb bone will be extremely painful and the child will be unable to move it; nor will she allow you to move even a fractured little finger. The affected limb will be swollen and may look misshapen (compare it with the other uninjured side). In the worst cases there may be a grating sensation as the broken bones rub against each other. In a more serious injury the thigh bone can break, in which case the child may be seriously ill due to the invisible loss of blood into the thigh muscle. If you suspect a break you should transport the child to a clinic or hospital. Keep her warm and as still as possible because the more the broken bone moves the more pain and shock the child will suffer.

When you arrive at the hospital the doctor will probably ask how the injury occurred; the position in which the child fell sometimes helps him set the bone correctly so try to demonstrate the position of the fall! Usually an X-ray will be taken; if the arm or leg is involved, the joints above and below the injury should also be X-rayed since they may also be damaged.

In a simple undisplaced fracture, the bones will still be in their correct position and will heal well provided they are kept still in a cast. Usually a broken limb is too swollen to apply complete plaster immediately, so a 'back slab' or half-plaster is applied. It is important to avoid flying with a new fracture in a complete plaster so this might be the time to go home or go somewhere with good facilities to amuse an immobilised child. Then a few days later a full plaster is put on. Since this will immobilise the child for weeks it is important to ensure that the fingers or toes are kept open when the full plaster is applied. In addition check that the fingers or toes do not go pale, cold, blue or numb over the next 24 hours; this suggests that the plaster is too tight and could cause permanent nerve damage; in this case return immediately to the clinic to see if it needs to be cut open. A plaster will probably need to stay on for a month to six weeks but the times vary according to the nature and position of the break and the age of the child. If the skin is broken close to the fracture (a compound fracture), antibiotics will be given to avoid the serious risk of osteomyelitis; such injuries should be seen by an orthopaedic surgeon.

If bones are displaced from their natural position they will need to be moved back, usually under anaesthetic. In the worst cases badly damaged joints may require metal pins and plates to hold them in place during healing. This is rarely necessary in an emergency and you should consider where the right place is for your child to undergo this complex and specialised surgery.

Pulled elbow

This is a very common injury in children between the ages of two and four. It is caused by a sharp pull on the toddler's arm, usually by a parent trying to raise up a child or take her in one direction whilst she has other ideas. The child cries immediately and will refuse to move the elbow. The problem is minor and at home would be treated by a casualty officer or in an emergency room; but if it happens when you are days from a clinic you may wish to treat it yourself, so that your child will become comfortable again as quickly as possible. You need to be firm but do not need to use any force.

With one hand, steady the child's upper arm by holding it (between the shoulder and the injured elbow) so that she does not wriggle away. Then, using the other hand, gently move her arm so that the elbow is bent to 90°, and then turn the forearm so that the palm of her hand is facing down towards the floor. Next, holding the forearm near the wrist, gently but firmly rotate the forearm (with the elbow kept at 90°) until the palm is facing upwards. If you get it right the elbow will click home and the child will be comfortable again. No further treatment is required. If the child still refuses to move the elbow either it is still dislocated or there could be a fracture. Seek medical help and perhaps an X-ray.

Head injury

All children bump their heads, but be reassured that the parts of the skull which are bashed most often are the thickest and strongest. Toddlers especially often fall forward and bring up a huge purple goose-egg on the forehead, but no other damage is likely to have been done. The worry is whether the bang has been hard enough to cause bleeding inside the skull; this is not likely if the child cried immediately after the fall and was not knocked out. Unconsciousness implies a significant head injury and the longer the child is unconscious the greater is the damage likely to be; more than a few minutes is worrying. If an internal bleed happens you will recognise it because the child will become increasingly drowsy and unresponsive. They must then be taken urgently to a doctor. Children commonly vomit after a fall, but vomiting by itself is not a sign of serious head injury unless it persists or worsens hours after the injury. After any fall when a child has banged her head be more aware of her and if she seems lethargic or unduly whingy get a doctor to check her over. Bleeding into the brain after a head injury is most likely within hours. Any child who has suffered a head injury in the afternoon or evening (and this is when most happen, because the child is tired and more prone to make mistakes) is always likely to want to go to sleep after all the upset has settled down. It is not necessary to keep her awake all night, but she should be checked at least once (two hours after the accident) to ensure you can wake her.

DANGEROUS MARBLE BATHROOM

When Alexander was two years old we lived in Hyderabad in Pakistan where, because it was so hot, we spent a lot of time splashing water around in the bathroom. One evening he went trotting into the bathroom and slipped on the wet marble floor, fell backwards and the back of his head hit a narrow but sharp marble edge. He cried immediately (a good sign) but seemed disorientated and his cry sounded more high-pitched than usual. Then suddenly he was asleep. Although if we pinched him he would open his eyes, he was not really conscious and I was worried, pacing about, my stomach in knots, unable to think clearly. Expatriate friends lent us a car, a driver and a fistful of rupees; we fled south to Karachi. As we drove out of Hyderabad about 45 minutes after the fall, Alexander suddenly woke up, pointed to the driver and said, 'That man no hit his head. I hit my head.' He continued to prattle happily on about the cars and trucks he could see out of the window. He was now well, but he had had a significant head injury and it would be wise for us to stay close to a decent hospital for the night. By the time we reached the Agha Khan Hospital in Karachi two and a half hours later Alexander was so happy, the trip seemed a crazy waste of time. The X-ray showed a small skull fracture, though, and we settled down in a plush private room in the hospital.

Alexander was terrified by the aggressively affectionate Pakistani nurses and their threatening thermometers. I was also slightly surprised to realise that they did not understand about the neurological observations that he needed. He did not need hourly temperature measurements but only checks on conscious level. I took over nursing duties, set my alarm clock for 02.00 and tried to get some sleep; he was easy to rouse and there seemed no reason to worry further. Since he was as bright as a button the next morning too, we sped back to Hyderabad the next day.

Care after a head injury

- Crying immediately after the fall is reassuring.
- A child who was knocked unconscious has had a significant head injury and must be watched.
- A child who does not respond to pain after a head injury needs urgent medical help.
- Drowsiness at a time when it is not normal to be sleepy is worrying.
- New headaches or drowsiness even days after a head injury should make you seek a check-up.

Swallowed something?

Non-poisons

Antibiotics, vitamin pills not containing iron, simple antacids for indigestion and oral contraceptives are not harmful; homeopathic preparations are harmless but herbal cures may contain toxic substances. Mild diarrhoea may result after a child has eaten garden plants but most are non-toxic. Berries which are harmless include berberis, Chinese lantern, cotoneaster, hawthorn, mahonia, mountain ash (rowan), pyracantha, skimmia and japonica. Most flowers are harmless, for example antirrhinum, daffodil, bluebell, daisy, dandelion, fuchsia, geranium, rose, violet and stock. Soaps, bubblebath, carpet cleaner, scouring powders and washing-up liquid are not toxic, although dishwasher powders are corrosive. Water-based paints are harmless but need to be distinguished from solvent-based paints which may be harmful. Water-based glues are also innocuous. Nail varnish and remover and perfumes should theoretically be harmful but are hardly ever swallowed in any significant quantity. Anticoagulant rat baits such as warfarin are toxic only in massive or repeated doses and poisoning with warfarin is therefore unusual.

Poisonous plants

As a general rule toddlers are unlikely to eat enough toxic leaves to poison themselves, because leaves tend to be bitter. Fruits, berries and seeds are more of a risk, but even so most are harmless. Many of the plants within the potato and **tomato family** (Solanaceae) are very poisonous; and they are perhaps more dangerous than most because some toxic fruits look like little tomatoes. The family includes aubergines, but also the deadly nightshade and the poisonous **angel's trumpet**, *Datura suaveolens*: those evening-scented shrubs with spectacular 30cm-long dangling white flowers which are common in gardens of tropical hotels. *Datura stramonium*, the thorn apple, is also very poisonous.

Angel's trumpet

All parts of the **yellow oleander** (*Thevetia peruviana*) are poisonous, and it is likely that one fruit might be enough to kill a child; prompt treatment with *atropine* (given by injection) is likely to save them, however. The plant is a native of Central and South America (where the large flat seeds are often worn as ornaments) but is cultivated in many tropical gardens. Aconites are also poisonous. The flesh of the bright-red berries of **yew trees** and hedges is harmless but all other parts of the plant are poisonous, *including the seed inside the berry*. Toxic effects usually start within 40 minutes of swallowing the berries and cause abdominal pain and often vomiting and diarrhoea. You must then seek medical advice. If no such symptoms have started within four hours it is likely that insufficient poison has been swallowed to do any harm. If in doubt seek help.

Corrosive or oil-based poison

Swallowing something poisonous is a particular hazard of travelling, even if the trip is only to go and stay with Granny. Other peoples' homes are unlikely to be child-proofed and children swallow all kinds of substances, most often a relative's medicine or cleaning fluids. In the developing world it is commoner for kerosene/paraffin to be swallowed. The stomach is remarkably resilient so the main worry after a child has drunk kerosene, petrol or any oil-based or corrosive poison is that it will end up in the lungs where it may cause a very nasty inflammation; with these, it is important to avoid vomiting since this increases the risk of the poison entering the lungs. The treatment then is to neutralise the poison in the stomach by getting the child to drink milk or yoghurt; if this is not available, nibbling on biscuits and drinking plenty of water will help.

Medicine or non-corrosive substance

Most tablets are not tasty enough to be eaten in any great amount: antimalarial medicines are especially bitter. Tablets which are particularly dangerous in overdose are iron, antimalarials, *aspirin*, *paracetamol* and some antidepressants and sleeping tablets. Significant overdose with any of these medicines requires hospital admission and monitoring for dangerous side effects. Count the remaining tablets and compare with the number there should have been. If your child has taken less than five times the adult dose, it is extremely unlikely that any harm will befall him. If the dose is worrying then he should be made to vomit. In some emergency departments, children are given *ipecacuanha* syrup but this is not available in some countries (eg: Indonesia); give the child a drink of water and then push a teaspoon handle sufficiently far down the throat to induce vomiting. Stomach pumping in hospital is the other option. Overdose 'remedies' like salt solution, copper sulphate, apomorphine and mustard are dangerous and should never be used. If in doubt a medical

SHE'S SWALLOWED SOMETHING POISONOUS

- Try to discover exactly what it is and how much she has really swallowed.
- If she's drowsy take her to hospital. Don't try to make her vomit and don't give her anything to drink. If there's room in the vehicle lay her in the unconscious position.
- If she's fully conscious and has swallowed petrol/gasoline, kerosene/paraffin or any other corrosive or oil-based fluids give her lots of milk to drink. If this is not available yoghurt will do fine. Otherwise give her a lot of water to drink and biscuits to nibble on.
- If she has swallowed medicines amounting to more than five times the adult daily dose, it's probably best to empty her stomach. The easiest technique is to push the handle of a teaspoon down her throat until she vomits. Otherwise give *ipecacuanha* (up to 18 months 10ml; older children 15ml; over 12 years 30ml) followed by a large glass of water. Wait 20 minutes and, if she hasn't vomited, repeat the dose. If *ipecacuanha* is not available, stomach 'pumping' may be necessary.
- Usually it is not worthwhile giving *ipecacuanha* or stomach 'pumping' more than four hours after taking the poison UNLESS the medicine is *aspirin* or a tricyclic antidepressant which stay in the stomach longer.

BITS OF TOYS

Karl was usually a fit and very active 15-month-old but had been increasingly unwell since getting back from a holiday in Morocco two weeks before. There seemed to be an infection in the lungs and a chest X-ray revealed that he had inhaled a small piece of metal; the piece was removed with a bronchoscope (a fibre-optic grope-a-scope) under a general anaesthetic. It proved to be the axle and wheels of a cheap little toy car that the family had bought while away. His pneumonia settled with antibiotics.

opinion should be sought. Iron tablets (perhaps originally prescribed for mother) are particularly nasty and are commonly taken by children, perhaps because they look like sweets; iron must be removed from the stomach if any number have been swallowed.

Alcohol

Finally it is important to be aware that alcohol is a dangerous substance for children, and not only because of the irresponsible state induced by drunkenness. Children under 16 who drink large quantities of spirits experience a dangerous lowering of their blood sugar which can cause fits or worse. Make sure the culprit consumes plenty of sugary drinks in the next 12 hours. If she has a fit or convulsion she needs an intravenous drip in hospital.

Accidental swallowing of poisons or other people's medicines or drinking large amounts of alcohol are perhaps the most preventable of all accidents that can befall your children. Keep the hazard in mind and it will not happen.

She's swallowed an object

It is difficult to prevent children swallowing things. Blunt objects like coins are harmless and small toys pose a threat only if inhaled rather than swallowed. If your child is breathing easily after some object has disappeared down her throat, it is pretty safe to assume she's swallowed it. Once in a while children will inhale small objects unbeknown to their parents.

Small objects may slip down into the lungs and cause a chest infection starting up to a month after the object was inhaled. Investigation and removal are best done in a larger paediatric centre; waiting a day or two is unlikely to make things any worse.

Eye problems

If there is some question of an injury to the eye it is important to try to work out what happened and in particular whether the eye may have been penetrated by a sharp object; it is possible for the child to have a significant injury without much discomfort if for example an object was fired into the eye at high speed, as can happen if metal is banged on metal. Find a witness if possible, otherwise look out for danger signs: does one eye look different from the other; is the eye becoming cloudy in appearance; can the child see normally out of both eyes? If the pupil (black part of the eye) looks ragged or has changed shape, or is different in size from the other pupil, these are signs of serious eye injury and a specialist should be consulted.

Something in the eye

If something is protruding from the eye, you need a doctor. Large objects which have penetrated the eye tend to fall out and small objects usually allow the eye to close. Generally the child's instincts will protect the eye sufficiently but, if a long and difficult evacuation is foreseen, it may be sensible to protect the eye. A cone-shaped shield can be made out of a piece of cardboard, stiff paper or thin plastic. Cut a circle which is larger than the eye socket and then cut a radius (like the first cut when slicing a round cake). Overlap and stick the edges of the cut to form a short, flat cone. Many first-aid texts suggest gently packing around the eye with bandages so that the injured eye is covered *without* any pressure on it. This can be very difficult to do in practice – especially with a distressed child – and may do more harm than good. If in doubt do nothing except get to competent medical help.

If there is something small in the eye, like a grain of sand or even an eyelash, ensure that the outside of the eye is clean by wiping with a damp cloth. Also wash the child's hands so that they do not rub more grit into the sore eye. If the child is older and co-operative you may be able to sweep out whatever it is with a twist of wet cotton wool or the corner of a clean handkerchief. Or, whilst getting the child to look up, grasp the eyelashes of the top lid and pull it over the bottom. Encourage the child to blink a great deal too.

If this does not work, or you have a small and/or distressed child, try laying her on her back, face up, and pouring lots of water into the eye. Use tepid water and pour from close to the eye, or gently trickle water from a syringe without a needle. The coloured part of the eye is very sensitive so pour gently on to the white part. If these attempts do not work, there may be something stuck under the lid. Grasp the top eyelashes, roll the lid over a cotton bud and inspect under the upper lid where grit often lodges. The eyeball surface should be checked too and any particles gently brushed away with another cotton bud. Even the tiniest of foreign bodies can be very painful and a magnifying glass will aid the search. If all this fails, a doctor may be more successful since he will be able to put local anaesthetic in the eye, and unco-operative children are sometimes less so with strangers.

Black eye

This is simply bruising around the eye so the treatment is cold compresses, as for bruising anywhere else. If there seems to be any injury to the eye, or if headaches or serious and sustained whinginess or unwarranted drowsiness begin after whatever caused the black eye, seek medical help immediately. If a child sees double when she looks up after an eye injury, seek a medical assessment reasonably promptly.

Blood-red eye (subconjunctival haemorrhage)

See description on page 140. This is generally harmless; but if there is bleeding in the white part of the eye after a fall or an accident, check for possible unrecognised injuries elsewhere in the body, and see a doctor.

Insects and irritation of the eye

A burning sensation or swelling around the eye can be caused by insects flying in and being damaged as the child rubs her eyes in response. The treatment is to flush out any remaining bits of the insect with plenty of water, apply cold compresses and give antihistamine syrup or tablets if it seems very uncomfortable. **Conjunctivitis** (pink-eye), **styes** and **yellow eyes** are covered on pages 140 and 170.

Ear problems
Something in the ear

Inexpert attempts to remove objects or insects from the ear may only push the offender further in; this could damage the eardrum. Lie the child on her side with the problem ear uppermost and fill the ear with water; the object should float out. In the event of a particularly stubborn insect, warm oil might prove a more effective sluicing agent. Soaking in a bath with ears underwater may also help. If this does not work you will need medical help. A medical worker with an ear syringe may be able to flush the foreign body out, but many need to be removed in a hospital Ear, Nose and Throat department.

Nose problems
Broken nose

If the child has received a substantial blow on the nose (eg: during a fist fight or hockey match or after a car accident) there will be a lot of bleeding (treatment is below). Check the shape of the nose: if it looks crooked it's broken. The treatment is to try to straighten it as best you can and before the full pain sensation has returned. Give a painkiller: *paracetamol* or an anti-inflammatory medicine like *ibuprofen*. Apply a thumb to each side of the hard bit of the crooked nose and straighten it as best you can. If you can get the nose reasonably straight (and don't struggle for long with this – a quick tweak should do the trick) nothing more needs to be done, and going to a hospital will probably only produce more pain. Cold compresses and *paracetamol* or an anti-inflammatory medicine like *ibuprofen* is the convalescent treatment; the sooner you give the first painkiller the better.

Something up the nose

Objects stuffed up the nose may come out by getting the child to blow, otherwise they can be difficult to retrieve without the right equipment: you will probably need medical help, but not urgently unless the child is uncomfortable. Meanwhile try Dr Deborah Mills's solution. Tell the child that they are going to get a big kiss. Close the unaffected nostril with one finger, seal the child's lips with your own and give a short sharp blow into the child's mouth. With a bit of luck the offending object will pop out of the nostril. It doesn't always work but might save a trip to hospital. Recurrent or persistent discharge from one nostril may indicate that something is stuck inside – toddlers love planting orange pips and beads in their noses!

Nose-bleeds

Pinch the soft part of the nose and apply a cold compress (wet cloth) over the nose. If the child has been rushing around and is very hot, sponge her down to cool her off too. Blood in the wrong place is irritant and if swallowed will probably provoke vomiting, which can look really alarming. And if the blood stays in the stomach and is digested, it will eventually emerge as black faeces, which can also look alarming. Nose-bleeds are common in dry and high places; grease anointed inside the nostrils helps prevent them.

Bleeding under a finger- or toe-nail

Injuries to fingers or toes can cause bleeding under the nail and even a tiny amount of blood trapped in such a confined space is intensely painful. Heat the end of an uncurled paper clip over a flame or hot-plate. When it is red hot place it firmly on the black nail, at right angles to the nail, so that it burns through the nail but not to the nail bed. Don't use a pin or needle; it's too sharp and you will push through to the sensitive nail bed before making a big enough hole to let the blood out. As the blood is released, there is immediate relief of pain. The nail may come off eventually, but a new one will grow in its place.

Toothache

Few family remedies for toothache work well for the kinds of tooth problems children are likely to have, although teething gel might be worth a try if you have some to hand; putting *aspirin* against the gum is a bad idea – the best way to get a night's sleep is to give the child some *paracetamol* to swallow. Then, if the pain doesn't settle, you will need to find a dentist; they seldom work at weekends. Dental services abroad may be less sophisticated and the emphasis is rarely on conservation: tooth extraction may be the preferred treatment.

Infection, such as a root abscess, will usually show itself with heat and swelling in the affected gum, as well as a throbbing toothache which won't easily go away; and sometimes there is also a horrible taste. More rarely a niggling toothache may be the only clue to a root abscess. Occasionally a swollen face may suggest trouble but it should be fairly obvious that the tooth is the cause of the pain. Don't put a hot-water bottle or other heat source against the face to relieve pain as this can encourage infection to spread. Hot salt-water mouthwashes are very useful with any infection in the mouth as they will prevent spread and help any abscess to come to a head. An abscess needs antibiotic treatment (*penicillin* or *erythromycin* tablets or syrup work well usually) and occasionally drainage by a dental surgeon. Start an antibiotic whilst trying to find a competent dentist.

Occasionally a simple cavity can cause significant pain whilst eating or drinking. In the absence of infection, the mouth will be free of pain in between meals. The short-term answer is to avoid eating on the painful side, and to avoid especially hot or cold food or drink.

Knocked-out teeth

The front teeth are most likely to be knocked out in an accident. If the tooth is part of the permanent dentition (more likely after two and a half years of age) then it must be reinserted within two hours if it is to have a chance of growing back into the gum. The sooner it goes back in the better: you shouldn't wait for a professional to replace it. You need to clean the tooth

CHILD-FRIENDLY NEPAL
We were shopping at Kathmandu's plushest department store; the two-year-old soon homed in on some shiny exercise bicycles and treadmills for the opulent of Kathmandu to work off their fat. Embarrassed that he might spoil these decadent toys we dragged him away. A smiling shop assistant approached to chastise us:
'If the baby wants to play here, you must let him! I will watch him whilst you shop. Isn't he cute!'

thoroughly, preferably in the child's saliva, or failing that, in a glass of milk. Then insert it and try to keep it in place until you find a dentist.

Finally, unless your children drink large quantities of water when brushing their teeth, you can use tap water. We do in Kathmandu.

Illness in Infants 1–12 Months: Is My Baby Ill?

This chapter is about illnesses in children up to the age of 12 months. It will help you work out whether symptoms and other changes you notice in your child indicate a significant disease or not. New parents will have many more anxieties than most and this is normal and healthy. Talk to other parents, particularly those who have more than one child, and they will reassure you. At home, children up to the age of six months rarely get ill, but thereafter they get colds, diarrhoea and vomiting and ear infections galore; they are likely to experience four or five illnesses between the ages of six months and their first birthday. Travelling children might expect more episodes of diarrhoea and, if they are in touch with local children, more colds. The safest time to start travelling with a baby is any time after the age of one month and while entirely breast-fed. We have assumed that parents are unlikely to be travelling with a child under a month; those giving birth abroad or travelling with a baby under four weeks should take special advice. Even the most serious problems in newborn babies may not emerge for a few weeks and a doctor's assessment is wise before you travel.

The signs of illness are covered under the following headings:

- Fever, lethargy, unconsciousness, fits, crying, jaundice (see below)
- Top to bottom: mouth and tummy problems (page 132)
- Breathing and the chest (page 138)
- Ears, eyes and noses (page 139)
- Rashes and other spots (page 141)
- Lumps, bumps and swellings (page 144)

Childhood infectious diseases are covered at the end of *Chapter 10*, page 172.

FEVER, LETHARGY, UNCONSCIOUSNESS, FITS, CRYING, JAUNDICE
Fever
Fever means a raised body temperature above the normal of 37.5°C or 99.5°F. Taking a child's temperature will distinguish a simply hot child from a child with a fever, which indicates infection. Methods for measuring temperatures are described on page 130.

Feverish babies may be lethargic and uninterested in feeding. These two symptoms – **fever with lethargy** – may be signs of serious illness such as meningitis. If after a dose of *paracetamol* the child does not perk up within 30 minutes, seek an immediate medical assessment. Not all causes of high fever

DANGER SIGNS

If you find any of the first seven danger signs (**) in your child you must seek a doctor urgently even in the middle of the night. The other four danger signs (*) may indicate urgent action is required but read the relevant section; you may be able to wait until morning. The *Baby Check* system on pages 145–7 will help you to decide whether a baby under six months is ill or not.

Always urgent

** Stops breathing or goes blue – flick the soles of the feet or pick the baby up; if no response start resuscitation (pages 107–9)
** Has had a convulsion or fit; place on tummy (page 131)
** Is unconscious (cannot be woken) or lethargic or shows no awareness of what is going on (page 130)
** Has glazed eyes and is not focusing on anything; doesn't seem to know you (page 130)
** Is unable to drink or feed or cry (page 131)
** Has a purple-red skin rash which does not blanch when pressed and is spreading rapidly (page 142)
** There is chest indrawing and/or fast breathing or grunting breathing (page 138)

Sometimes serious

* Vomits everything he drinks or eats; or vomits green material (page 133)
* Inconsolable continuous crying for an hour without a break (page 131) or a cry of a different kind
* Inside of the mouth is dry, not glistening with saliva – assess to see if dehydrated (page 132).
* Fever of more than 38.5°C/101°F

are dangerous but dangerous causes need to be excluded by a doctor. Illnesses causing rashes are described at the end of this chapter, pages 141–4.

If you have been in a malarious area for more than a week (or have left one within the past three months) you must assume any new fever to be a serious form of **malaria** until proved otherwise. This is a nuisance but, since malaria can rapidly be fatal, there is really no alternative to extreme caution. Fever in a baby in a malarial region means a trip to a doctor; if the blood test shows malaria parasites the child will be treated; if the blood test is negative other tests will be necessary or the malaria test will be repeated.

Treatment of fever

If your child seems hot, has a fever and is generally miserable, the treatment is to cool him. It is best not to take an ill and feverish baby into the parents' warm bed since this will make him still hotter. Strip off most of his clothes and sponge him with a cloth dipped in tepid water. Give him a dose of *paracetamol*

(Calpol) which is called *acetaminophen* (Tylenol) in North America; give 60mg for a child up to nine months and 120mg from 9–12 months, every six hours or so. *Ibuprofen* can be used instead or alternated with *paracetamol* since the two medicines control temperature in different ways. Generally children with some trivial problem like a cold will get considerably better half an hour after a dose of *paracetamol* or *ibuprofen*. If a dose does not perk him up, seek medical advice; or in a child under six months do *Baby Check* (page 145). Meanwhile keep him cool (minimal clothing) and wipe him over every few minutes with a wet cloth. See a doctor if the fever persists for more than 24 hours.

Measuring temperature

Well children maintain their body temperature between 36.5°C and 37.5°C but, the smaller they are, the less efficiently they keep this temperature balance right. A high body temperature in a child can warn of an infection.

The most reliable way of measuring body temperature is a mercury-in-glass thermometer, or digital device. See also page 32. First make sure the reading is at least below 36°C. Mercury thermometers need to be shaken down as done by TV nurses. For measuring armpit temperature take the child's arm out of his sleeve. Holding the arm away from the body, place the thermometer bulb high up in the armpit with the thermometer shaft pointing out forwards. Bring the child's arm back to his side so that the thermometer is held in place between the arm and the body. Hold the child's arm in place (gentle pressure on the upper arm is usually enough) for two minutes; time it with a watch.

In very young and wriggling infants it may be easier to measure temperature with a rectal thermometer. Place the child on his back, take the nappy off and, by grasping both ankles with one hand, hold the legs up and out of the way. With the other hand gently insert the thermometer 2cm (the breadth of your thumb) and hold steady for two minutes before reading. Be careful not to go too far in and to hold the thermometer still relative to the anus.

Temperature strips are liquid-crystal thermometers which can be a useful guide but since they are less accurate than other thermometers, check again with a mercury or digital thermometer if there is any doubt. Digital thermometers occasionally record some crazy temperatures (eg: an impossible 47°C!), especially if the battery is running out, but usually are excellent and may be carried on aeroplanes. Thermometers which measure temperature in the ear are the easiest and quickest to use.

Sweating

It is common for infants to have a sweaty head and hands and this does not indicate illness. More generalised sweating suggests a fever, and beads of sweat on the head imply a significant temperature; so check with a thermometer.

Lethargy, floppiness, looking glazed, unconsciousness or coma

If a baby is unresponsive, or unconscious, or floppy or drowsy so that he will not respond to you normally, he needs urgent medical attention. If you are uncertain whether or not a child is floppy or drowsy he probably isn't: it's obvious if there's a problem, and if he takes milk happily he's certainly all right.

Unable to drink or feed

If the baby cannot drink because he seems too weak or seems frightened of drinking or is too breathless to drink, he needs urgent medical assessment. Try not to communicate your anxiety to him because if he becomes anxious this may make any breathing difficulty worse.

A fit, convulsion, seizure, funny turn or going blue

A convulsion, seizure or fit causes a baby to go rigid and unresponsive; he may also go blue; and there may be shaking or strange breathing or grunting noises, followed by floppiness. This is an emergency and requires urgent medical intervention. If the baby is hot, sponge him with tepid water. While travelling to see a doctor, place him on his tummy or side and never leave him alone. Any fit must be assessed by a doctor since it could be caused by meningitis, malaria or other serious diseases of the brain. From the age of about six months, breath-holding attacks can cause 'turns' which can look like fits; these are described in *Chapter 10*, page 154.

Inconsolable crying

A child who is inconsolable, does not want to feed and cries incessantly for more than an hour without a break, or whose cry sounds different or higher-pitched than normal, needs prompt medical assessment. Babies over the age of three months occasionally get episodes of crying when they are obviously in pain, go very pale and draw up their knees. The episodes last up to a couple of minutes and then there may be a lull of 20 minutes; between attacks the baby may lie abnormally still, pale and quiet. This may indicate a telescoping of the bowel which is called **intussusception** and, if this is the diagnosis, the baby needs an operation urgently; the commonest age is 3–11 months. In a more advanced stage of this problem, the stools resemble redcurrant jelly. Up to the age of about four months, well babies get symptoms that are described as 'evening colic'; but are pink and lusty, and usually distractible: colicky babies are well between attacks and will continue to take feeds. Colic is described on pages 67–8. Other rare but serious causes of crying are a strangulated hernia (page 165) or torsion of the testicle (page 165). A look in the groin/scrotum area will reveal painful swelling and redness and the child will need an emergency operation.

Pale baby

Any major disease can make a baby go pale. There will almost always be other clues that something serious is going on. Occasionally a lightening of the baby's complexion can signify blood loss. The commonest cause of hidden blood loss in infancy is inflammation of the bottom end of the gullet where it enters the stomach. Has he been vomiting a lot? Have you seen blood in the vomit or dark sticky altered blood in his poo? If so, he needs to be checked out by a doctor. Do not self-treat.

Yellow baby

Jaundice is the yellow discoloration of the body caused by liver disease, most easily seen in the eye when the white part turns yellow. It is common in newborn babies (when the liver is just starting to function properly) but should fade by the age of two weeks; and jaundice which persists longer or affects older infants is abnormal and needs investigation by a doctor within a day or two, or sooner if the baby seems feverish or unwell. Dark urine and pale stools accompanying jaundice in the first six weeks of life requires especially prompt medical appraisal. There are many causes of jaundice after six weeks; the commonest is infection. In the really young baby, urine infection is probably the most common cause; whilst as he gets older, hepatitis and malaria become more likely. In a black baby jaundice at around six months may indicate a sickle-cell crisis which is an emergency.

Sunken eyes, dry mouth and wrinkly skin (dehydration)

If anyone is dehydrated the inside of the mouth will look dry. A baby may be dangerously dehydrated if he also has sunken, hollow-looking eyes or his skin has lost its normal elasticity. This can be checked by pinching a good chunk of the skin of the belly. It should spring back when you let go and within two seconds there will be no sign that the skin has been pinched. If it stands up in a little ridge, he is badly dehydrated; check the other signs of dehydration listed on page 135. Also redouble your efforts to get the child to take even sips of clear fluid or more breast-milk. Give drinks whilst setting out to seek medical help.

TOP TO BOTTOM: MOUTH AND TUMMY PROBLEMS
Mouth infections
Sore or white mouth

Babies may develop 'thrush', a fungal infection of the mouth, which can make the mouth sore enough to put them off feeding. In a breast-fed baby the infection can ping-pong between the baby's mouth and mother's nipples which become sore and may bleed. In the baby's mouth (especially inside the cheek) there are often white plaques which – unlike milk – do not wipe or scrape off easily. The area around them may look red and angry, and the baby may cry when starting to feed. This is easily treated with a suspension of *nystatin* or *miconazole* (or less effectively with gentian violet). Treatment should be given after each feed for a week; mum's nipples need the same treatment.

Blistering around the mouth

Herpes infections are quite common in babies and cause painful mouth blisters which may extend on to the cheeks. By the time the blisters have formed, antiviral treatment with *aciclovir* doesn't help and you have to sit out an unpleasant and painful illness. Give plenty of drinks using a spoon if the baby's mouth is too sore to suckle, and give regular *paracetamol*. If you find yourself in a place well stocked with pharmaceuticals ask for an analgesic mouth spray such as *benzydamine hydrochloride* (Difflam).

Gastrointestinal and tummy problems
Burping up milk and rumination

Most babies effortlessly regurgitate milk after a feed. Babies' disproportionately large stomachs are prone to over-flowing in milky 'burps' or milk may be effortlessly regurgitated during a feed or up to two hours later. This is normal; it is messy, but it is not vomiting and there is no cause for concern.

Vomiting

Babies vomit a great deal and it often looks an impossibly huge amount; if it worries you, get the baby weighed in a clinic to check that he's absorbing some food. In younger infants (below six months) vomit which is projected forcibly 30cm/1ft or more out of the mouth is also worrying. Such projectile vomiting does happen in normal children but it can be an early sign of a narrowing of the stomach outlet in which case the baby (often a three-month-old first-born boy) has a ravenous appetite, but seems worried by eating since he continues to vomit profusely and forcefully. He will become ill within 24 hours or so. This condition is called pyloric stenosis and he will need intravenous fluids followed by an operation. As with all surgery in young babies, this is best performed in a specialist centre.

When your child vomits, do not automatically think that he has a tummy problem: ear or urine infections often cause vomiting too. Get a doctor to check the baby over if he seems unwell or is feverish.

Green vomit is worrying at any age (unless the child has just eaten spinach soup). It may indicate a blockage or twist in the gut and prompt medical assessment is needed. Vomited snot in a child with a cold, however, is nothing to worry about.

Vomiting blood usually indicates irritation at the point where the gullet joins the stomach. The baby will have a tendency to vomit after meals for many weeks before you notice the blood. Small quantities of blood will be mixed in with whatever he has eaten. The blood is of little significance but the cause of the vomiting must be pursued. If there are large quantities of blood there is some more severe problem and urgent medical care is needed. Vomited blood can look like coffee grounds: this is also a sign of serious bleeding which needs urgent medical attention.

Vomiting everything When children vomit it always looks more than it is; everyone overestimates the volume vomited and so it is best to check for signs of dehydration (see page 135) in order to work out whether the amount is dangerous. Count the number of times a child has vomited in an hour; this figure will help a doctor assess the severity of the problem. Further notes on vomiting are on page 157.

Nappy/diaper contents
Normal poo

Babies produce a fine array of poo-types. Bottle-fed babies are fairly consistent in what they emit; breast-fed babies often produce something like whole grain mustard, but it can range through to sloppy green stuff which looks like freshly liquidised broccoli. It may vary with mum's diet so may change according to the culinary delights of travelling. The frequency of poos can range from once every four days to 12 a day. If there is some consistency to the poo (that means it has to be scraped rather than poured off the nappy), this is normal. If the poo is very hard, and especially if the baby seems to be in pain when pooing, he may need more to drink. Offer more breast-feeds or, if the baby is bottle-fed, recheck that you are making the formula properly and offer additional boiled and cooled water or dilute juice. Young babies in particular usually poo while they are feeding; this is a normal – if messy – reflex. Once you start offering solids, the poo changes and becomes smellier and less pleasant to travel with. Parents are sometimes alarmed to see undigested vegetable matter in the poo of older infants; this is because small children have relatively short intestines, so it is nothing to worry about as long as they are growing normally. If it worries you see *Toddlers' diarrhoea* on pages 161–2.

Diarrhoea

It can be surprisingly difficult to define diarrhoea in babies, but you will know what is abnormal for your child. Don't be concerned about one loose stool; but, if you think your baby has diarrhoea, look to see if he remains bright-eyed, moist-mouthed, interested and happy to feed, in which case you need only worry about the mess. Large quantities of watery diarrhoea are obviously always abnormal.

He has diarrhoea. What do I do?

Diarrhoea can be dangerous because of the out-pouring of water that it provokes. The smaller the baby the less fluid he can afford to lose. The four important rules to follow are:

- Keep offering the baby breast-milk at frequent intervals and seek help if he does not want to feed. Bottle-fed babies should be given clear fluids.
- Assess whether the baby is dry/dehydrated.
- If the baby is dry/dehydrated give oral rehydration solution.
- Assess every few hours whether he is getting dry.

Oral rehydration solution

When diarrhoea and water are pouring out of the baby's bottom, fluid needs to be poured in at the top to keep up with the losses. But when a baby has diarrhoea the gut cannot absorb food and water well. Mixing water with a little sugar and salt improves absorption efficiency enormously: put two heaped teaspoons of sugar or glucose plus a thumb and two-finger pinch of salt (less than a quarter-teaspoon) of salt into a glass of safe water, and mix. The solution must taste no more salty than tears. Commercial oral rehydration solutions (ORS) are slightly improved sugar and salt mixtures. ORS is not a medicine but a means of preventing dehydration, so that you must give enough to compensate for all the fluids leaving from the baby's bottom for as long as he has diarrhoea. ORS is widely available and the powder should be made up in boiled and cooled water. The instructions will be on the packet so check with the shopkeeper if you cannot read the directions.

If you are giving ORS to a baby under two months of age, use twice the standard amount of water for each sachet; this half-strength ORS will prevent too much salt overwhelming immature kidneys. Small babies with diarrhoea should also be heading for a doctor, since they can get into trouble very easily.

DEHYDRATION CHECKLIST
- Is the inside of the mouth and the tongue dry? Does the mouth lack the usual glistening layer of saliva? This is the easiest sign to assess and it is also a very good indicator of the beginnings of dehydration; it is also present in severe dehydration.
- Does the child seem thirstier than normal? If she is thirsty, offer her more to drink. And always check the other items below.

Danger signs
** Drowsiness; the child is listless, unresponsive and unable to drink. This is the **worst** of the danger signs – GO TO HOSPITAL IMMEDIATELY.

If the child has any of the next three signs he is seriously dehydrated and needs medical attention as soon as possible and at least within a couple of hours:

** The child is passing less urine than normal. Normally a child will pass urine very frequently, at least every four hours. Children who are becoming significantly dehydrated pass less urine and it is dark or tea-coloured. (Watery diarrhoea can be hard to distinguish from urine – if in doubt smell it.)

** The eyes look sunken within the surrounding bony ridge and there are dark rings.

** The child's skin loses its natural elasticity. Pinch a fold of skin on the belly. When released the skin should immediately spring back to the normal smooth surface of the belly. If it continues to stand proud after two seconds this is a serious danger sign. Go to hospital.

How much ORS to give
Giving ORS early will generally avoid severe and dangerous dehydration, so, if in doubt, give it. Offer ¼ to ½ a cupful (50–100ml) of ORS after each loose poo. If the child is thirsty and wants more, give more. You cannot give too much ORS. Encourage your baby to drink and drink until those early signs of dehydration disappear. If the baby vomits, wait ten minutes, and continue offering ORS more slowly – perhaps as slowly as one dessertspoonful every five minutes. Breast-milk is therapeutic so also ensure this is given first, followed by ORS with a cup and spoon.

Drinking too much too fast may induce a vomit. This doesn't matter; slow down, but continue offering ORS by spoon.

Bloody diarrhoea
The commonest cause of blood with the stools is constipation; smears of blood will then be on the outside of a hard stool. True bloody diarrhoea (which means blood mixed in with loose or watery faeces) should always be taken seriously and medical opinion sought. Bloody diarrhoea with mucus and fever indicates

dysentery or rarely the serious haemolytic uraemic syndrome. Both conditions result from bacterial infection in the gut and require treatment with antibiotics and careful administration of fluids. The next chapter contains a fuller discussion of bloody diarrhoea. In any kind of diarrhoea, if the child loses interest in drinking she will need hospital or clinic treatment perhaps with intravenous fluids. Young children are not only more likely to suffer travellers' diarrhoea but they are also more likely to suffer difficulties and complications, so seek a doctor's help sooner rather than later in this age-group. Some conservative doctors say that families shouldn't travel to unsanitary countries with children under three but we encourage travel amongst well-prepared families.

When to seek help

If you are worried about the baby or if he refuses feeds, or if you don't feel confident about managing, seek medical advice. If you are happy that the infant is only mildly dehydrated, that he is taking ORS nicely and that any signs of dehydration are getting better, then carry on. Always seek help if he has any of the signs of serious dehydration (see page 135).

Even if you decide to seek help, continue to give ORS (and/or any other fluids that you can see through). When you get to a clinic or hospital it is likely you will be asked to continue giving ORS yourself in a special room reserved for rehydrating babies. In many good hospitals now, intravenous drips are reserved for only severely dehydrated, drowsy babies.

Drugs to avoid in diarrhoea

Drugs which stop diarrhoea work by paralysing the bowel. These are dangerous in babies for three reasons: a slight overdose can also paralyse the breathing muscles and kill the child; if the child has dysentery the bowel may rupture; paralysing the bowel keeps toxins inside and does not stop crucial fluids leaking from where they are needed. The main villain-drug is *loperamide hydrochloride* (marketed as Loperamide or Imodium), but *codeine* and Lomotil are also dangerous. Unfortunately these drugs are still prescribed in some developing countries especially India and Pakistan. Don't give them to your baby even if they are prescribed.

Getting back to normal

Once the diarrhoea is drying up and you are happy that the baby is well hydrated, you can stop the ORS. Breast-fed babies continue as normal. In the infant who has started solids be sensible at first. Avoid wheat-based foods and very greasy heavy foods. Bananas and rice-based weaning foods are perfect for rehabilitation. Recovering children will have huge appetites and should be fed as often as they ask. Offer food at least five times a day, plus extras like bananas, yoghurt and biscuits.

If the diarrhoea doesn't settle down?

If the baby continues to be unwell with diarrhoea for more than two or three days, go to a clinic. There may be persisting infection and tests are worthwhile. Some babies continue to have loose stools for days or even weeks following a bout of diarrhoea; they remain well in themselves, but the lining of the gut is still recovering and has temporarily lost the ability to absorb the natural milk-sugar lactose. The treatment is to avoid cow's milk for a few days although yoghurt is therapeutic. Then, after some days, see if reintroducing cow's milk makes the symptoms return. If it does, the baby's bowel needs a further holiday from it. Medical supervision will help you with diagnosis and management if in doubt.

If your child continues to have diarrhoea you may find more frequent weight checks helpful. If she is continuing to put on weight this is very reassuring. Conversely if the weight gain doesn't pick up again two weeks after the initial diarrhoea episode you should seek help.

Distended abdomen or tummy

Infants' stomachs swell considerably when filled with milk, and swallowing air can distend the whole abdomen, but the child remains well. The most serious cause of abdominal distension is obstruction of the gut, when there will be no (or a minimum) poo or farts coming out of the bottom end and eventually the infant will start vomiting. This needs an operation. Worms rarely cause abdominal swelling.

Bottom problems
Constipation
Constipation is only a problem if your child seems unhappy when doing a poo. The actual number of times a baby poos is far less important than whether the poo seems hard and scratchy, or has blood on the outside. Fresh blood smeared on the outside of a hard stool may mean that there is an **anal fissure**, which is a small crack in the lining of the anus caused by passing hard abrasive stools. The treatment is to give extra drinks; offer boiled and cooled water with a pinch of brown sugar in it. If this does not help you may need to give a laxative such as *lactulose*. In the meantime a local anaesthetic (such as *lidocaine/lignocaine* ointment) smeared inside the anus with a little finger may help.

Threadworms
These tiny white thread-like worms may either be mixed in with the baby's poo or squirm around the anus. They emerge at night to lay their eggs, when they cause intense itching. This may be a reason for a baby to howl in the night and when you catch them you will understand why. They are highly contagious and lurk under fingernails. Everyone in the family needs treatment, everyone's nails need to be cut short and meticulous hand-washing before eating (even snacks) is needed. Children under two years need *piperazine* taken as two doses 14 days apart; treatment of older children is discussed in the next chapter, along with descriptions of other worm types (pages 165–6).

Nappy (diaper) rash
A red and sore genital area is a hazard of wearing nappies. There are two common kinds of nappy rash. One is a simple chemical irritation when the groin creases are spared from inflammation. This should settle down with more frequent nappy changes and application of lots of greasy cream. Travelling distracts the best of parents from the routine tasks of baby care and

nappy-changing; it is easy for quite severe nappy rash to set in before you realise it, especially if faeces are left in contact with the skin for a while.

If the rash goes into the skin folds of the groin, where the skin may appear raw with a covering of what may look like cream cheese, and/or it looks rather spotty, it's likely to be caused by a fungal infection. Apply an antifungal cream such as *miconazole* (Daktarin in UK; Monistat or Micatin in US), *nystatin* (Nystan), or *clotrimazole* (Canesten). Alternatively gentian violet solution has some antifungal properties and is cheap and widely available; it will give your baby a bright purple bottom though. Apply the greasy waterproofing cream on top of any antifungal treatment too. Tea tree oil has some antifungal action and may also help.

The best treatment for the worst nappy rash is to expose the bottom to the air. This may be difficult to arrange if you are determined to carry on travelling at all costs, but in most places with a warm or hot climate, the baby can lie or crawl around with a naked bottom for a day or two. If the rash is severe, it may be necessary to apply a steroid cream (see page 9) sparingly for a few days. Steroids should not be used for more than a week without medical advice. Many antifungal creams now include a steroid and these will be available from pharmacies.

Urine
Babies normally pee very pale yellow urine frequently (often hourly). If the nappy is stained with tea-coloured wee, the baby is not getting enough to drink. Red wee is abnormal (ask a doctor to check), unless the baby has been eating beetroot. Occasionally babies get urine infections; urinary symptoms may not be obvious, but they will make the child unwell with a fever and/or vomiting. Girls are more likely to suffer than boys. Such urinary tract (UTI) or kidney infections happen at home too. The urine may look normal, or it may look cloudy. The child may have tummy ache or pain when she urinates. Pain on urination in a girl can be caused by a UTI or thrush which causes soreness in the genital region. If a doctor suspects a UTI he should ask for a urine test before starting antibiotics. Ask for a copy of the urine test result and show it to your own doctor when you get home, since urine infections in babies need careful monitoring and sometimes long-term antibiotics. Probably the best antibiotic for immediate treatment is *trimethoprim* (doses on page 36).

Laboratory test for a urine infection
If you are asked to provide a urine sample to a laboratory, ask the lab to give you a sterile container. Clean your baby's nether regions with soap and water, then dry him but do not replace his nappy. Encourage him to drink copiously whilst sitting him on your knee, then try to catch a dribble of the urine. It does not need to be a large quantity. Stroking the inside of the upper leg may help induce the child to wee. Keep a copy of the lab report.

BREATHING AND THE CHEST
Lungs, breathing problems and difficulties feeding
Breathing quickly, noisily or abnormally
Young children have small air-passages which can make a range of noises. Most commonly a baby with a chest infection may wheeze: a musical whistling

sound on breathing out, or grunts on breathing out are not danger signs in themselves but imply a problem which needs a doctor's opinion. Occasionally, you may hear a harsh low-pitched rasping noise when the child breathes in; this is called **stridor**. It is serious and needs urgent medical assessment; it's commonest in toddlers and is discussed in the next chapter (pages 166–7).

If there is serious infection in the lungs, the breathing rate will increase substantially although it is difficult to count this rate unless the child is asleep or very still. Babies under two months breathe at up to 60 breaths (in and out is one breath) per minute, slowing to 40 per minute by the age of one year. If the rate is faster than this there is probably a chest infection. Breathing rate is best counted when a baby is calm and not crying, with his clothes removed and lying flat on his back in a good light. Laying your hand on his chest will help you feel each breath. While you are counting the breathing rate, look for indrawing. There is indrawing if:

- the whole of the lower part of the chest (not just between the ribs) moves in when the child breathes in and
- the inward chest movement is clearly visible and happens with every in-breath.

If there is indrawing, the baby probably has a chest infection. The commonest cause of indrawing with fast breathing in children under one year of age is a viral infection called bronchiolitis; the baby may get over this by herself but if she is having trouble feeding then she requires medical help. Pneumonia causes similar symptoms but the baby will feel hot and look ill and will need antibiotic treatment probably via an intravenous drip in hospital. A doctor will need to make the diagnosis and decide on treatment.

Coughing spasms with a whoop

Whooping cough has a very characteristic pattern and can even occur in a child who is protected by pertussis immunisation. The child, generally a young infant, usually has repeated coughing spasms lasting up to a couple of minutes. Each spasm is followed by a loud inspiratory whoop. The coughing may be severe enough to cause small blow-outs of the blood vessels of the skin and the whites of the eyes. These appear as non-blanching reddish-purple spots on the upper chest and face; and the whole white of the eye may become blood-shot. The danger with whooping cough is the lack of oxygen during a coughing fit, indicated by the child turning blue. If during the coughing spasm the child remains a normal colour there is nothing to worry about. *Erythromycin* given very early in the course of the illness may help.

EARS, EYES AND NOSES
Ears
Sore ears

The baby's ear canal can become sore and itchy, due to a mild superficial infection which will be cleared easily with antibiotic ear drops. This is common at home and is commoner still in hot moist climates. It does not lead to hearing problems nor does it damage the ear. An unwell, hot baby who is pulling at one ear may have a middle ear infection. Get it checked at a clinic.

Discharging ears

Discharge from the ears is uncommon in infants; but if greenish-yellow gunk appears to be coming out of the ear, there may be a middle-ear infection. Sometimes when the child has a fever this causes ear wax to melt and trickle out; this looks like brown discharge and does not indicate a problem in the ear.

In a young child a middle-ear infection might cause fever, discomfort and whinginess, or even vomiting followed by a sudden discharge of foul-smelling yellow stuff on the pillow. This relieves the pressure and cures the problem and generally no further treatment is necessary. If an ear discharges material for more than two weeks it might indicate either something stuck inside or a long-standing infection which needs clearing with antibiotics. Both will require expert medical assessment, but not urgently unless the child seems distressed. Very rarely a middle-ear infection spreads to the mastoid area of the skull directly behind the ear lobe. The skin over this bony point will be red and painful: the problem requires an urgent operation.

There can be infection of the skin of the ear canal, which tends to cause swelling and itching in and around the ear-hole; sometimes the inflammation makes the ear canal appear to close up. The usual treatment is antibiotic ear drops (eye drops will also do fine if they're all that's on offer). Medicines dropped into the ear do no harm so buy some local preparation.

Eyes
Sore or watery eyes

Young babies often get sticky eyes but if they are not red it is more likely to be a drainage problem rather than infection. Wash your hands and then clean the eyes with cotton wool dipped in water (a little salt makes the water antiseptic). Then several times a day massage the corners of the eyes nearest the nose to help clear any gunk in the tiny duct which should drain tears from the eyes into the nose; many babies rather enjoy the massage.

If the eyes are stuck together (especially in the morning) or are pink or red, this is probably **conjunctivitis** which may need treatment with antibiotic ointment or drops: *tetracycline, gentamicin, framycetin, neomycin, chloramphenicol* and *ciprofloxacin* are the usual antibiotics for eyes. Place the baby on his back and put a drop in each eye (it doesn't matter if the eyes are shut: drops go in as the baby struggles or seep in if he is asleep). Apply every two hours at first (or at every nappy change if that is easier to remember), then reduce the frequency of drop-administration to three to four times a day; give the baby at least five days of antibiotics. Some doctors prefer ointment, while others like drops. Ointment put close to the eye will probably be rubbed in pretty much as required.

Blood-red eye (subconjunctival haemorrhage)

Bleeding into the white part of the eye looks horrendous but in itself is harmless; blood never covers the coloured part of the eye. It usually happens spontaneously or is caused by a coughing spasm (see whooping cough on page 139) and needs no treatment. However, if it has come on after a fall or an accident think again about possible hidden injuries elsewhere in the body; perhaps the fall was more serious than it seemed.

Swelling around the eye

The most likely cause of swelling around the eye is mosquito bites on the eyelids, or possibly conjunctivitis. If your baby's eye(s) looks swollen, take his temperature and also look to see if the white part of the eye is red. Red eyes and no temperature means conjunctivitis (see page 140). Swollen eyelid but with the white of the eye remaining white and no temperature is probably a mosquito bite. Red eye with a temperature may be a serious infection of the tissues around the eye when the whole area becomes swollen, hot and red. The eyeball itself may be either red or normal-looking while the baby will be feverish and unwell. This could be orbital cellulitis which needs intravenous antibiotic treatment urgently in hospital. For styes, see page 170.

Yellow eyes and yellow babies See pages 131–2.

Noses
Blocked nose

Young babies cannot breathe through their mouths, so if the nose is blocked with a cold it may be difficult for them to feed. A drop of boiled water up each nostril will usually make a baby sniff in or sneeze out the offending snot and temporarily help the breathing. It may be necessary to do this several times a day for a few days, after which time the baby will be back to normal. If the mucus is very thick, clean the child's nose using a soft clean cloth dipped into slightly salty water; a corner can be twisted to a point and then gently inserted into each nostril and turned to remove the snot. We do not recommend nose drops containing *ephedrine* because of its significant side effects; there can also be a rebound congestion of the nose after you stop giving them. Water has no side effects and works well.

RASHES AND OTHER SPOTS

Babies get spots, blotches and rashes which appear and disappear without apparent reason, but if they continue to feed and burble, there's no need to worry. Do a *Baby Check* (at the end of this chapter on pages 145–7) if in doubt.

Eczema

Eczema (see pages 175) and nappy rash (pages 137–8) are the commonest rashes of infancy. Eczema is a dry scaly itchy rash. Most often it affects the fronts of the elbows and backs of the knees, but it can appear anywhere. In this age-group the rash comes and goes unpredictably, but sunshine can make it worse. Treat the problem by avoiding too much soap, baby bath and other cosmetics and applying lots of moisturising creams. Keeping fingernails cut short will reduce skin damage from scratching. Many children will also need some steroid cream from time to time; 1% *hydrocortisone* is the weakest and is available over the counter; ointment works better than cream since it is more moisturising. Stronger steroid types should be used under medical supervision. Some children are driven to distraction and misery by the itching; a sedating antihistamine at night and a non-sedating one during the day may help and these are listed under motion sickness medicines in *Chapter 4*, pages 50–1. If your child has eczema, ensure you feel confident to cope with a flare-up while you are away and discuss with your family doctor before travelling. Moisturisers and emollients are often difficult to find abroad.

Eczema easily becomes infected when it weeps, then the redness spreads and the child may even be feverish. Antibiotic treatment with *flucloxacillin* (or *cloxacillin*) and *ampicillin, amoxicillin* or *erythromycin* syrup will then be needed (doses and cautions are on page 36).

Red rashes all over the body
Reddish-purple rashes which do not blanch
If your child has a purple-red skin rash, try pressing on it to see if it goes white (see page 173); if it does not blanch this implies that tiny amounts of blood have leaked out of the blood vessels into the skin. Particularly if he has a fever this may be the first sign of meningococcal septicaemia (even if he has had the meningococcus immunisation) and you should get him to a doctor fast. If you foresee any delay arrange for a paramedic or pharmacist to give 300mg of *penicillin* immediately by intramuscular injection. There are other causes for a non-blanching rash but a doctor needs to distinguish them.

Red rashes which blanch and temporarily disappear when pressed
These are common when there is a mild fever (up to 38.5°C) or a slight cold or slight diarrhoea. Any viral infection can cause red spots or larger blotches which are either flush with the skin surface or slightly raised. The rash usually starts on the baby's trunk but over the course of the day disappears or reappears elsewhere. When you press a finger on the blotches they will go pale and disappear until you take your finger off. Another way to check whether rashes 'blanch' or not is to apply a clear glass (bottom down) on the rash. Whilst you are pressing down, the rash will be colourless, but when the pressure is released the red colour will return. These rashes need no treatment apart from *paracetamol* if the baby seems unhappy.

Roseola is a common viral infection causing a red blanching rash and high fever (at least 40°C); this and other childhood infections are described in the next chapter, pages 172–6.

A widespread rash may indicate allergy for instance to baby-bath products; stick to warm water for a while and see whether avoiding cosmetics improves things.

Blistering rashes
There are four possible blistering rashes that can occur in infancy; the commonest by far is impetigo.

The weeping crusty golden rash of impetigo
Children of all ages and in all countries get impetigo, but it is commonest in hot moist climates. It is a bacterial infection of the surface of the skin causing a scabby golden crust that weeps; sometimes there are minuscule blisters within the scab which ooze clear fluid. There may be one scab in one place, such as at the corner of the mouth or at the site of a mosquito bite, or they may be quite widespread and some of the areas look like small boils. The treatment depends

upon how widespread the impetigo is. One or two small patches will be treated easily by smearing on an antibiotic such as *neomycin* or *fucidin*; gentian or crystal violet solution works quite well too (but should not be used on broken skin) or a dilute solution of potassium permanganate or iodine or red mercurochrome are also effective if rubbed briskly in with some cotton wool or gauze. Ideally you should get the scab off, but what is more important is to douse the area in lots of antiseptic three or four times a day. Antiseptic **creams** (eg: Savlon) are not good since the greasiness of such preparations can promote bacterial growth in humid climates. If the problem is widespread, or if redness is spreading out from any of the patches, or the child has a fever, then he will need some antibiotic syrup or tablets by mouth. The recommended medicines are *flucloxacillin* or *cloxacillin* (but these taste disgusting and it is hard to get babies to take them) or you may give *erythromycin*; doses are on page 36.

Scalded skin syndrome
An unwell child with fever, a widespread and rapidly blistering rash and a scalded appearance to the skin (the skin even peels off in sheets) has a serious infection that needs oral antibiotic treatment in hospital. If you are a long way from help you should probably start a broad-spectrum antibiotic – *flucloxacillin, amoxicillin* or Augmentin (*co-amoxyclav*) would be best, but you may not have a choice. Evacuate as quickly as you can.

Chickenpox
Crops of small blisters first appear on the chest and there is a mild fever; this is described in the next chapter. You may not fly with a child with active chickenpox. It can be a very serious illness in young infants: seek medical help.

Hand, foot and mouth disease
This causes blisters to appear in those three sites. It is a mild viral illness that causes a slight fever and may make the baby off colour. This is nothing to do with the outbreaks of foot-and-mouth disease of farm animals.

Other spots etc
Measles and other childhood infections are described in the next chapter since they are commonest in school-aged children. There can be a mild attack of measles after **MMR immunisation**, when the baby will have a low-grade fever and perhaps a slight rash. This is most noticeable about ten days after the injection.

Mosquito bites in infants look very different from the itchy red lumps that older children and adults get; they appear like little pinpricks and are not raised. If you notice them, think about protecting your child from further mosquito attack.

Cradle cap Even older children get dry scaly patches on the top of the head which look unsightly. Apply oil, massage in and then shampoo out at bath time; nit combs help with cradle cap removal. Repeating this weekly for several weeks should clear the problem.

LUMPS, BUMPS AND SWELLINGS

Boils are covered in the next chapter, page 179.

Tummy button is sticking out

In many babies, especially those of African descent, the tummy button sticks out and may bulge impressively when the baby cries; sometimes the skin looks stretched and bluish as if it is about to burst. It will not; it causes no discomfort and will not create problems later. This phenomenon usually fades away by the age of one as the baby's tummy muscles grow stronger.

Swellings around the groin

There are two common kinds of swelling in the groin of a young baby: a hernia and a hydrocele. Hernias are common, can affect boys or girls and often appear at around two months of age or at a year. Older children and adults also suffer from them. A hernia is a painless lump at the bottom of the abdomen, on one side, and it may extend into the scrotum if the child has one. It is due to a weakness of the muscle wall of the abdomen which allows a segment of intestine to bulge out under the skin. It may come and go, and usually will be more obvious towards the end of the day: it gets bigger when the baby cries. The danger is that the intestine may get trapped and so it is best to have the operation to repair the hernia shortly after diagnosis. This should be done by a team experienced in operating on babies. If the intestine is twisted or obstructed in the hernial sac the lump will not disappear; and the baby will be unhappy, cry a lot and start vomiting. At this stage surgery is urgent.

Hydroceles, which are also common, affect only boys; fluid accumulates around the testes so that one or both sides of the scrotum look swollen, but do not change in size when the baby cries. This swelling will go away by itself and needs no treatment but it can be difficult to distinguish from a hernia. Seek prompt medical opinion to be sure.

A third swelling in the groin area is commoner as the infant grows older and is due to swollen lymph glands fighting infection, often in the leg. The glands are usually tender and lie in the middle of the groin crease (midway between the private parts and the bit of the pelvic/hip bone which will later hold up the trousers). Look for a sore area or redness in the leg below the swollen glands; antibiotic syrup (probably *flucloxacillin* – see page 36) may be needed to clear infection in the leg.

Finally a testis can twist and become acutely swollen and inflamed even in the first year of life. Like an obstructed hernia this is a surgical emergency.

Swellings in the neck

Hot or tender swellings in the neck usually indicate an infection in the mouth, ear, throat or tonsils. If the baby does not seem unwell wait a few days to see whether the lumps will start to disappear without treatment. *Penicillin* or *trimethoprim* syrup for five days should clear this (doses on page 36). If they persist for more than a week, seek medical advice, although if the baby seems well in herself there is no urgency. It is common for babies to have painless little (3–5mm) bony lumps under the skin at the back of the neck; these are not a sign of disease.

COMMON CHILDHOOD INFECTIONS

These are discussed at the end of *Chapter 10* along with more exotic and rare diseases. The *Baby Check* below is a good way to decide how ill your baby is.

IS MY BABY ILL?
Baby Check for infants up to six months

Dr Colin Morley and colleagues working both in Cambridge, UK, and in Australia have developed a scoring system to help parents gauge the severity of illness in infants up to the age of six months. This is called *Baby Check*. In an emergency, or if faced with one of the danger signs listed on page 129, don't waste time performing *Baby Check*. It is most useful when the baby is not right but you are not sure how seriously 'not right'. Especially on a short trip the last thing you want is the hassle of tracking down a doctor at night. On the other hand you want to be sure that the baby really is well enough to be managed in your hotel room. *Baby Check* asks you to assess 19 points. For each check you select the description that matches your baby best and each description gives a score, but only score if it is obvious; the scores do not expect any subtlety of observation. As you work through the checks you add up the score. The higher the score the sicker your baby is. Each scoring band indicates a course of action which we have adapted slightly for the travelling parent.

The Checks			**Score**
1	Unusual cry	Cries the same as usual when hungry or tired	0
		Unusual cry (weak, high-pitched, moaning, etc)	2
2	Fluids taken (drinks) over last 24 hours	Usual amount taken	0
		Has taken a little less than usual	3
		Has taken about half as much as usual	4
		Has taken a lot less than usual	9
3	Vomiting (being sick); most vomiting is not important	None/brought back only small amounts after one or two of the last few feeds	0
		Vomited at least half the feed after EVERY one of the last three feeds	4
4	Green vomit	None	0
		Some green vomit	13
5	Wet nappies/ diapers	Normal	0
		Has passed less urine than usual	3
6	Blood with motions	No blood or small flecks of blood on the nappy/diaper or on the outside of the motion (faeces)	0
		Large amount of obvious blood in the baby's dirty nappy	11

			Score
7	Drowsiness	As alert as usual when awake	0
		Slept more than usual but alert when awake	0
		Occasionally drowsy	3
		Drowsy most of the time	5
8	Floppiness	Strong as usual; holds head up in the normal way	0
		More floppy than usual	4
9	Watching (talk to the baby)	Watches you in the normal way	0
		Watches you between cries	0
		Watches you less than usual	4
10	Awareness (watch the baby)	Aware as usual; interested and responding to you	0
		Crying but interested and responsive between cries	0
		Less aware or less responsive than usual	5
11	Breathing difficulty (look for indrawing as described on page 139)	Indrawing just visible with each breath	4
		Obvious or deep indrawing with each breath	15
12	Looking pale (is most of your baby's body paler?)	Same colour as usual	0
		Much paler than usual now	3
		Much paler than usual at any time over the last 24 hours	3
13	Wheeze (listen to the baby)	No unusual noises when breathing	0
		Snuffly or throaty noises	0
		Whistling sound or wheezing noise when breathing out	3
14	Blue fingernails or toenails	Baby's nails are similar colour to your own (pink or white)	0
		Baby's nails are blue or slightly blue	3
15	Circulation (gently squeeze baby's big toe for 2 seconds to make it white)	Toe returns to normal colour within 3 seconds	0
		Colour did not return in 3 seconds	3
		Toe was completely white before the squeeze and remains white	3

			Score
16	Lump in the groin	Has an inguinal hernia (a swelling of at least 1cm in the groin)	13
		No such swelling	0
17	Rectal temperature (see page 130)	Below 38.3°C/101°F	0
		Above 38.3°C/101°F	4
18	Rash (check the baby all over for a rash)	No rash	0
		Few spots or a small area of rash	0
		Large area of rash bigger than the palm of your hand	4
19	Crying (during the checks)	No crying or only grizzling	0
		Crying (more than a little grizzle)	3

What your baby's total score means

The higher the score the sicker is the baby.

0–7 Your baby is well, or only a little unwell. Relax and enjoy the trip.

8–12 Your baby is unwell but not seriously so at present. Consider seeking medical advice at your convenience but in the meantime watch your baby closely. Repeat *Baby Check* if there is any deterioration or you suspect any change.

13–19 Your baby is ill but is unlikely to be seriously ill. Consider how and where you will find a doctor if the baby deteriorates. Repeat *Baby Check* in an hour.

20 or more The baby is significantly ill and should be seen by a doctor. The score is a guide to the urgency. A score of 40 says you must go immediately whilst one around 20 suggests that you must go soon.

Remember that the score only measures the baby's condition at one point in time and does not predict whether the baby will improve or deteriorate. If in doubt recheck hourly.

A full version of *Baby Check* can be obtained from PO Box 324, Wroxham, Norwich NR12 8EQ, UK; tel: 01603 784400 or on the net at www.nicutools.orcon.net.nz/MediCalcs/BabyCheck.html. This information has been gleaned from *Baby Check* and Dr Colin Morley; it is reproduced here with kind permission of *Baby Check Ltd*.

Illness in Children over One Year: Diagnosis and Treatment

It can be difficult, particularly with younger children, to decide whether they are unwell or not, but it gets easier as they get older and are more able to communicate. If you become concerned, note any sign of illness (like vomiting, rash or a temperature) and then think whether they are also behaving in a way which is unusual for them. Is your son crying a lot? Is your daughter irritable or refusing food? Are they drowsy and lethargic? A single sign of illness on its own without a behaviour change should not alarm you. There are very few signs which may indicate serious illness; if you identify any of these you should act quickly and go to the best medical facilities you can find locally. If your child's symptoms do not appear under the danger

DANGER SIGNS

If you find any of the first five danger signs (**) in your child you must seek a doctor urgently even if this is in the middle of the night. The other five danger signs (*) may indicate urgent action is required but read the relevant section; you may be able to wait until morning.

Always urgent

**Has had a convulsion or fit (page 153)
**Is unconscious (cannot be woken) or lethargic (page 153) or delirious
**Is unable to drink or speak (pages 149 and 166)
**Has a purple-red skin rash which does not blanch when pressed, and is spreading rapidly (page 173)
**There is chest indrawing and/or breathing is fast (pages 137 and 166–7)

Sometimes serious

* Vomits everything he drinks or eats; or vomits green material (page 157)
* Severe abdominal pain which is not relieved by opening the bowels (page 163)
* Inside of the mouth is dry, not glistening with saliva – assess to see if severely dehydrated (page 159)
* Severe pain in the scrotum (page 165)
* Fever of more than 38.5°C/101°F (page 149)

signs section, though, you have plenty of time to think what to do next, and maybe even continue to enjoy your journey. Finally keep in mind that when children get ill, particularly pre-school children, they appear to lose a frightening amount of weight. As they recover, their appetites will be huge in order to compensate, and you will be amazed just how fast they grow chubby again. Feed children five times a day when they are recovering from diarrhoea or flu, or if you are worried about their weight.

Unable to drink or too breathless to speak
This may be because the child is too weak or because swelling in the throat or airways prevents her swallowing. Either way it is an urgent medical problem and you must find a doctor fast. Try to pretend that you are calm. If the child realises you are scared, she will become anxious and this is likely to exacerbate any breathing problems.

The other signs of illness are covered under the following headings:

- Fever, pallor, facial swelling, lethargy, faints, fits, headache (below)
- Top to bottom: mouth and tummy problems (page 156)
- Breathing and the chest and throat (page 166)
- Ears, eyes and noses (page 169)
- Joints and aches (page 171)
- Rashes, spots and other common infections (page 172)
- Notes on rare and exotic diseases (page 179)

FEVER, PALLOR, FACIAL SWELLING, LETHARGY, FAINTS, FITS, HEADACHE
Fever
Dangerous fever?
Notes on how to measure temperature are on page 130. Fever, a body temperature greater than 37.5°C/99.5°F, is common in children. Are there any hints of the origin of the fever, such as earache or a cold with runny nose and sore throat? If you have been in a malarial area for a week or more or have left such an area in the last three months, you must assume any new fever is caused by a serious form of malaria until proved otherwise. Flu-like symptoms, being off colour, and feeling alternately hot and sweaty then cold and shivery usually occur in malaria, as can diarrhoea, vomiting, headache and a cough. Since malaria can be rapidly fatal in children there is no alternative to extreme caution; and a small sample of the child's blood needs to be examined for malaria parasites. Even a negative result does not necessarily prove there is no malaria, though; so if the child remains unwell and feverish, get another blood test done.

Any high fever can cause hallucinations, especially in younger children. These are not dangerous in themselves, but the fever causing them needs prompt diagnosis and treatment. See also meningitis (page 156).

Malaria
This is a disease common in the tropics and subtropics which is caused by parasites taking over the red blood cells; when the parasites have taken all they

FUNNY FEVER

An Australian family was working in a remote part of Flores in Indonesia; the solid healthy toddler had been off colour and cranky for ten days but the parents could not identify anything specifically wrong and they were not worried. The older sister developed a mild fever and became lethargic and unusually uninterested in life. Next morning they could not wake her. The family rushed down to the capital where malaria was confirmed in the girl and intravenous treatment soon returned her to normal. As an afterthought they also took a blood sample from the toddler; he too had malaria. The family had been given confusing information about the malaria risk in their area and were not taking prophylaxis. The children liked playing outside in their shorts and T-shirts in the cool of the evening; they seldom used repellent since it was not available locally.

can from their blood-cell home they burst in unison, liberating parasites to colonise new blood cells and incidentally causing a fever. Red blood cells form nearly half of the volume of human blood. In severe malaria up to 60% of red blood cells may be parasitised and so synchronised bursting is disastrous. Of the four kinds of malaria which commonly infect man, only *Plasmodium falciparum* can cause this level of destruction and this is why it is so dangerous; *falciparum* parasites can also cause cerebral malaria. The disease is spread by mosquitoes which bite from dusk until dawn. The incubation period is usually from one week to three months, but occasionally symptoms can appear up to a year after exposure. Worldwide around two million people die of malaria and more than 10,000 travellers bring it back to Europe each year. There is no screening test.

Typhoid fever

In children over two years, vague flu-like symptoms and a fever which continues for more than a week may, rarely, be the early stage of typhoid. It can be mild in children, although usually it causes a sudden onset of high fever (39–40°C) with a bad frontal headache. Other symptoms may include disorientation, drowsiness, abdominal pain and distension, cough, diarrhoea, or even constipation. There is sometimes an irregular fine rose-coloured rash on the abdomen and back. The most serious complication, perforation of the small intestine, typically does not occur until the second or third week of the illness. Typhoid is more likely in the Indian subcontinent, Egypt, Central and South America; and less likely in sub-Saharan Africa and Southeast Asia. Immunisation gives only about 60% immunity against typhoid. The disease is uncommon before the age of two. Early in the illness typhoid is diagnosed by a blood culture test or later by a stool test in a specialised laboratory. These tests should be arranged on any child suffering a fever for a week or more in a risk country. Treatment with *trimethoprim* (12mg/kg/day) for ten days or high-dose *amoxicillin* (100mg/kg/day) for 14–21 days is usually effective; *ciprofloxacin* is also a good alternative. Typhoid can be serious and drug side effects can cause problems, so medical supervision is needed.

Other fevers

A very common dilemma is what needs to be done for a child who is off colour with a mild fever (less than 38.5°C) with no obvious cause. The diagnosis usually reveals itself: there may be a runny nose, perhaps slight diarrhoea and often a fleeting pinkish rash (which blanches when you press on it) to suggest a viral illness, which will not respond to antibiotics. If the fever persists for more than four days without an obvious cause then it is time to seek medical advice. If in a malarious region or there are other worrying symptoms get a medical opinion sooner. Meanwhile give *paracetamol* regularly. Fever following a recent tick bite – even in Britain and Ireland – needs a medical assessment since there is a risk of Lyme disease and other unpleasant illnesses. Unexplained fevers that last more than four days require laboratory tests. Roseola (page 174) can cause high fever for three days; tonsillitis (page 169) causes high fevers and so does pneumonia (page 167).

Treatment of fever

If your child seems hot and miserable, cool her. Strip off most of her clothes and sponge her with a cloth dipped in tepid water. Give *paracetamol* (Calpol) which is called *acetaminophen* (Tylenol) in North America; doses are on page 36. Generally children with some trivial problem like a cold will get considerably better half an hour after a dose of *paracetamol*. If a dose does not perk them up, seek medical advice, so that you can also give specific treatment for the illness if possible. Meanwhile keep them cool (minimal clothing) and wipe them over every few minutes with a wet cloth.

Hallucinations

In young children these are usually caused by a high fever and infection is the cause; this could be a range of readily treatable infections (pneumonia, dysentery, tonsillitis) and seeing a doctor should speed up diagnosis and treatment. Occasionally migraine or rare types of epilepsy can make the child think he has seen or heard something out of the ordinary. Older children and adolescents may have taken some mind-altering 'magic mushrooms' or other local equivalents.

Pallor
Pale child

If your child is always pale, as many are, it means nothing. However pallor can be a sign of illness. If a child suddenly becomes pale, there may be an infection or she may be bleeding internally, or else she may be dehydrated (page 159). Old blood in the gut comes out of the bottom end as a dark, sticky, smelly stuff which can constipate. And vomited blood can look like black coffee grounds. If there is massive breakdown of blood cells as can happen in malaria then the child will be pale and will pass dark urine. All these conditions are rare; and a simple cold, a tired child or a late night are the likely explanations!

Pale and crying

Children under two may have an attack when they go very pale with severe pains and crying bouts lasting 1–2 minutes which come on every 20 minutes or so; this could be an **intussusception** (see also page 131). Such children are initially well but pale and subdued between the spasms and then become increasingly ill and distressed; the treatment is an operation.

Yellow child

Yellow discoloration, best seen in the whites of the eyes, often accompanied by varying degrees of dark urine and/or pale stools, is jaundice. The commonest cause is infective hepatitis (A), but hepatitis E is increasingly recognised as a cause in travellers particularly to South Asia. In children hepatitis is usually mild and no special treatment is required.

Jane believes that traditional South Asian Ayurvedic or Tibetan cures can help. Often the child will be unwell (with headache, nausea, lack of appetite, tummy ache and perhaps a mild fever) for some days before you notice the yellowness. The jaundice of hepatitis A lasts for 8–11 days, so if it persists for more than two weeks or if the child seems very unwell seek medical help. When the jaundice is due to hepatitis A the patient is infectious for no more than a week after its onset. The incubation period for hepatitis E is 2–9 weeks. If jaundice comes on quickly with a high fever (above 39°C) and you have been to a malaria zone within the last three months a serious form of malaria could be breaking down blood cells and medical treatment is urgent.

Facial swelling

The most common cause of a swollen face is mosquito bites, especially first thing in the morning after a bad night under attack; it looks worse in the morning since lying down tends to make the face puffier. Swelling will start to settle over 12 hours but you should reconsider your insect protection measures.

Occasionally the whole face can swell up in an allergic reaction, the cause of which is often never identified. It is not painful but very rarely the swelling can also affect the windpipe leading to breathing difficulties. If your child develops a face swollen all over you should take him to a doctor who will prescribe an antihistamine medicine to control the reaction. Some people can become especially sensitised to the sun by taking certain medicines or contact with plants (see page 93) or other substances including citronella-based 'natural' sunscreens. The treatment is to stop taking the medicine or avoid the substance and meanwhile stay out of the sun.

Uncommonly, facial swelling may simply be the most noticeable part of a widespread swelling of the body caused by a kidney problem. The doctor will want to check your child's urine and measure his blood pressure. The findings may indicate one of two conditions confusingly called nephrotic syndrome and nephritis. They generally respond to treatment but can be dangerous. If the local doctors are having trouble controlling the child's blood pressure or balance of body fluids you need expert help and at the very least your child's doctors should be in touch with experienced paediatricians.

Swelling around the angle of the jaw spreading up towards the ear may be due to **mumps**, although there are plenty of other causes of swellings in this region; a doctor may help with the diagnosis. The MMR immunisation protects against mumps. In mumps the child may be somewhat unwell and complain of pain around the ear or on chewing. Sometimes there is also some tummy ache. Give regular *paracetamol* and he will be better within a week. Swollen testicles are not a problem in childhood mumps; it is not dangerous during pregnancy. The incubation period is 16–18 days; the feverish phase of the illness lasts about six days. Patients are infectious until nine days after the arrival of the swelling.

Lethargy, coma and irritability
If your child is unusually lethargic or you cannot wake her at all, seek immediate emergency medical attention. A lethargic toddler does not respond to you, is limp and has no interest in play or food. Try to rouse her, by talking to her or by pulling her by the arms up into the sitting position. A lethargic child will not make any response to your efforts and will usually be very floppy. If you are unsure whether your child is or is not lethargic she probably isn't. Older children and teenagers who seem drowsy or disorientated may have experienced a head injury (see *Chapter 8*, pages 119–20) or may have been experimenting with alcohol or other drugs.

Irritability, the opposite extreme, can also be a sign of severe illness if a young child is unremittingly miserable for several hours. A cranky child who is merely 'off colour' will settle within a couple of hours, whilst a truly irritable child is unhappy for hour upon hour and is inconsolable (despite being offered treats). If you feel your child is abnormally irritable something probably is bothering her and she should be seen by a doctor.

A fit, convulsion, seizure or funny turn
Whatever you call them these are worrying events during which parents often think their child is dying. Yet fits are common in childhood with nearly one in 20 children experiencing one or more fits at some time. The vast majority will have no ill effects, so try to keep calm and remember these attacks are common and usually benign.

A rapidly rising temperature can cause a fit in a child under the age of five. Typically all four limbs shake and the child is 'not with it'. Since the breathing muscles also go into spasm she may go blue. When a child has a fit she suddenly appears vacant or distant, becomes rigid, falls, often starts to shake and may urinate. Clear away furniture to avoid injury. Never force anything into the mouth. Open her clothes and fan and sponge her if she feels hot. Fits last from a few seconds to ten minutes, but occasionally go on for much longer. Don't wait for the convulsion to subside. Don't leave the child alone. Send someone to arrange immediate transport to a place where emergency care is available. If you can, sit with the child on your lap in the back seat of the car as you travel to hospital. Unless you know that your child is epileptic, fits are always worrying and you should seek medical help urgently since they can indicate serious illness such as meningitis or cerebral malaria. The doctor may perform a lumbar puncture/spinal tap to be sure; but the vast majority of fits are harmless febrile convulsions (see below). First-aid measures are described on page 112.

DISTINGUISHING A FAINT FROM A FIT
(after Dr D Chadwick, 1993)

	Faint	Fit
	Common	*Less common*
Position	Upright initially	Any position
Skin	Pale and sweaty	Usually normal or bluish
Comes on	Gradually; often dizzy before	Sudden or preceded by crying
Vision/hearing	Greying out	Suddenly unaware
Injury, tongue bitten	Rare	Quite common
Convulsive jerks	Rare	Common
Incontinence	Rare	Common
Unconscious	For seconds	For minutes
Recovery	Rapid	Often slow; usually sleep it off
Confusion afterwards	Rare	Common
Frequency	Infrequent	May be frequent
What brought it on?	Stress; lack of food; emotional distress pain or fear	Rare to have a 'cause'

Febrile convulsions

The brain of young children is especially sensitive to temperature so that they hallucinate when they are feverish and about 5% of children under the age of five may experience a fit in response to a fever; the peak age is in the second year of life. Usually a close relative had the same sensitivity. There is no increased likelihood of epilepsy or other long-lasting problems, after you have all got over the shock of witnessing a frightening event. Rarely a fit can be a sign of serious illness so all first fits must be investigated in hospital.

Faints

These are common in children from about ten years, especially adolescent girls; they can be worrying events. The stresses and disruptions to routines of eating and sleeping mean that children may be more likely to suffer while you are away. Faints are harmless, but there are a few illnesses which might cause your child to pass out and even have a fit. The table (above) will help distinguish a benign faint from a more worrying fit.

Breath-holding attacks

These are common (1–2%) in children up to the age of three and often continue up to five years of age; they scare the living daylights out of parents. The 'turn' is often precipitated by something which upsets the child: temper at being told off, a skirmish with another child or a painful injury. The child emits a lusty yell after the insult and then, after two or three breaths, holds his breath with a lung full of air. He then goes red in the face and then may go blue and briefly lose consciousness; he may twitch a few times just like a fit.

He then starts breathing again and soon is back to normal. The best action is to do nothing (the more attention that is paid, the more likely it is to happen again); but if there is a worry that these attacks are something less benign, discuss them with a paediatrician, preferably of your own culture.

An alternative type of turn follows an accident, typically in the same age-group, when the child turns a deathly shade of pale and collapses; again there may be a few twitches. This is really a kind of faint; but again they never cause any lasting damage and children 'grow out' of both kinds of attacks, usually by about five.

Tingling in the hands and feet

There are two common causes for this in children. If your child is on medication this may be the cause: *mefloquine* (an antimalarial), *nalidixic acid* (antibiotic) and *acetazolamide* (Diamox, used to speed acclimatisation to high altitude) are the commonest culprits in travellers and you should find alternative medicine. In the older child, attacks accompanied by light-headedness and symptoms of panic are all due to hyperventilation or over-breathing. This is stress related (such as wandering around in a strange bazaar without your parents) and the answer is to learn to relax and not over-breathe. As a short-term treatment an affected child can breathe in and out of a paper bag; this makes the symptoms disappear and reassures everyone.

Headaches

When should you worry about headaches? Any illness causing a fever is likely to cause a headache. The commonest cause in travellers to hot places is dehydration; try getting the sufferer to drink at least one large glass of water and see if the headache improves. In any environment, headaches become increasingly common as the child grows up, but headache in a child who usually doesn't suffer from them or a different type of headache from normal may suggest illness. Early-morning headaches and headaches that wake a child at night should always be taken seriously and need to be checked out by a doctor. Headaches that start after a head injury (see pages 119–20) or period of unconsciousness – even months after the injury – should be a reason for seeking a competent medical opinion.

Migraine headaches

These are throbbing and can last anything from a couple of hours to a couple of days. They may be one-sided or feel as if they are coming from all over the head. One in ten sufferers experience strange disturbances of vision or hearing just prior to the attack. The headache is relieved by sleep and in between attacks the child is perfectly well. Migraine is common and may begin well before puberty especially in boys. In many cases the child suffered from recurrent vomiting or tummy ache in the pre-school years. Many factors can trigger attacks – fatigue and long car journeys among them. If your child suffers with migraines you should have his medication with you. A first attack should be treated with regular 4–6-hourly doses of *paracetamol* (doses on page 35) and enforced rest in a darkened room will help.

Headache and neck stiffness

Meningitis begins as an apparently mild malaise but there will be a fever, which you may not be aware of until you measure her temperature. The child with meningitis quickly becomes obviously ill, often with vomiting; she will not want to get out of bed and lies with her chin up to reduce any stretching of her intensely painful neck. If there is neck stiffness she will be unable and unwilling to place her chin on her chest. In meningitis, children often complain of headache, particularly around the back of the neck; if the child can kiss her knee she does not have the neck stiffness of meningitis. She will lie turned away from the light (looking at light hurts). In the most dangerous type of meningitis you may see a red rash, which often starts on the legs and does not disappear when you press on the skin. If you suspect that your child may have meningitis, get her to a hospital urgently. If you foresee any delay in getting to hospital, ask a local doctor, paramedic or pharmacist to give a first dose of *penicillin* by intramuscular injection (600mg *benzylpenicillin* or *penicillin* G for any child aged between one and nine years; children of ten years and over need the adult dose of 1.2g *benzylpenicillin*). Not many children are allergic to *penicillin* and, unless you know the child is allergic, it is best to give the injection in this emergency situation.

The commonest cause of **neck stiffness** is a throat infection with swollen painful glands in the neck. In tonsillitis you should be able to make the child wince by pressing on the glands. Look inside the mouth and feel around the neck. If you have any doubt seek an urgent medical opinion.

Other causes of headaches include dental abscess (see *Chapter 8,* page 126*),* sinusitis (see page 168) and nephritis – a serious but rare kidney condition causing high blood pressure, smoky urine and severe headache.

Toddler paralysis

There is an extremely rare syndrome which might afflict travelling toddlers between the age when they have become mobile enough to explore scrub and jungle and the age when they can communicate effectively, around two and a half years. A tick climbs up to feed in an inaccessible nook (often near the genitals or in an armpit). As certain ticks feed, they secrete a toxin which affects the nervous system; 4–6 days after the tick attaches, the toddler starts to experience paralysis of the hands and feet; next there is lack of co-ordination, paralysis of the face, slurring of speech and uncontrolled eye movements. If no-one has realised what is happening, by about the eighth day breathing stops. However, once the feeding tick is found and removed (see page 83) the symptoms begin to disappear in the reverse order of their appearance and there are no long-term effects. Only in Australia are continuing problems likely but an antidote is available. This strange syndrome is most often reported from northwest America but it is known from all continents.

Other tick-borne illnesses are discussed on pages 181 and 182.

TOP TO BOTTOM: MOUTH AND TUMMY PROBLEMS
Refusing food

The commonest reason for a child under three to refuse food and drink is tonsillitis (see page 169), which also causes a fever; in small children it may be soreness caused by thrush in the mouth (see page 132). Have a look at the inside of the mouth and throat. Otherwise all kinds of illnesses can ruin a child's appetite, but she will not starve and will make up for it once she feels better.

Vomiting

Children vomit readily and a couple of stomach-emptying chucks are nothing to worry about. Sometimes a mere cold and a stomach full of snot can cause a bit of vomiting (when the vomit will look slimy). There are three reasons to worry when a child vomits:

- Is the vomiting so frequent and profuse that the child is getting dehydrated? (see page 159)
- Is there blood or 'coffee grounds' in the vomit?
- Is the vomit green?

Vomiting green material

Provided the child has not recently eaten green vegetables the green stuff is bile. Its presence in vomit suggests intestinal obstruction. Go to hospital within the next hour or so.

Vomiting blood

Fresh blood may be seen in the vomit if a child is repeatedly retching for any reason, or has tonsillitis or a nose bleed. Small amounts of red blood need not concern you. Swallowed blood from a nose bleed can cause children to vomit blood, and in this case you need not worry. If a child vomits a large quantity of bright-red blood or material that looks like coffee grounds she needs to go to hospital urgently. Seek urgent medical advice and meanwhile give the child sips of clear fluid only.

Vomiting everything

Repeated severe vomiting will quickly lead to dehydration especially in a young child. It is difficult to estimate how much a child has vomited; everyone over-estimates the volume. Consider the number of glasses of fluid the child has drunk during the day. Now assess the actual volume the infant is vomiting. If it approaches the intake volume then take this seriously and seek medical help soon; she may need intravenous fluids. Start giving sips of clear drinks or ORS and assess whether she is becoming dehydrated (see page 159).

Vomiting with fever

The sudden onset of fever and vomiting is a sign of infection, but this may not necessarily be in the gut. Infections of the urinary tract or the ear are common causes; and meningitis is a possibility. If there is no cause found but the local doctor is keen to start antibiotics, and your child is under five, collect a fresh urine sample for laboratory testing before starting the antibiotics. A confirmed urine infection should be further investigated once you get home.

Diarrhoea

Any kind of diarrhoea can cause dehydration and you must be able to assess whether your child is becoming dry, using the list given next. The easiest and most sensitive sign of dehydration is whether the tongue and inside of the mouth are wet. A dry mouth indicates that up to 5% of the body water has been lost. Quantity drunk is more important than constituents and the child's usual drinks of water, juice or fizz are good; cow's and formula milk should be avoided. If there is profuse watery diarrhoea or signs of dehydration offer oral rehydration solution (ORS). If she does not like that, give a cup of any clear fluid (a drink that you can see through) after each loose stool. If she refuses solid foods don't worry providing she continues to drink. However keep offering her light, non-greasy snacks. Often she will enjoy nibbling on dry biscuits and if taken with lots of drinks these will aid fluid absorption and keep her morale up too.

Dehydration and rehydration

Profuse watery diarrhoea and/or severe vomiting can dehydrate a child fast and the smaller the child the less fluid she can afford to lose. You should not hesitate to seek medical help if you are not confident of managing, especially if the child is under three.

There are four rules to follow when children have diarrhoea:

- Keep offering favourite drinks and food. Children should be offered plenty of clear fluids (juice and/or oral rehydration solution, ORS). Give children below two years half a cup (100ml) after each loose stool and children 2–10 years one cup (200ml) after each loose stool.
- Assess every few hours whether she is getting dry. Use the checklist on the next page.
- Under twos who refuse to drink or feed for more than three hours are probably getting into trouble so seek help.
- Don't starve a child who wants to eat, but stick to crackers and bland carbohydrates.

Oral rehydration solution (ORS)

Fluid lost as diarrhoea must be replaced. ORS and mixtures of water, sugar and salt are absorbed more efficiently than plain water. All travellers should carry a few ORS packets, plus a water bottle of the required volume to make it up in. Remember that different ORS brands are designed to be made up with different volumes of boiled and cooled water.

ORS is the perfect biochemical mix to make your child feel better but it tastes ghastly and many children – particularly if they are not especially ill – refuse it. The body is quite clever at sending messages about what it needs and often people who are salt-depleted will have a craving for salt. And children who are in need of the constituents of ORS will drink it uncomplainingly. If the child won't take ORS, find some other clear fluid to tempt her: green coconut 'milk', rice water, clear soups, even the ubiquitous Coca-Cola, preferably with an added pinch of salt, will do the job. Otherwise mix eight level teaspoons of sugar (18g) and one level teaspoon of salt (3g) in one litre (5 cups) of safe water. Alternatively, add a four-finger scoop of sugar and a thumb and two-finger pinch of salt to a glass of safe water. Add a squirt of citrus juice too if it is available.

When anyone has an upset stomach, very hot and very cold drinks (or foods) provoke a more pronounced gastro-colic reflex. This reflex results in

DEHYDRATION CHECKLIST

- Is the inside of the mouth and the tongue dry? Does the mouth lack the usual glistening layer of saliva? This is the easiest sign to assess and it is also a very good indicator of the beginnings of dehydration; it is also present in severe dehydration.
- Does the child seem thirstier than normal? If she is thirsty, offer her more to drink. And always check the other items below.

Danger signs

** Drowsiness; the child is listless, unresponsive and unable to drink. This is the **worst** of the danger signs – GO TO HOSPITAL IMMEDIATELY.

If the child has any of the next three signs she is seriously dehydrated and needs medical attention as soon as possible and at least within a couple of hours:

** The child is passing less urine than normal. Normally a child will pass urine very frequently, at least every four hours. Children who are becoming significantly dehydrated pass less urine and it is dark or tea-coloured. (Watery diarrhoea can be hard to distinguish from urine – if in doubt smell it.)

** The eyes look sunken within the surrounding bony ridge and there are dark rings.

** The child's skin loses its natural elasticity. Pinch a fold of skin on the belly. When released the skin should immediately spring back to the normal smooth surface of the belly. If it continues to stand proud after two seconds this is a serious danger sign. Go to hospital.

the bowel opening a few minutes after something arrives in the stomach. Giving hot or iced drinks to a child with diarrhoea on a bus is therefore exceedingly unwise. The lag time in the reflex will just about give enough time for the bus to start again.

Drugs to avoid in diarrhoea

In many regions less well-trained practitioners will give drugs which stop diarrhoea by paralysing the bowel. The main culprits are *loperamide hydrochloride* (marketed as Loperamide or Imodium), *codeine* and Lomotil; these are dangerous for children. Fluids (ORS), and in some instances antibiotics, are the only medicines needed in diarrhoea; do not give anything else.

Symptoms of different kinds of diarrhoea

If you can you should seek medical help if diarrhoea goes on for more than three days and/or there are very frequent watery bowel movements, blood in the stools, repeated profuse vomiting or fever. If you cannot seek help the notes below will help you decide what to do. Diarrhoea is caused by a range of microbes and the symptoms point to appropriate treatments.

Explosive diarrhoea with fever (there may also be obvious blood)

Bacillary dysentery comes on suddenly, dramatically and often explosively (literally); vomiting and abdominal cramps are common but not invariable. Sometimes blood and usually mucus is visible in the watery faeces which are pouring out, and blood cells will be seen if a sample is examined under a microscope. The most important part of treatment is to tempt the sufferer to drink. And keep checking that the mouth remains moist-looking. If the child seems to be becoming dry you may need help in a clinic or hospital. Never give blocking medicines (eg: Imodium, Lomotil) to anyone with dysentery since they can cause a perforation of the bowel. Antibiotic treatment should improve the symptoms, but many antibiotics are ineffective because the bacteria are fast at developing resistance. At the time of writing *nalidixic acid* is very effective; doses are in *Chapter 3*, page 36. If the child is not significantly improved within 36 hours, the microbes are probably resistant and you may wish to weather the last couple of days of the illness or reconsider the choice of antibiotic; *ciprofloxacin* or *norfloxacin* antibiotics often work well. Local doctors should know what works best. And even if you do choose to give antibiotics, rehydration is ESSENTIAL. Seek medical help if possible.

Rarely bloody diarrhoea with fever is complicated by bleeding elsewhere such as into the skin (easy bruising) and into the urine (smoky or red urine) and with jaundice (see page 152). This a very serious disease called haemolytic uraemic syndrome and needs urgent management in hospital.

Diarrhoea with fever and no blood

This is a common way for all kinds of diseases to start. Could it be malaria? (See page 149.) Since both trivial and serious infections can begin with diarrhoea and fever, start by giving fluids and a dose of *paracetamol* to see if the child perks up; if he doesn't, visit a doctor.

Diarrhoea with blood and no fever

This is most likely to be amoebic dysentery, but laboratory examination of a fresh (still warm) stool sample is the best way of confirming the diagnosis. Despite the dysentery label the disease can be mild, and the child remains quite well, rarely vomits and is unlikely to complain of cramps. But since the amoebae can be troublesome it is worth treating, and medical guidance is wise if available. *Metronidazole* for five days is the usual treatment: 1–2+-year-olds need 200mg three times daily; 3–6+-year-olds need 200mg four times daily; 7–10-year-olds need 400mg three times daily; and anyone over ten should take 800mg three times daily. It tastes vile, with side effects of nausea and an unpleasant metallic taste in the mouth. The newer but less readily available *tinidazole* has the advantage of a single daily dose of 50mg/kg bodyweight for three days only. A ten-day course of *diloxanide furoate* (Furamide in the UK) is also needed to clear the cysts from the intestine; the dose is 20mg per kg of the child's bodyweight per day but divided into three daily doses.

STOOL TESTS IN FOREIGN LABORATORIES

Medical laboratories abroad may be poorly equipped but they are usually very practised in looking at stool samples! Make sure the sample is fresh – preferably still warm. The simplest investigation that almost any laboratory can manage is to look at the sample under a microscope. If they see mucus or red blood cells (which is often written RBC; a following '+' indicates some RBC have been seen; '++' quite a few; or '+++' means lots) this indicates dysentery which requires antibiotic treatment. The kind of antibiotic depends upon the nature of the symptoms and not the laboratory result. Presence of worms' eggs may be another finding, but these do not do any harm (and do not usually cause diarrhoea) so you can wait for treatment until it is convenient and you trust the doctors. More sophisticated laboratories can identify bacteria and work out which antibiotic will kill those bacteria most effectively. This process takes some days, and often the child will be better by the time you get the result ... or you will be in the next town. A simple look under the microscope is all you need unless some serious problem like typhoid is suspected.

Diarrhoea, no fever and no blood

Apart from the usual attention to giving the child lots to drink, this is unlikely to need any special treatment. Even such 'uncomplicated' diarrhoea may sometimes cause a profuse watery out-pouring and occasionally abdominal cramps. Many episodes will be caused by viruses so antibiotics will not help. If the symptoms are severe take a fresh sample to a laboratory and ask them to look for blood cells under a microscope. If blood cells are seen treat this as dysentery. And don't forget to give lots of clear fluids.

Diarrhoea plus a cold and mild fever

In the common viral forms of diarrhoeal disease there is often a cough or cold a day or two before the diarrhoea starts. These may be a fine raised pimply rash, mild fever (below 38.5°C) and vomiting. The child is not particularly unwell and there is no blood in the stool. This sort of upset will settle down by itself within a week. There is unlikely to be any advantage in treating mild diarrhoea with antibiotics, and indeed they may make it worse.

Diarrhoea lasting for more than three days

Seek medical help if diarrhoea goes on for more than three days and/or there are very frequent watery bowel movements, blood in the stools, repeated profuse vomiting, or fever.

Toddlers' diarrhoea

Many toddlers pass faeces which appear to comprise undigested food. It is commonest in boys between the ages of six months and two years but can persist until the age of five. The bowel is relatively short at this age and young children are usually too busy to chew. As long as the child seems active and is not becoming skinny (weigh him) this is nothing to be concerned about. Sometimes the food can be in such a rush to get through (carrots can reappear in 20 minutes!) that the consistency is rather loose; then it is described as toddlers' diarrhoea. Avoiding high-fibre foods and also 'squash'/coolaid-type drinks may help a little.

Lactose intolerance

Diarrhoea that persists for longer than two weeks is not uncommon in babies and toddlers even at home. The bowel usually makes an enzyme called lactase without which the sugar in cow's milk (lactose) cannot be processed. A temporary lactase deficiency can follow a bad bout of gastroenteritis, when milk will tend to go straight through and come out at the bottom end as a gassy explosive diarrhoea with abdominal cramps. Avoiding milk-based products should cause a dramatic improvement within a day or two, and if the child seems much better give her bowel a rest from milk products for a few days. If despite this the diarrhoea continues, seek help.

Persistent diarrhoea with weight loss

This may indicate *Cyclospora* (see next paragraph) or rarely even tuberculosis or tropical sprue. Troublesome diarrhoea often mysteriously improves on returning to the comforts of home; if you are not on your way home, consult a gastroenterologist who should do some tests and may then give the locally appropriate treatment for tropical sprue.

Cyclospora and Cryptosporidium

There are a couple of inconvenient parasites which are common worldwide. *Cryptosporidium* gets into water supply systems in Britain and elsewhere. It causes an unpleasant diarrhoea with abdominal cramps which lasts ten days or so. There is no treatment except fluids. *Cyclospora* (see also *Chapter 6*, page 73) causes a less dramatic diarrhoea which seems almost to get better but then comes back repeatedly over 6–12 weeks. *Co-trimoxazole* clears the infection. Both can be diagnosed from microscope examination of a fresh stool but non-specialist laboratories may not detect it.

Mild but prolonged diarrhoea, or gassy diarrhoea

In children under the age of two, lactose intolerance (see above) is the most likely cause of diarrhoea which goes on for more than two weeks with explosions into the nappy. In older children the commonest culprit is *Giardia*; symptoms include being off colour, usually watery smelly motions, lots of burping and flatulence and the child may go off her food. *Giardia* can be identified by a simple stool test involving the microscopic examination of a fresh stool. One negative result does not rule out the diagnosis though since only about 80% of samples from people with *Giardia* will get a positive test result; so take two more samples collected several days apart. Various worms (see pages 165–6) may also cause mild bowel disturbance and this is another reason for taking at least two samples to the laboratory. The treatment for *Giardia* is either *metronidazole* for three days (1–2[+]-year-olds need 500mg daily; 3–6[+]-year-olds 600–800mg a day; 7–10-year-olds 1g a day; and people over ten years 2g a day). These amounts can be divided so that you give the medicine two or three times in the day. The newer *tinidazole* is a single dose of 50mg/kg bodyweight. Side effects are fewer at these lower doses (compared with treatment of amoebic dysentery).

Passing blood with the faeces in absence of diarrhoea

Occasionally a child may pass blood with her stool. Check for a source of the bleeding at the anus; anal fissure is described on page 137 and will require the same treatment as below for constipation. If there is no obvious cause this may indicate a serious problem. In a very young child (less than two years) consider intussusception (see page 131). There are several rarer causes for blood loss in the gut which require prompt investigation and possibly surgery.

Constipation

Travelling children may become constipated for several reasons. Changes of diet may slow the passage of food through the bowel or a mild bout of diarrhoea might upset the usual routine. Hot weather may make a child mildly dehydrated; this tends to harden the stool and make it slower in transit. A change in the frequency of needing the toilet is in itself nothing to worry about. But if the stools become uncomfortably hard, take some action. First make sure the child is drinking plenty and at regular intervals and see if you can increase the amount of fibre in the diet. If you are in a rice-eating culture this may be difficult; wholemeal bread will not be available but in India chapatis are made with wholemeal flour, and fruits and perhaps sweetcorn should be available. Beware, though, that some children become more constipated if they eat bananas – a tea made from boiled banana skins is actually a diarrhoea cure in Africa. If drinking more and eating more fruit does not help, try some bulking agent like bran, ispaghula husk or methylcellulose. Running about also stimulates the bowel! Otherwise see if *lactulose* syrup is available at the pharmacy, and take as recommended on the bottle (1ml/kg/day).

Abdominal problems

Abdominal distension or a swollen tummy

A normal toddler's belly protrudes because of the shape of the lower spine; worms are rarely the cause of a swollen belly. A swollen tummy is not a cause for concern unless it is painful on prodding or there is also constipation and vomiting. This suggests there may be an obstruction: seek urgent medical advice.

Abdominal pain and appendicitis

Most causes of abdominal pain are trivial but pain on movement (coughing, turning in bed or while out driving in a car over a bump) suggests the lining of the abdomen is inflamed (peritonitis) which occurs in appendicitis, and necessitates an operation. Abdominal pain which wakes a child at night often indicates a significant problem. How do you tell the difference between a tummy upset and early appendicitis? A child with an appetite, or who can be tempted to play or eat something, does not have appendicitis. In appendicitis the child will almost certainly have taken to his bed and refuse all food, and typically the pain moves from the tummy button down towards the right groin. If pain makes the child reluctant even to roll over, then appendicitis is a strong possibility and you need to consult a doctor to see whether an operation is necessary. Occasionally the early signs of appendicitis are not recognised by even the best doctors; so, even if someone has previously reassured you, if the child is not improving or seems to be deteriorating seek a second opinion (perhaps in a bigger town). Intussusception is a cause of crying and pain in children under two; this is discussed on page 131.

Tummy aches

Tummy ache is a common complaint of young children when they are feeling unwell and it may be an expression of almost any physical or psychological ill! Children under the age of three may point to their tummy when they have a sore throat or earache! The pre-schooler who is anxious about being in new surroundings, with parents distracted by the practicalities of travel, may take refuge in the attention a bout of tummy ache is likely to earn her.

One-tenth of schoolchildren suffer from repeated tummy aches and this is at least as likely to come on during a trip abroad as at home. The pain is typically right in the centre of the belly – children often point to the tummy button when asked where the pain is. The attack should settle within a few hours and no treatment is needed. If the child experiences a mild fever and sore throat, this indicates a slightly different illness which is probably a viral infection and this is unlikely to recur. A dose of *paracetamol* may cheer the child up in any case. Pain which centres on the belly button is generally benign whilst children pointing to another part of the abdomen are more likely to be significantly ill. There are plenty of causes of tummy ache but you may need a doctor's help to sort out the trivial from the serious. Severe pain persisting for more than half a day is worrying.

Viral illnesses may cause enlarged tender glands in both the neck and the abdomen, and this can cause a rather more prolonged attack of tummy ache and mild fever: this is mesenteric adenitis. The pain will come and go, the child will be able to get out of bed if encouraged and she will eat snacks. Another cause of tummy ache is a urine infection which is more likely in girls than boys (see below).

There are many other rarer causes for abdominal pain. If the symptoms do not fit the common causes described above, the child appears generally unwell, or the pain is continuously present for six hours or intermittently present for more than 24 hours then seek a medical opinion promptly.

Urinary symptoms
Pain on urinating

This is a common problem, especially in girls. The commonest cause is irritation where the urine leaves the body via the short urethra. This is commonly red and angry-looking due to irritation caused by a combination of factors. If this is the case start a regime of frequent washing in warm, non-salty water without soap or any other chemical irritant and don't let the child spend all day in wet, sandy nylon swimwear. If she insists on hanging around the water's edge let her go without clothes if necessary. The irritation will settle down on this regime in the vast majority of cases. Pain without irritation may be a sign of a urinary tract infection; it is more likely in a hot climate when a girl is not drinking enough. Ideally urinary infection needs to be confirmed by a laboratory test before commencing treatment.

Discoloured urine

Small amounts of blood make the urine appear smoky. If this is due to a kidney problem there may be a puffiness of the face and the child may complain of a severe throbbing headache. This is called **nephritis** and requires early medical help to control the high blood pressure which results.

Truly bloodstained urine is more likely to be due to a urinary tract infection. Other causes of red urine are having eaten beetroot, blackcurrants, blackberries and rose-hip syrup. Eating lots of carrots (or other orange foods) may turn the urine yellow whilst several drugs can turn urine funny colours.

Vaginal bleeding

This (sometimes) smelly discharge suggests something has been pushed up inside. This is common in inquisitive toddlers but requires delicate examination to extract the offending object – a non-urgent procedure best left to a doctor in an emergency room when you find one.

Scrotal pain and swelling

Torsion of the testis can occur at any age but peaks around the age of ten. The boy will complain of pain (in the scrotum or possibly lower abdomen) which may come and go over a period of several hours. He may have had similar episodes of pain before. A surgeon should be consulted without delay; the problem requires an operation within a few hours.

Worms

Threadworms (Enterobius vermicularis)

Threadworms (also called pinworms) cause intense itching around the anus especially at night; the consequent scratching helps to spread the eggs around the home and thus infect the rest of the family. The worms are white and thread-like and measure 2–13mm. They are highly contagious and lurk under fingernails. The best drug for anyone over the age of two years is *mebendazole*: one dose followed by a second after 2–3 weeks; this is not safe in pregnancy. Children under two should take *piperazine*: two doses 14 days apart. Everyone in the family needs treatment; nails should be cut short; and meticulous attention to hand-washing before eating (even snacks) is also needed. Expatriates may need to treat the household staff too.

Roundworms (Ascaris lumbricoides)

Roundworms are big: they look like whitish-pink earthworms; they can cause mild abdominal discomfort but rarely do any harm. If your child passes one it may be worth getting a stool sample checked before treatment since sometimes only one lonely individual is present. Treatment of roundworm in the over twos is with *mebendazole*: 100mg twice daily for three days. Children with roundworm aged 1–3 can take *piperazine*: 10ml/1.5g dose (containing

750mg/5ml) repeated after two weeks. Older children need bigger doses if you use this medicine: 4–5-year-olds take 15ml/2.25g; 6–8 years 20ml/3g; 9–12 years 25ml/3.75g; and over 12 years 30ml/4.5g. Avoid *albendazole*. This drug should only be used to treat the dangerous infestation with the very rare hydatid worm or troublesome strongyloides worms (a doctor or laboratory might give these diagnoses). In these cases, or if you suspect tapeworm, take expert advice rather than treat your child.

BREATHING AND THE CHEST AND THROAT
Breathing and the chest
Breathing problems are probably the most alarming conditions encountered in children. Communicating your distress to your child will worsen the situation, so stay outwardly calm whilst assessing the situation. Decide which description below is most relevant and follow the advice accordingly.

Unable to drink or talk due to breathlessness
A child who is too breathless to talk may be having an asthma attack. She is in serious trouble and should be taken to a hospital immediately. Meanwhile give any asthma medicines previously prescribed for her. If you are uncertain how ill the child is count the breathing rate and look for indrawing. See *Chapter 9*, pages 138–9. Asthma usually starts with coughing and **wheezing** over a few hours or days; wheeze is a high-pitched musical whistling sound on breathing *out*. Asthma is common in children; perhaps 20% are affected so it is a possibility even if no-one has made the diagnosis before, and especially if any relatives suffer from asthma or eczema. It can be dangerous so seek help early especially if you do not feel confident about dealing with an attack.

Difficulty breathing
Several childhood infections can cause difficulty in breathing but the danger signs are similar. Breathing rate is an excellent indicator of how ill a child is and any child breathing at more than 40 complete breaths in and out per minute needs urgent medical assessment and treatment. If the breathing rate is variable, time it for one to two minutes, and repeat the count a second time. Sudden difficulty breathing happens when a child chokes on any small object ranging from a peanut, coin or a piece of meat to a toy animal; see page 109 for first aid.

The most serious breathing problem is **epiglottitis** which is most likely to affect children over the age of two years. The illness usually comes on rapidly over a few hours, often during the early evening or night. The child will be hot (feverish), obviously unwell, drooling, and unable to swallow. She anxiously sits upright. Her breathing is usually noisy with a harsh sound on breathing in; in severe cases the breathing can be noisy on breathing in *and* out. This noisy breathing is called **stridor** and is a danger sign. Other related danger signs are fast breathing (40 a minute or more), and chest indrawing (see pages 138–9). In really severe cases the child will have noisy breathing with rapid respirations but will tire so that the respiratory rate becomes slower, the noisy breathing less obvious and she will go blue. Any child with stridor must be seen urgently by a doctor but do not let anyone examine her throat until safely in a well-equipped accident department or emergency room! Ideally you should get her to sophisticated medical facilities where artificial ventilation is possible ... just in case. If hospital admission is not possible, the local physician or paramedic may need to start treatment with *adrenaline* (by injection initially) which will have to be given repeatedly to reduce airway obstruction. The good news is that your child will be largely protected against this particular disease if she has had the Hib immunisation.

Croup also causes stridor and a barking cough. It can cause serious problems in children from six months to three years, although usually it is a less serious condition than epiglottitis. Children with dangerous croup will also have the danger signs of rapid breathing and indrawing. A child under three with stridor should be taken to hospital or if hospital is too far get into a steamy environment; a boiling kettle in a small room or running a hot shower in a hotel bathroom will help. Keep the air conditioner off. Check for the danger signs of stridor (noisy inhalations) and fast breathing (more than 40 a minute) and look for indrawing (pages 138–9). Finally check she is well enough to drink. We personally know of two deaths from croup in expatriate children: it can be dangerous and must be treated seriously. Any danger signs mean you should evacuate to a hospital, preferably one where they can perform operations on children.

If she has a croupy cough but is breathing and drinking normally you can be reassured, but sleep in the same room as her and check there is no deterioration in the night. Croup, like all respiratory illnesses, is typically at its worst in the small hours of the night. In school-aged children croup is noisy but unlikely to cause problems.

Chesty cough with fever
A cold that drags on and goes 'on to the chest' is quite common and suggests pneumonia, which is infection of the lungs. There may be a persistent cough with or without wheeze (see below). Pneumonia is severe when it causes rapid breathing, fever and chest indrawing. This is a reason to go to hospital for antibiotic treatment urgently. Antibiotics may initially be given intravenously via a drip. Many clinics take a chest X-ray. Differentiating pneumonia from asthma can be difficult, especially as infections often trigger asthma attacks. Productive coughs will not be improved by taking cough remedies, but drinking plenty will help loosen the phlegm.

Long-lasting cough with or without wheeze
A cough which drags on for more than two or three weeks, or which is worse during/after exercise or at night, may indicate asthma; it is a very common problem of childhood and about one-fifth of children suffer from it. Children with close relatives who have had asthma or eczema are more likely to suffer. Asthmatics often turn out to be children who suffer from frequent 'chest infections' and the most common trigger bringing on an attack is a common cold. In very young toddlers a cough, which is worse at night, may be the only symptom of asthma. As asthmatic children get older a musical expiratory wheeze usually becomes more obvious. Urban pollution (common in burgeoning big cities), wood-smoke in poorly ventilated rural houses, summer pollen and autumn fungal spores are all possible new triggers; air conditioners or smoking in the hotel room can bring on an attack too.

If your child is asthmatic you should carry suitable medicines, but if you have forgotten or he does not respond to these do not delay seeking help simply because you are abroad. The most commonly used asthma medicines are given in inhalers. Even adults find inhaled medicines difficult to use, and the best way around this problem is to acquire a polystyrene coffee cup, and push the delivery end of the inhaler through the bottom of the cup. By placing the cup over the child's nose and mouth and activating the inhaler the child can breathe in the fine mist of medicine from the cup. Asthma is safely and effectively treated with a five-day course of steroid syrup or tablets. The other treatment which may be required for severe asthma is nebulised medicines through a mask in hospital.

A rarer cause of a persistent cough is a small object inhaled accidentally. Was there an episode of choking which may have preceded the illness? Nearly half of all inhaled objects are nuts. It is not unusual to find an object in the lungs despite no-one realising the child has even choked: recently Matthew was surprised to see an X-ray reveal a clothes peg in a toddler's lungs, yet mum had noticed nothing!

Runny nose with cough

Children suffer from lots of coughs and colds wherever they are. Children get 5–8 episodes of respiratory illness (coughs and colds) a year, or about 50 days annually. The average rate is even higher, rising to 11, in the first year of school. On average half of all illness in the under twos is respiratory (coughs, colds, etc) while in the 5–12-year age-group respiratory illness accounts for 30%. Many families develop colds after a long flight too: it is prudent to travel with your *paracetamol* or Tylenol ready.

Tickly cough

Tickly dry coughs (without fever) are common and can be very troublesome; honey helps relieve the symptoms. Half a teaspoonful taken neat seems to help children tortured by a relentless cough at night or you can make a honey drink with lemon or other goodies. Cough remedies have no proven therapeutic effect and in some instances they will contain dangerous cocktails of drugs. Gargling with warm water or with solutions of soluble *paracetamol* can also be soothing.

Colds and congestion

The common cold is common wherever you go. Children's tubes are small and so relatively little congestion can cause problems and pain especially if it prevents a child equalising pressure in the ears during flying (or diving into a swimming pool). *Pseudoephedrine* (Sudafed) taken two hours before a flight will help, as can inhaling steam; put boiling water into a bowl and get the child to lean over it with a towel over her head if she is old enough not to tip it over herself. Plenty of grease on the nose will help it stop getting sore, and so will using cloth handkerchiefs; paper 'tissues' are made of pulverised wood and are very scratchy indeed. If you don't possess handkerchiefs buy a quarter-metre of some soft cotton and use that. Sinusitis occurs in older children with a blocked nose and aching around the nose, cheeks and forehead. Steam inhalations should also help.

Sore throat or tonsillitis

School-aged children will often complain of a sore throat; if they also have a cold, the illness is probably caused by a viral infection and antibiotics will not help. The sore throats which are most likely to respond to antibiotics are those causing a high fever (39°C or more), enlarged and painful red tonsils covered in white pus and also painful enlarged glands at the side of the neck just in beneath the angle of the jaw. There is no reliable way to distinguish a viral from a bacterial sore throat without taking a throat swab, but the laboratory will take a couple of days to produce the result. The same bacteria can cause scarlet fever, a high fever with an impressive bright-red rash which accompanies the sore throat. The correct treatment for all bacterial sore throats is a ten-day course of *penicillin* or, if your child is allergic to *penicillin*, *erythromycin* (doses are in *Chapter 3*, page 36). The long course of treatment is required to clear streptococcus bacteria, and if you opt to treat with antibiotics you must ensure you finish the course.

Lumps in the neck

Lumps in the neck, particularly beneath the ears, are common in children with infections of the throat or ears: most swellings in the neck are NOT due to mumps (see pages 152–3). Sometimes a swelling persists after the obvious infection has passed; if it has not gone in a month see a doctor but remember, unlike in adults, cancer almost never presents itself in this way. Lumps in the neck can follow head louse infestation.

EARS, EYES AND NOSES
Ears and earache

Infection of the middle ear is common; it is a frequent problem in pre-schoolers and 20% of two-year-olds will suffer. Ear infections sometimes cause temporary hearing loss. There is a build-up of secretions behind the eardrum which becomes excruciatingly painful, causing the child to wake up in the night. If the eardrum bursts there is a smelly discharge and the pain goes away; and usually the problem settles without further treatment. If the drum has not burst treatment with *trimethoprim* syrup or tablets for five days should speed recovery; alternatively *amoxicillin* is often effective. *Erythromycin* or *clarithromycin* may be given to children who are allergic to *penicillin*. Further notes on giving antibiotics are in *Chapter 3*, pages 35–7.

Occasionally after a burst eardrum the drum fails to heal by itself and there is persistent discharge from the ear. This requires the attention of an Ear, Nose and Throat (ENT) specialist, but not urgently. It is also worth seeking a specialist ENT opinion if your child suffers frequent ear infections: six or more a year.

The outer-ear canal often gets infected, especially in hot humid countries. A sore, oozing or scabby area extends from the ear canal. This can be treated with any one of a variety of antibiotic eardrops. If the discharge is particularly nasty and long-lived do see whether the child has pushed a small pellet into the ear-hole. If you suspect an object is stuck, seek medical help. If the child gets a series of infections of this kind watch to see whether she is sticking things into the ear canal – and try to discourage the habit. Nothing should be poked into the ear – not even cotton buds.

The eyes
Conjunctivitis or pink-eye

Infections which turn the eye red are very common, especially in children and especially in the tropics. The infection usually starts in one eye, but rapidly spreads to the other and makes the eyes feel sticky, gritty, red and sore; often the child's eyelids are stuck together with green gunk in the morning. Start by mopping this stuff off with plenty of water – warm with salt in it is best, but plain cold water is also fine. Conjunctivitis like this is usually caused by bacterial infection and requires treatment with antibiotic drops into both eyes every 2–3 hours at first. Most antibiotics are fine; newer, fancier antibiotics cost more, but are no more effective. If the symptoms do not improve after 36 hours, try *tetracycline* drops or ointment. If this does not work seek medical help. Avoid eye preparations which contain any extras especially *hydrocortisone, betamethasone* or other steroids.

With small unco-operative patients drops are the easiest way of giving antibiotics. Lie the child on her back and put an antibiotic drop into each eye. It does not matter if the eyes are closed, for the medicines will seep in between the closed lids, or be rubbed in as the child struggles.

Viral conjunctivitis causes less inflammation, irritation, discharge and green gunk and there is usually a cold and/or sore throat. This will get better without treatment (although antibiotic drops will do no harm). Conjunctivitis is highly contagious so be careful about washing your hands after bathing the patient's eyes. Conjunctivitis can also be caused by getting noxious chemicals in the eye including slug slime, cicada spit, whip-scorpion squirt or centipede ooze (see pages 86 and 87). Bathe the eye in warm, slightly salty water and if the inflammation is very bad, tape or pad the eye closed and see a doctor.

Finally some children suffer from allergic conjunctivitis: the white of the eye is pink but there is very little sticky stuff. Sometimes drops can help (try *sodium cromoglicate* drops four times a day) and see a doctor if this doesn't alleviate the symptoms. See also hay fever in *Chapter 1* on page 9.

A single painful red eye implies a foreign body in the eye or a more serious problem. Seek help.

Styes

Styes are small boils on the eyelid; they are best treated by applying a hot compress (use a face cloth dipped into water which is hot, but not uncomfortably hot). If the infection starts to spread elsewhere on the face or the whole eyelid is becoming hot and inflamed a course of antibiotics (*flucloxacillin, cloxacillin, co-amoxiclav* or *erythromycin*) by mouth may be needed. Treat as for any skin infection (see pages 114–15; and see page 36 for doses).

Recurrent 'styes'

If your child gets a stye which does not discharge and go away or if one keeps recurring in the same place, a course of antibiotics (*flucloxacillin, cloxacillin, co-amoxiclav* or *erythromycin*) will be needed to clear the infection; the lump will probably remain but needs no further treatment unless it is causing recurrent problems, when a simple minor operation under local anaesthetic to remove the cyst can be done at leisure when you get home.

The nose
Nose bleeds
These seem to happen most dramatically whilst away on holiday. They often result from the combination of a cold and nose-picking nicking an inflamed nasal vein. The nose should be firmly pinched; a cold compress over the nose also helps. This will almost always succeed in stemming the flow provided sufficient patience is exercised. A full half-hour of pressure may prove necessary. Further nose-picking will provoke another nose-bleed! In high altitude or very dry, arid environments the inside of the nose can become very dry and sore. Smearing vaseline up the nose (on the end of your little finger) solves the problem. Persistent green or smelly discharge from one nostril may mean something is stuck inside (see page 125).

JOINTS AND ACHES
Perhaps the commonest cause of aching muscles and joints is the body's reaction to a fever. Usually this is a viral flu-like illness, but there are some more serious causes such as dengue (page 179) or brucellosis (below). *Paracetamol* will help reduce the fever and relieve the pain, whatever the cause.

Painful joints
It is not unusual for a well schoolchild to develop hip pain or pains in other joints with no injury or other obvious cause. The problem is not well understood but it settles down by itself after a few days; bed-rest speeds recovery. If the child has a fever and a painful joint, serious joint infection must be suspected and hospital investigation should be sought. Unusually several joints at the same time may become hot, painful and even swollen. This may follow, or be part of, a more widespread illness and should be fully investigated within a few days.

Brucellosis
This can cause a hot painful joint or joints; it is most often acquired either from direct contact with goats, sheep or pigs or from unboiled or unpasteurised milk or cheese. Cow's milk can also be a source. It is a rather evasive disease which lingers but can be difficult to diagnose. In the most dramatic cases there is a sudden onset of fever, shivering and sweating; but more often there is a rather vague fatigue, odd aches and pains and mild fever which comes and goes for weeks. There can be constipation or diarrhoea. Diagnosis is usually made after a blood test and then treatment is at least a three weeks' course of antibiotics.

Limping
If a child develops a limp which lasts more than a day or two or comes back from time to time, it is worth checking out. Limping usually indicates pain somewhere. Verrucae or something embedded in the sole of the foot can cause a limp. Even early appendicitis can cause a younger child to limp, or complain of hip pain.

First check the child's shoes for a protruding nail and her feet for blisters or puncture marks where a piece of coral, splinter or thorn might have entered. Pressing over a puncture mark ('ouch!') should tell you whether something remains inside. Next examine the affected leg looking for any signs of local heat, redness or tenderness. Check the ankle, knees and hip joints to ensure they are not hot or swollen and that they are moving freely. Finally check the groin for tender, inflamed glands. If you cannot decide whether there is a problem, compare with the other side. Most sites of infection are obvious and will require antibiotic treatment. If you suspect infection in a joint, this is serious and you should go to a hospital for intravenous antibiotics. Hip problems can cause a limp and can cause pain in the knee. Between one and seven years an 'irritable hip' is the commonest joint problem. For reasons that are not understood the child gets hip pain and starts limping. She remains well in herself and any fever is slight. She will be back on her feet within a few days. If she is unwell and you are concerned that she may have a true joint infection then she should be promptly checked out by a doctor.

'Growing pains'
Any flu-like illness or cold will bring with it fleeting joint aches and pains. In the absence of any signs of joint inflammation these are merely a nuisance and will be controlled by *paracetamol*. It is not unusual for children between five years of age and puberty to experience vague leg pains especially around the knees. These are not understood but are called 'growing pains' and require no treatment except rest and *paracetamol* or *ibuprofen* if they interfere with sleep.

Cramps and other muscle aches
Pain that follows or accompanies vigorous exercise is almost always benign. Common sites are the tendon at the back of the ankle, the knees, small bones in the feet and the elbow. Pain comes on only during use of the affected part and disappears with a judicious balance between exercise and rest, which is the remedy for all these minor ailments.

RASHES, SPOTS AND OTHER COMMON INFECTIONS
The classic childhood diseases don't take a holiday and may accompany the family to spoil yours! These days you can prevent your children from catching measles, mumps and rubella by ensuring that they have been immunised. In case you have not taken this sensible precaution here are some ways of recognising these diseases and suggestions for what to do. Remember that reddish/purplish rashes which do not fade when pressed are a danger sign (see below).

If your child comes up in spots or a rash, decide whether she is off colour; if she remains well it probably does not matter what the diagnosis is. Mosquito bites tend to be few and on the exposed parts of the body (especially the face) after attack at night; in infants mosquito bites look like pinpricks. Fleas snack under the clothes and feast in lines so that there are breakfast, elevenses, lunch, tea and supper bite-marks. Flea bites are raised and itchy like mosquito bites, but sometimes they have a centre which looks filled with pus. Put bedding and clothes out in the sun to get rid of them. If the child is off colour too, or the itching is driving her mad try giving her *paracetamol* and dab the rash with *calamine* if you have it.

All itchy rashes become itchier when the skin is hot so tepid baths, *calamine*, loose cool clothes, and *paracetamol* if there is fever will all help relieve the misery. Bad reactions to **insect bites and stings** can be treated with antihistamine by mouth such as *cetirazine*, or *hydroxyzine* if sleep is needed; 1% *hydrocortisone*, 0.25% Betnovate RD or some such mild steroid may be required on the skin too.

Rashes and eruptions
The only dangerous rash: a purple-red rash which does not blanch
If you notice a reddish-purple skin rash check to see if it will blanch (go pale) when pressed: most rashes will go white when pressed. Put a glass over a spot to see whether it blanches on pressure. If the rash stays red this indicates that tiny amounts of blood have leaked out into the skin. This implies a blood-clotting problem and can be the first sign of a life-threatening infection with meningococcal bacteria, so if you find such spots get the child to a doctor fast. If there is likely to be any delay in getting to a clinic ask a paramedic or pharmacist to give an immediate intramuscular injection of *penicillin* (a child aged 1–9 years needs 600mg *benzylpenicillin* or *penicillin G*; anyone over ten years needs 1.2g).

There are less dangerous reasons for a rash which does not blanch. Small non-blanching spots on the front of the legs and the backs of the arms are usually accompanied by some mild swelling around the eyes and perhaps some discoloration of the urine with blood and often arthritis. This condition also requires prompt medical assessment. Non-blanching spots limited to the head and neck in a child with severe cough or retching are the result of the blowout of small blood vessels due to the high pressure involved in these manoeuvres and can safely be ignored. No treatment is necessary.

Unexplained bruising
More extensive bleeding into the skin may result from a shortage of platelets: the blood cell components responsible for clotting; there is usually a cold followed by bruising at the slightest touch. This condition usually only needs to be monitored but it is vitally important to get the diagnosis correct since leukaemia, the commonest (but still very rare) form of childhood cancer, can announce itself in this way.

Measles
This begins like a bad cold with a cough and sore eyes. The child gradually becomes more unwell with a fever and after a couple of days salt-grain-like spots can be seen on the inside of her mouth near the molar teeth. On the third or fourth day the rash appears on the skin. The spots begin on the forehead, behind the ears and on the neck from whence they spread downwards. The rash is red, slightly raised and rather than being discrete spots it tends to merge. It begins to fade five days after appearing. Ear and chest infection and diarrhoea are all common aspects of measles. Occasionally fits occur and may indicate serious complication. For these reasons if you think your child may have measles you should consult a doctor. Incubation takes 10–14 days; the illness lasts about ten days; and the patient is infectious until seven days after the appearance of the rash.

A very mild form of measles (with a slight rash) can occur 8–12 days after the measles immunisation; treatment is with *paracetamol*. It is best to get the routine immunisations over three weeks before travel or you could have a miserable child on your hands.

Rubella (German measles)

This is a trivial illness for a child but can harm unborn children. If you are in the first three months of pregnancy and unimmunised, then keep away from a child suspected to have rubella until at least a week after the first rash appeared. The illness begins like a slight cold with a mild fever for 1–5 days, then a pinkish, flat rash appears on the face and spreads downwards. Often lymph nodes can be felt at the back of the neck at about the hair line. No treatment is necessary. Incubation takes 14–21 days. The feverish part of the illness lasts perhaps five days; lymph nodes may be inflamed for 12 days. The patient is infectious until seven days after the appearance of the rash.

Roseola

This causes high fever (at least 40°C) and irritability for 3–5 days without anything else apparently being wrong. The fever fades on the fourth or fifth day as a blotchy rash appears on the trunk, spreads but then fades within 1–2 days. The commonest ages affected are six months to two years. The incubation period is nine days. *Paracetamol* is the treatment.

Erythema infectiosum or 'slapped cheek' syndrome

This parvovirus infection causes a mild illness without much of a fever. The main feature of the illness is a rash which is often most vivid on the face so that

---

SPOTS!

The phone rang. It was about Andrew, six-year-old son of a good friend.

'When he woke this morning there were spots!'

'What kind of spots?' I asked.

'Well ... just spots! I wondered whether he was getting chickenpox or whether they were mosquito bites? They're kind of normal pink bumpy spots! Most of them are on his face and chest; there aren't very many.' It hadn't occurred to me until then just how difficult it is to describe spots! I asked 'How is he? Any fever? Good appetite?'

'He seems fine; he ate a huge breakfast and is playing with his Lego now.'

'If he's well in himself, it's either something mild which doesn't need treating, or it's mosquito bites which don't need treating ... with chickenpox you'll notice that the child is a little off colour and mildly feverish before the rash starts. I don't think you need to worry, but phone me again if he becomes ill or you notice anything else. You've got mosquito nets, haven't you?'

'Yes, and I must put them up tonight: it looks as if the mosquito season is in Kathmandu again already!'

it looks as if the child has been slapped on both cheeks. The redness can also occur on the forehead and chin, with a contrasting whiteness around the mouth. There is a rash with a lace-like appearance on the arms and trunk then lower limbs. The illness most often affects school-aged children and there is no special treatment, although some *ibuprofen* can be given if the child is suffering from some aching of the joints. About half of adults are immune but the virus can cause problems in an unborn child if the mother catches this for the first time during the first 20 weeks of pregnancy; in this case a doctor should be consulted. The incubation period is 7–14 days.

Scarlet fever
This almost always accompanies a sore throat (see page 169), headache and fever. The rash looks like red pinpricks and appears a day or two after the beginning of the illness. It starts in the armpit or groin but rapidly spreads to the rest of the body. The tongue is often swollen, looks like an unripe strawberry and is heavily coated with a whitish fur. The illness responds to a ten-day course of *penicillin* (see treatment of sore throat) or *erythromycin* if allergic to *penicillin*.

Incubation is 2–4 days but can be seven; the rash lasts about six days and then peels; the fever lasts about five days. The child is infectious until she has been taking antibiotics for three days.

Fine pimply rash
A common cause of a fine pimply rash is prickly heat (see page 98) when the rash will be itchy and is most likely to be on the neck, back and chest. A more widespread and less itchy rash may be caused by a viral infection, which often also causes mild diarrhoea. In this case the child is only slightly off colour and requires no treatment.

Eczema
Eczema is a problem of the skin, especially the skin in the crooks of the elbows and back of the knees becoming dry and sore. It is commonest in families with members who also have eczema and those with allergic problems including asthma. It gets considerably better with liberal use of moisturisers (but beware of any that contain components to which your child is sensitive) and the avoidance of soap and other cosmetics. Soap dries the skin and is not needed much except for the dirty 'edges' of children – feet, knees and hands particularly. Aqueous cream and some of the other moisturisers can actually be used as soap substitutes. Eczema is unpredictable; it may get better or worse in hotter climates. Non-allergenic moisturising creams may be difficult to find while travelling so if your child suffers from eczema make sure you pack enough. Mild steroid creams are also needed from time to time; never put steroid creams on the face unless guided by a competent doctor. As with all continuing medical problems it may be worth discussing your travel plans with your doctor before you leave home.

Hives (urticaria)
Hives is common in children under five; it is a rash of red blotches and white raised weals that itch. Sometimes it is precipitated by an allergy to a medicine

or food, but often no cause can be identified. It disappears and reappears over hours or days. Treatment is to ease the itching with a soothing lotion such as *calamine* and antihistamine syrup such as *chlorphenamine* (Piriton). Rarely a more serious allergic rash develops with widespread blistering all over but especially of the mouth. This is a serious illness and requires hospital admission and treatment with high-dose steroids.

Acne

Acne, spots or zits torture innumerable teenagers: it afflicts 88% of people in the UK between the ages of 12 and 25, yet there is now a range of very good treatments. Sufferers should consult their family doctor. If one treatment does not help, go back to the doctor and ask for another. If acne is a problem, it can get considerably worse in strong sunlight. Sunbathing is therefore an extremely bad idea for those with acne, and precautions like staying out of the midday sun and wearing a hat are doubly necessary. Infected acne is best treated with *oxytetracycline* antibiotic capsules: 500mg twice a day for a week followed by 250–500mg daily for as many months as is required – this should control and clear the acne.

Cold sores

Cold sores are crusty eruptions on the lip which tend to recur in teenagers when they are run down, having a period, under stress, etc. This is another problem which may re-emerge after exposure to strong sunshine. If someone with an active cold sore kisses another, they may catch it. Sufferers should pack *aciclovir* cream; the cream works best if applied *before* the cold sore appears, but when the tingling in the lip indicates it is about to erupt. The cream is now available over the counter in the UK and in India. If a cold sore appears for the first time when you are travelling it may be impetigo (see opposite).

Scabies

This is an especially distressing, excruciatingly itchy rash caused by minuscule mites mining beneath the skin; itching is worse at night. It often starts between the fingers but can be very widespread and because it induces children to scratch the rash quickly becomes infected. The whole family and anyone in close contact needs to be treated; unfortunately the itching may persist for a week or so after successful treatment. As the mites do not survive away from the body, there is no need to treat bedding or clothes; just wash them as normal.

Malathion 0.5% is probably the best parasiticidal preparation widely available for treatment of scabies. *Permethrin* can be used in children over two. The older *lindane* carries a greater risk of side effects and is best avoided in children and breast-feeding or pregnant women. *Benzyl benzoate* is effective but more irritant to the skin. Aqueous lotions are preferable to alcohol-based which are more irritant and to creams which achieve lesser coverage. All members of the family should be treated simultaneously. Apply the lotion all over in children under two years, sparing only the mouth and eyes. Pay particular attention to the web spaces between the fingers. In older family members you can stop at the neckline. Be sure to get the lotion under finger nails and reapply if the hands have been washed. Leave the lotion to dry and wash off 24 hours later.

SOME COMMON CAUSES OF ITCHING IN THE TROPICS
- Insect bites – raised bumps (pages 143 and 172–3)
- Heat rash – often on front of upper chest (page 98)
- Eczema – dry patches of red flaking skin (page 175)
- Scabies – dry excruciatingly itchy patches classically initially between the fingers and at the wrists (page 176)
- Fungus infections – dry whitish patches between toes and elsewhere (pages 178–9)
- Geography worm – migrating worm-like track often on feet or buttocks (page 89)
- Onchocerciasis/river blindness – parts of Africa and tropical America only (page 96)
- African sleeping sickness – parts of tropical Africa only (page 85)

Moles and bumps on the skin

White children who are exposed to the sun a great deal – especially tropical and subtropical sun – are at increased risk of developing skin cancer in adulthood. This is most likely to look like a dark brown or black mole that changes in colour or shape, or grows or starts weeping, bleeding, itching, oozing or sprouts hairs. A changing or growing patch on the skin or an ulcer must be checked by a doctor. Skin cancers are extremely rare in children; commonly they occur after the age of 30 years.

Blistering rashes
Impetigo

Impetigo looks rather like a cold sore but spreads and weeps and can be anywhere on the body. It is exceedingly common, especially in travellers to warm moist climates. It is highly contagious and can be spread by fingers, shared bath sponges and face cloths. The infection often begins in a crack at the corners of the mouth or in a mosquito bite. If you catch the infection early you will control it by rubbing with cotton wool or gauze soaked in plenty of a drying antiseptic like potassium permanganate solution, dilute iodine, red mercurochrome or gentian violet. Ideally you need to get the scab off, but what is more important is to douse the area in lots of antiseptic three or four times a day. Weepy rashes get worse if moisturised, so antiseptic creams are not good for impetigo; but antibiotic cream or *neomycin* powder works well. If the problem occurs in more than one or two wounds, antibiotic syrup or tablets will be needed; *flucloxacillin* or *clarithromycin* are best.

Even the smallest graze or mosquito bite is a break in the skin which can lead to a troublesome wound infection which in hot, moist or unhygienic environments can spread to make the child quite ill. Clean and dress all wounds promptly and thoroughly follow the guidance on pages 114–15.

Scalded skin syndrome

A rash which spreads from the skin folds of the neck and armpits and blisters rapidly suggests a serious infection which needs treatment in hospital. In this condition the child's skin may look as if she has been badly scalded and the skin peels off in sheets. There will be high fever, but no blisters in the mouth. Evacuate to hospital and, if there is going to be any delay reaching medical help, start antibiotics by mouth: *flucloxacillin* or other *penicillin, erythromycin,* or *clarithromycin* would all be good.

Chickenpox

The illness begins with the child feeling unwell with a slight temperature. Within 1–2 days the spots appear on the chest and back and are initially red and flat. Within hours the rash becomes raised and then starts to blister. Over the next couple of days other similar blisters appear on the trunk but they also spread over the face, upper arms and legs. One characteristic of the infection is that the blisters come in crops; usually three crops in as many days, and once these crust the child is no longer contagious. The rash is itchy and the commonest problem is skin infection due to scratching. Keeping the skin cool reduces the number of spots and relieves the itching so give frequent tepid baths, daub liberally with *calamine* lotion, and keep the child stripped or put on loose-fitting 100%-cotton clothes. Give regular *paracetamol* and plenty to drink while the child is feverish and do not put on too many bed-covers. Keeping fingernails short will help reduce the scarring. Difflam spray (*benzydamine hydrochloride*) will soothe any blisters inside the mouth. Eventually the skin spots dry into scabs which drop off. Adults who have had chickenpox can catch shingles from a child with chickenpox and there is a risk to the unborn child during the first ten weeks of pregnancy and if the baby is delivered during or soon after the mother has had chickenpox. Incubation is usually 14–16 days but can be 20. The fever goes on for about a week. It is infectious (airborne spread) before the rash appears and then contagious (spread by touch) until the last crop of blisters have crusted; complete crusting occurs 5–10 days after the first appearance of the spots. You may not fly during the infectious phase of the disease. Chickenpox is not covered by the currently advised immunisation schedules in Britain, but immunisation is given in the US and can be arranged now in Europe.

Shingles

Painful blistering limited to a single strip of skin on one side of the body is shingles. The pain may precede the blistering by some days. Keep the rash clean and provide plenty of regular pain-killers; it occurs in older children and adults.

Hand, foot and mouth disease

This causes blisters to appear in those three sites. It is a mild viral illness causing the child to be a little off colour for 7–10 days; there are summer epidemics of the illness in temperate regions. No treatment is necessary. Foot-and-mouth disease of livestock is an entirely different infection that does not affect people except in extremely rare instances amongst farm workers.

Miscellaneous
Athlete's foot

Cracking and soreness between the toes is caused by a fungal infection and the treatment is an antifungal cream like *clotrimazole* (Canesten) or others listed on page 32. Allowing air to the feet and avoiding nylon socks helps clear the problem. There are now socks impregnated with antifungal chemicals. Tea tree oil has some antifungal action and should also help.

Boils

The normal treatment for these large, hot red tender swellings under the skin is to wait until they burst spontaneously. Otherwise when they are 'ripe' a doctor drains the pus with a scalpel. A pleasanter alternative is to buy some *magnesium sulphate* paste from a pharmacy; often it will need to be prepared especially by a pharmacist so simple medicine shopkeepers may not know about it. Apply a blob of the paste to the boil, trying to put the paste only on the inflamed skin; then cover with a waterproof dressing, Band-aid or Elastoplast; repeat every 12 hours or whenever the dressing comes off. After a few days the boil should discharge yellow pus and everyone will feel better.

NOTES ON RARE AND EXOTIC DISEASES

Rather than describing each and every enormously rare exotic disease we present a few notes on the most talked-about pestilences. Although not all possible diseases are mentioned by name in the text, prevention strategies will protect the family from almost all problems. Taking precautions against malaria, for example, will protect you from Japanese encephalitis; and avoiding mosquitoes which spread yellow fever will also protect you from dengue.

Cholera is a disease which causes profuse watery diarrhoea but rarely any lasting damage in well-nourished healthy people. There is usually no need to immunise against it for normal travel but the new cholera vaccine (Dukoral) gives some protection to the diarrhoeal diseases so is useful. It is avoided by observing precautions against other filth-to-mouth diseases (see page 71).

Dengue fever which is also called 'break-bone fever' is spread by day-biting *Aedes* mosquitoes (see page 80), most often in tropical and subtropical urban environments; it is an unpredictable illness which breaks out in epidemics all over the world where the climate is warm, although outbreaks in Europe are exceptional. In seasonal regions (such as in India) the disease is most prevalent around October. The illness comes in two forms, one of which is dangerous, but the commonest form is fortunately the only form likely to afflict travellers originating from countries free of the disease. This causes high fever, headache (especially behind the eyes), backache, joint pains and often a faint red rash on the trunk. The incubation is 3–10 days after the bite and the illness usually lasts 3–6 days and then settles by itself. There is no specific treatment, except *paracetamol* for the fever and pain. It is usually a mild disease in children. Many kinds of illnesses cause fever and aches so it would be wise to get a doctor to check your child.

Diphtheria has almost completely disappeared in the West but persists in many countries, both tropical and temperate, especially those with ongoing political or infrastructural problems. It starts with a sore throat and can progress rapidly to cause difficulties with breathing; it can also damage the heart and nervous system and if untreated can kill. Immunisation gives excellent protection but even so prophylactic *erythromycin* is advised if there has been close contact with someone with diphtheria.

Ebola virus was first recognised in Sudan and Zaire and half of the victims died. It makes people very ill suddenly with a high fever, after an incubation of about seven days. It is highly infectious and is untreatable.

Elephantiasis (filariasis) is the disease which adult males fear, but in travellers and expatriates the fever and illness caused by the first attack will precipitate a trip to the doctor long before the scrotum grows so large a wheelbarrow is needed to transport it. It is spread by night-biting mosquitoes so sleep under a permethrin-impregnated net.

Filariasis is the medical name given to tropical diseases caused by minute worms and spread by biting flies. Elephantiasis and loa-loa are two filarial diseases. There is a screening blood test which needs to be done more than six weeks after leaving a risk area.

Giardia is probably the most over-diagnosed and inappropriately treated disease of travellers; if you think someone in the family has it get a stool check before starting your own treatment. It causes smelly gas to issue from both ends of the intestinal canal but otherwise does little harm. The full Latin name of this protozoan is *Giardia lamblia* and it causes giardiasis.

Hepatitis means inflammation of the liver and the commonest cause in travellers (both children and adults) is from three kinds of viruses: hepatitis A (= infective hepatitis), hepatitis B (serum hepatitis) and the recently recognised hepatitis E. There are vaccines against A and B, and one under trial of E. A and E are transmitted by the filth-to-mouth route of infection so can be avoided by taking care in what you and the children eat. Hepatitis causes jaundice: the yellow discoloration of the whites of the eyes and the skin. Hepatitis E is sometimes dangerous in pregnancy.

Japanese encephalitis is a dangerous untreatable viral illness spread by night-biting mosquitoes which fortunately is virtually unknown in travellers and tourists. It may be a risk in families staying in poor rural conditions in endemic areas (a travel clinic will say if you are at risk). There is a vaccine.

Lassa fever is a West African disease which starts with a sore throat, aches and pains but then the victim suddenly deteriorates after 3–6 days into a very serious condition. It will come on within 3–30 days of being in a risk region. Avoid it by eating thoroughly cooked food.

Legionnaires' disease More than 95% of people infected suffer no symptoms whatsoever; so don't worry about this now well-understood and treatable condition.

Leprosy is one of the conditions causing loss of fingers, toes and sometimes the nose. It is not very contagious and you will not contract it by brushing past people in the bazaar nor by being touched by lepromatous beggars.

Loa-loa (loaisis) is caused by minute (filarial) worms spread by biting mangrove-flies in forest areas of central and western Africa; infestation causes local itching, prickling, swelling and aches and pains. See a doctor for the correct treatment.

Lyme disease is one of several **tick-borne** illnesses: a flu-like feverish illness after a tick bite should precipitate a trip to the doctor. Lyme disease begins a week to ten days after a tick bite. In 70% of victims there is a slowly enlarging raised red non-itchy weal spreading from the bite site and it reaches a diameter of 15cm (six inches) or so after a couple of weeks. Aching joints occur in 80% of victims and other common symptoms are fever, aching muscles and headache. If treated (with a three-week course of *penicillin* or *erythromycin*) within four weeks further more serious stages of the illness will be avoided. *Oxytetracyline* and *tetracycline* are also good antibiotics to use in children over the age of 12. Lyme disease occurs in the British Isles including Ireland, especially in deer country, and also in the US, tropical Africa and many other places wherever *Ixodes* ticks occur. To find out how to get ticks off, see page 83.

Meningitis means inflammation of the lining of the brain. This serious infection can be caused by a range of bacteria, TB bacilli, viruses and even protozoa. Immunisation is only possible against some strains of the meningococcus bacteria and TB. Viral meningitis is untreatable but is unlikely to be serious.

Plague is an enormously rare flea-borne disease of very poor communities; even during an epidemic normal travellers are unlikely to be at risk.

Rocky Mountain spotted fever is a **tick-borne** disease of the New World including **east** of the Rockies (it has even been recorded in New York City) and in Central and South America. Like many tropical illnesses, it starts with fever, aches and pains. There is usually a dark reddish-purple rash which starts on the arms and legs and later spreads to the trunk; it is treatable with antibiotics.

SARS (Severe Acute Respiratory Syndrome) was first recognised in 2003 when significant numbers of people in Southeast Asia became seriously ill with a kind of pneumonia. The infection is airborne but it is not as infectious as was first feared. Although the disease probably continues to simmer in overcrowded regions of China and neighbouring countries the risk to ordinary travellers is minute. People going to stay with relatives in Southeast and East Asia may be at some risk.

Sleeping sickness See tsetse flies on pages 85–6.

Tick-borne encephalitis is a very nasty viral infection acquired from **tick** bites in temperate forested areas of eastern Europe and Scandinavia, and also in parts of temperate central Asia. It is a risk during summertime and families who are camping, orienteering or walking in forested areas should protect themselves with long, loose clothes and also the vaccine. Anyone who develops a fever after a tick bite should consult a doctor. This infection is sometimes called European tick-borne encephalitis and the vaccine does not protect against tick-borne infections caught in the New World.

Tuberculosis (TB) is a disease common amongst poor people living in overcrowded conditions. It is not very infectious, and to catch TB you need to be in extremely close and repeated contact with an infected person: wandering through a crowded bazaar will not result in infection. Expatriates may be at risk if their household staff have the disease. If they have a chronic cough, unexplained weight loss or especially if they start coughing up blood they should be checked for TB at a clinic. TB and a few other infectious diseases can be caught from drinking unpasteurised cow's milk. Ensure all milk is boiled before consumption; powdered milk will be safe as long as the water used to make it up was clean. BCG immunisation gives some protection; see page 17.

West Nile fever is an infection transmitted by mosquitoes that are active from dusk until dawn; it can be mild but it can cause inflammation of the brain which is extremely serious. It occurs in Africa, the Middle East, west and central Asia and there have been sporadic cases in southern Europe since the 1960s. In 2004 two adults acquired the disease in the Algarve, Portugal. Recently it arrived in North America too where it is now a problem each summer. The virus affects birds and horses as well as humans.

Expatriate Life

EXPATRIATE FAMILY LIFE

The expatriate lifestyle can seem very attractive and it certainly has many advantages. But most expatriates are posted abroad, so may have little choice about where they are sent; some feel they have to choose between what they see as risking tropical diseases and splitting up the family. Yet educational psychologists list several advantages to children who are brought up abroad surrounded by people of other cultures.

Advantages of being brought up an expatriate...
• Tolerance and acceptance of difference
• Broader vision – global view
• Maturity of opinions
• Commitment to social service; wanting to do something worthwhile
• Ease of communication with adults
• Closer bonds within the immediate nuclear family unit
• At ease with social diversity.

...and disadvantages
There are challenges too. Playmates at home often don't understand (or care) what the child's family has been doing while away. Children can be isolated because of their different experience or may be labelled as 'know-alls'. Their maturity and sophistication make them different from stay-at-home contemporaries; so new returnees are teased and even accused of lying. Even children need to learn to 'edit' what experiences they talk about or be careful who they tell them to.

Children quickly pick up on all the enticing local stories featuring ghosts, curses and spirits, but sometimes these cause nightmares. Local people will have religious *pujas* and other defence mechanisms to deal with such fears; but expat kids have no access to such help, especially if the family's own religious affiliations keep them away from local belief systems. Perceptions and prejudices are presumably more important than actual belief bases. It was interesting talking to an American Buddhist about all this: spirits and curses posed no threat for her children because their beliefs could deal with anything that their religion raised.

ADJUSTING TO A NEW COUNTRY
It is perhaps dangerous to generalise, but some age-groups find up-rooting more difficult than others. Even so, as long as parents feel confident and

enthusiastic about a posting then the children too will be keen. The early teens may be one of the hardest ages for moving: children are often in turmoil then, anyway. Also the age of starting primary school can be an unsettled time, with children needing to find their identities and adjust to new social norms. Moving when children are infants or around three to four years of age is often relatively easy. Ideally, school should start straight after arrival in the new country so that the child is kept busy and quickly starts making friends. Then there's less time for brooding and homesickness.

The adjustment process

There are five transition stages of adjustment to a new country:

- Involvement and belonging in own native culture
- Leaving the home culture: celebration and excitement, but also distancing and denial
- Transition: chaos, anxiety
- Interim: superficiality, vulnerability
- Reinvolvement, intimacy, belonging: feels like home again.

The timescale of this process is highly variable; but knowing that the process happens can help families deal with the stresses of moving. If parents feel lost, insecure and anxious but recognise this as a temporary symptom of adjustment it is easier to cope and look forward.

Being a sedentary parent is a hard job and being a travelling parent is even harder, though it has its rich rewards. Many of us go through times when we might feel inadequate; if those feelings are getting you down be quick to seek help: talk it out with your partner or friends or seek professional counselling. Travel is stressful but the stresses can usually be put into context by talking things through.

Coping strategies

There are five key strategies for coping with the kinds of changes and challenges which travelling families, and especially expatriate families, encounter – the five Cs:

Communication – important for members of the family to talk through conflicts; there should be no taboo subjects.

Constancy and predictability – especially if the family is on the move children need reassuring rituals, particularly perhaps when they are settling down in the evening; such rituals as bedtime stories are readily transportable and you can even take them trekking!

Collaboration – involving the children in choices; planning together; consulting the children on what you and they need to take.

Closure – when the family is about to move on, allow time for genuine goodbyes and visiting favourite places; and talk about leaving.

Cultural confirmation – particularly when the family is living abroad long term, parents need to work on determining their identities and values, and ensuring that the children are similarly self-assured. Children like to know that they are not different from their parents in attitudes, affinities, affiliations. The nuclear (immediate) family is a much closer and more dependent unit when the family is travelling a lot or living an expatriate lifestyle; the children may lack geographical stability and so need more security from stable and predictable parents.

Education

Education and schooling is perhaps the biggest worry to expatriate parents or families travelling for long periods. Most capital cities will have a good international school, although good English-medium schools are not found everywhere. When choosing a school abroad, consider whether your child needs a British, North American or European curriculum. Many expatriate parents who are living in villages choose to send their children to the local school perhaps during the morning only and then teach them at home ('home-school') in the afternoon. This has the huge advantage of the child making local friends and learning the local language yet educationally keeping up with peers at home. The arrangement works well in young children up to the age of about eight, but thereafter the time becomes insufficient for progress both at the local school and in home-school. And, especially in Asia, local schools can impose terrific pressures on children to achieve at very young ages: there are even entrance exams for nursery schools! One child could read at the age of four but started bed-wetting and became miserable and withdrawn; the parents realised that she was not gaining any skills in problem-solving, but only excelling in areas which were rote-learned. The child became happier on changing schools. In Asia's best schools there is a surprisingly high suicide rate among older children who think they are failing. Parents need to be aware of these additional pressures and support their children as best they can.

Home-school curricula, teaching notes, books and teaching supervision can be bought; eg: from World-wide Education Service, Waverley House, Penton, Carlisle, Cumbria CA6 5QU; tel: 01228 577123; email: office@weshome.demon.co.uk; www.weshome.demon.co.uk. Before travelling, examine the contents carefully to determine what else you will need since the assumption is that you will have access to a photocopier and stationery. Nor is it cheap; the reception year (4–5-year-olds) for example costs over £1,500 including the recommended books. The great disadvantage of home schooling is that children can become socially isolated and the parents can have difficulties dividing parental from teaching roles. It is not an easy option; I have discussed home schooling now with dozens of parents and all say it is hard; children know how to manipulate parents in a way they never can with a teacher who is a relative stranger.

Avoiding illness

It is important to take precautions against mosquito-borne disease: fit screens to the windows and doors of the house and spray inside regularly, and dispose of or cover collections of water. Keep the main garden paths, especially the one leading to the outside toilet, clear of vegetation. And remember that keeping chickens and rabbits will attract rodents which in turn attract snakes. Ensure that all uncaged animals which are kept as pets are immunised against rabies. Any household staff who cough for more than a month and cough up blood probably have TB. Once a sufferer is on treatment they are no longer infectious.

Shoes

Finally, expatriate families with small children may have problems buying good shoes, especially for toddlers. We probably get a bit brainwashed in the West about the importance of children's footwear; indeed according to a paper in the *Journal of Joint & Bone Surgery* 77B 257–9 children who go barefoot until the age of six have healthy feet for the rest of their lives. Even so it is good to have decent shoes. Start-rite publishes 'Help for those living abroad' with notes on measuring children's feet and guidance on buying leather shoes by post. Styles are on their website at www.startriteshoes.co.uk. Write to Carol Monk, Start-rite Shoes, Peachman Way, Broadland Business Park, Norwich NR7 0WF, UK; tel: 01603 437909; email: carol.monk@start-rite.co.uk. Shoes are supplied by James Phillippo, tel: 01603 454967; fax: 506945; email: drummee1@aol.com. If you don't want to use this service and you wish to check whether shoe-size is correct, cut a strip of stiff paper to the length of the child's foot and see whether the strip fits inside the shoe.

VISITING FRIENDS AND RELATIONS

Families who have settled in another country often return home to stay with relatives and friends in the country of their birth. Or they may leave their adopted country to return home after decades away. From the point of view of illness, children of such resettled families are outsiders. The trip may involve, say, a British-born child going to stay with relatives in a big tropical city or in a remote and steamy village. The visitors will be welcomed back into the family and expected to behave like locals. With experience only of British illness patterns, they will have no resistance to local disease. Despite this, the visiting child will be expected to sleep out on the back verandah or in a bed with his cousins, will drink unsafe water or eat unsafe food perhaps, and will be bitten by malaria mosquitoes. For these reasons, this group of travellers are at much higher risk of going down with TB, dysentery or malaria after returning to their adopted home than are those without family links abroad. What little immunity people do acquire to malaria wanes within a year. In Southeast Asia there are unpleasant and very dangerous strains of dengue haemorrhagic fever; the way the disease attacks is not well understood but, unlike tourists, people who were brought up in the region and return in late childhood or adulthood are at the same risk as locals.

The inescapable fact is that whatever one's ethnic origins, adults returning 'home' after a long absence or children visiting grandparents have as much or even more risk of suffering from the local diseases than casual tourists. Visiting friends and relations need to be extra careful, get all their immunisations, take malaria prophylaxis, avoid mosquito bites and take all the precautions other travelling families have to take.

TRAVELLING WHILE PREGNANT
When is it safe to travel?

The safest time to travel while pregnant is between three and six months, but be aware that two diseases can be extremely serious if contracted during pregnancy: malaria and hepatitis E. During pregnancy it is probably unwise to travel to areas of high risk for malaria transmission or to areas where filth-to-mouth disease transmission is rife, for example the Indian subcontinent and Peru/Ecuador/Bolivia (see *Practical concerns*, page 6). It is not yet possible to immunise against hepatitis E or malaria. If pregnant (or planning a pregnancy) take special advice on malaria pills; some prophylactics are unsuitable and with Paludrine you need to take folic acid as well.

Miscarriages are common and perhaps one fifth of pregnancies miscarry. Most happen around the eighth or the 12th week and so you may wish to plan being close to a decent hospital at these times and not halfway to Everest base camp! Similarly you may wish to be close to medical facilities during the last two months of pregnancy. Many airline companies will not let women fly after the 36th week or after the 32nd week if carrying twins. Rules vary according to the length of the flight, the airline and your medical history so check before making your travel plans. Some airlines will ask for a medical check up and a fitness-to-fly certificate from your GP, for which there will be a fee. Pregnant women have a 60-fold increased risk of blood clots, so should wear flight socks on long-haul journeys by bus and plane. There are no medical contra-indications to flying whilst pregnant; it is just very inconvenient and unpleasant for everyone if a woman gives birth on a plane. And pain-relieving medicines and emergency care are difficult to arrange in the kitchen of an airliner.

Where to deliver

Maternity services in the West are good at identifying women who may get into trouble during labour and so in Britain the maternal death rate is about six deaths per 100,000 live babies born. In a country like Nepal where maternity services are not so good the death rate is over 500 per 100,000: nearly one hundred times greater. This kind of statistic hints at where may or may not be a safe place to have the baby. Giving birth to a child is one of the most dangerous things a woman will do in her life and it is illogical to think of it as a natural and therefore unhazardous process. The problem for many expatriate families, though, is that if mum opts to travel to have her child in a safe hospital she will often be separated from her partner; and baby-sitting the other children can be a problem. All these issues need to be considered during this anxious time when emotional support will be needed to allay maternal anxieties. We have said elsewhere (pages 7–8 and 128) that few people choose to go abroad before the baby is a month old and this is the earliest age we would advise you to go abroad with a new baby. By this time the baby will have put on weight above its birth weight, breast-feeding should be comfortably established and any problems present at birth will have been identified.

Returning Home after Travel Abroad

SCREENING AND SYMPTOMS

There was a vogue for returning travellers to go for a medical check-up after returning from an exotic trip or period of work overseas. Certainly, if anyone in the family has persistent symptoms or is worried they should see a doctor. As a general rule, however, routine check-ups are unnecessary. The reason for this is that almost all problems will cause some symptoms; there are very few illnesses which lurk unnoticed and then suddenly burst out and overwhelm the body. The very few exceptions to this reassuring fact are detailed below.

Malaria

Malaria is a dangerous disease that can kill rapidly, especially children and pregnant women. The severe and rapidly progressing illness is increasingly being imported into temperate developed countries. If you have been in a malarious region within the last three months any unexplained fever *could* be serious malaria and you should mention this fact to the doctor you consult. Malaria which has been partially treated or is one of the more benign forms may take up to a year to manifest itself. There is no screening test which can diagnose the problem so it is important for travellers and doctors to be aware of possible exposure. And don't forget to continue taking antimalarials for a month after return, unless taking Malarone.

Rabies

Rabies is acquired from the bite of a dog, monkey or other warm-blooded animal, or from a rabid animal licking broken skin. There are no symptoms initially, and no screening test. Injections are advised after any suspect bite. Once the symptoms of rabies begin, the disease is untreatable and invariably fatal.

Bilharzia

The African lakes are the commonest place to acquire this troublesome worm. Most travellers will get some symptoms (described on pages 96–7) but a few may not and a blood test *more* than six weeks after your last possible exposure will tell you whether you have the problem or not. The disease is readily curable.

HIV/AIDS

The human immunodeficiency virus may strike adolescents who have enjoyed sexual adventures without using condoms or have experimented with injectable recreational drugs.

Chagas disease

Chagas is a risk if the family has been staying in villages in South or Central America *and* has been bitten by assassin bugs; infection is most unlikely unless you have been sleeping on the floor in very poor wattle-and-daub-type ramshackle huts. If you are worried, there is some sense in getting a blood test to determine whether you have been exposed to the Chagas parasite. Very few travellers will have been exposed and it would probably be best to ask your family doctor to make enquiries at a specialist tropical diseases centre. See also page 88.

Worms

A large roundworm may be passed as much as 18 months after stowing away in your child's intestine. They are harmless although revolting. It is worth having a stool check before treating worms since sometimes the infestation comprises one lonely individual. If the thought of tropical worms really makes you feel squeamish you may want to send a stool sample off to the laboratory; otherwise do not bother. Unlike threadworms these large worms are not directly transmissible from one family member to another.

PSYCHOLOGICAL SYMPTOMS

Reverse culture shock can hit children, especially if the family has been abroad long term; and readapting to your own culture can cause problems, especially for adolescents who may also be going through their own identity crises. There are some special tips for expatriates in the preceding section (page 183). One important area to be aware of is the need for **closure**, that is allowing a comfortable separation from familiar places and friends when the family is about to move on. Goodbyes need to be said to both people and favourite haunts, and it is healthy to talk a little about leaving. The longer you have been based in a place, the longer the closure rituals should be; but even after a holiday, children like a 'last go' on this slide or a 'last visit' to that favourite rocky cove. Ensure they know it is a last visit. And when you get 'home' be prepared for all the adjustment problems you may have noticed when you first went abroad; these processes are mentioned in the previous section (page 183). Travel is stressful so allow all members of the family time to adjust.

Finally be aware that children are treasured and protected in developing countries in a way we have forgotten at home. Returning children who are not shy of strangers may be exposed to possible new hazards or even abduction. Expatriate children are more mature in many ways but they also may have been sheltered from the obscene aspects of 'civilised' countries.

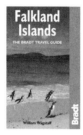

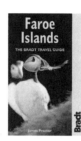

Appendix 1

USEFUL ADDRESSES AND FURTHER INFORMATION AND ADVICE
Health information and travel clinics
There are many travel health websites that supply up-to-date information on disease risks and outbreaks; none are perfect but the best is www.fitfortravel.scot.nhs.uk.

Other useful websites
www.who.int Information on tropical diseases but in rather over-technical language
www.fco.gov.uk/travel/countryadvice Security information
www.tripprep.com Not specifically for children but a good site for general and travel health advice, www.nathnac.org is also useful
www.cdc.gov/travel The scary but comprehensive American site

The Blood Care Foundation PO Box 588, Horsham, West Sussex RH12 5WJ, UK; tel: 01403 262652, or Chemin de la Petite Fontaine, 1261 Trelex, Vaud, Switzerland; telex: 427 172 CH; tel: 022 369 1904, fax: 022 369 2814. International agents are **SOS Assistance SA**, 15 Rue Lombard, CH-1205 Geneva, Switzerland; tel: 41 22 347 6161; fax: 41 22 346 2932. They promise to deliver blood of an appropriate type or quantity by courier to anywhere in the world; they offer a good deal for expatriate families.
MEDEX Assistance Corporation PO Box 5375, Timonium, MD 21094-5375, USA; toll-free: (800) 537 2029; fax: (410) 453 6301; tel: (410) 453 6300; email: medexasst@aol.com. *Also at* Victoria House, 5th Floor, 125 Queens Rd, Brighton BN1 3WB, UK; tel: 01273 223002; and Gotthardstrasse 17, 6300 Zug, Switzerland; and Regus Office 19, Beijing Lufthansa Center, No 50 Liangmaqiao Rd, Beijing, 100016, China. Offers cover for travelling individuals and families and also expatriates. They provide medical evacuation assistance, help in locating appropriate medical care while abroad, and sell safe medical kits.

Resources and contact details by country
UK
Foreign and Commonwealth Office Tel: 0870 606 0290; www.fco.gov.uk/travel
Hospital for Tropical Diseases Mortimer Market, Capper St, London WC1E 6AU; tel: 020 7387 4411; www.thehtd.org. Their telephone health line, 020 7388 9600, can give advice on specific destinations, while the clinic offers a comprehensive pre-departure service and also post-trip consultations.
Malaria Reference Laboratory Tel: 09065 508908. Country-by-country information line but there is a long list of destinations that cannot be short-circuited.

MASTA (Medical Advisory Services for Travellers) London School of Hygiene and Tropical Medicine, Keppel St, London WC1 7HT; tel: 09065 501402; www.masta.org. Phone for a personalised health brief. Or attend one of the 30 **MASTA pre-travel clinics** in Britain. Tel: 0870 241 6843 for the nearest. They sell some travel health products.

Nomad Travellers' Store and Medical Centre 3–4 Wellington Terrace, Turnpike Lane, London N8 0PX; tel: 020 8889 7014; www.nomadtravel.co.uk. Offers travel health advice, an immunisation service and sell *permethrin* clothes and bed-net treatment kits, repellents and a range of travel health products. They also have two other London shops/clinics and one in the STA shop, 43 Queen's St, Bristol; tel: 0117 922 6567. You can also call for information (particularly on immunisations) on the **Nomad Travel Health Line** Tel: 09068 633414 (premium rate).

Royal Free Travel Health Centre Pond St, London NW3 2QG; tel: 020 7830 2885 and 020 7472 6114; www.rfc.ucl.ac.uk/departments/TravelHealthCentre/about-us.htm. Immunisations, kits and returning travellers' clinic.

Interhealth Worldwide 157 Waterloo Rd, London SE1 8US; tel: 020 7902 9000. Profits fund health care for overseas workers on Christian projects.

Trailfinders Travel Clinic 194 Kensington High St, London W8 7RG; tel: 020 7938 3999; www.trailfinders.com/clinic.htm

Travel Clinic, Cambridge 48a Mill Rd, Cambridge CB1 2AS; tel: 01223 367362; www.travelcliniccambridge.co.uk

Australia

The Travel Doctor – TMVC have a network of clinics in Australia, New Zealand and Thailand; they are all members of IAMAT. Tel: 1300 65 88 44 which forwards the call to the nearest clinic, or check their website, www.traveldoctor.com.au. These clinics offer immunisations and advice and they also publish the TMVC *Travelling Well Fun Book*, aimed mainly at expatriate children to help them learn about prevention of illness. They are very child-friendly and might be the best first port of call if your child is taken ill in Australia with travel-related symptoms.

Africa

Johannesburg Travel Clinic (formerly run by British Airways) Tel: 27 11 807 3132; fax: 27 11 803 9562; there are also clinics in **Cape Town**, tel: 021 419 3172; **Knysna**, tel: 044 382 6366 and **East London**, tel: 0431 43 2359

AMREF (the **African Medical and Research Foundation**) 4 Grosvenor Place, London SW1X 7HJ; tel: 020 7201 6070; fax: 020 7201 6170; www.amref.org and www.passporteastafrica.com. Provides information for travellers to each East African country. Money spent funds work for community hospitals throughout East Africa. Subscriptions depend on where you are and the length of cover required.

USA

Centers for Disease Control Atlanta, Georgia (tel. 888 232 3228), are the central source of travel health information in North America with a touch-tone phone line and fax service. They publish each summer the invaluable *Health Information for International Travel* available from CDC (Attention Health Information), Center for

Prevention Services, Division of Quarantine, Atlanta, GA 30333. This is the best English-language publication for up-to-date international disease risk information. **International Association for Medical Assistance to Travellers** (IAMAT) 736 Center St, Lewiston, NY 14092, USA; tel: 716 754 4883; email: iamat@sentex.neta. A non-profit foundation that provides lists of English-speaking doctors abroad as well as foreign health information.

Nepal
CIWEC Clinic Durbar Marg, Kathmandu, Nepal; tel: 00 9771 228531 & 241732; www.ciwec-clinic.com. A travel clinic providing immunisation and other medical services. Experts at evacuation to Bangkok.

Vietnam
There are two American-owned, comprehensive 24-hour health-care facilities:
Columbia Asia Gia Dinh Clinic 01 No Trang Long, Binh Thanh Dist; tel: 84 8 803 0678; fax: 84 8 803 0677
Columbia Asia Saigon 24-hour Clinic 08 Alexandre De Rhodes, Dist 01, HCMC; tel: 84 8 823 8888; fax: 84 8 823 8454: email: medevacca@columbiaasia.com; www.columbiaasia.com

Some suppliers of equipment, mosquito nets, etc
Cotswold Outdoor PO Box 75, Malmesbury SN16 9WQ; tel: 01666 575575; www.cotswoldoutdoor.com. Sells a good range of water purification devices, first aid kits, nets, etc.
Field & Trek Langdale House, Sable Way, Laindon, Essex SS15 6SR; tel: 01268 494444; www.fieldandtrek.com. Sell net *permethrin*-impregnation kits, water filters, Macpac baby carriers and a good range of outdoor equipment.
The Great Little Trading Company 124 Walcot St, Bath BA1 5BG; tel: 0870 850 6000; fax: 01604 640107; www.gltc.co.uk. Sun suits, books, all sorts.
Homeway Medical West Amesbury, Salisbury SP4 7BH; tel: 01980 626361; www.travelwithcare.co.uk
www.kiddicare.com For carriers, buggies, sterilisers, etc.
Mountain Equipment Co-op 130 West Broadway, Vancouver, BC, Canada V5Y 1P3; tel: within North America 1 800 663 2667; local and international 604 876 6221; fax: within North America 1 800 722 1960; local and international 604 876 6590; www.mec.ca mail orders. Lifetime membership costs US$5.00. Good range of equipment for self-propelled wilderness activity. Good range of kids' clothing and bags for comfort down to −7.
www.safariquip.co.uk Sells DEET, Mosi-guard, nets and a good range of survival gear.
Yellow Cross PO Box 448, Farnham GU9 8ZU, UK; tel/fax: 01252 820321; email: info@yellowcross.co.uk; www.yellowcross.co.uk. Sells a range of bags – safe, secure travelling containers for personal medicines particularly for those required in emergency situations with personal identification included. Translation cards available in many languages (including both Thai and Malay) for travelling safely with allergies and other medical conditions.
Young Explorers The Minories, Stratford-upon-Avon CV37 6NF; tel: 01789 414791; www.youngexplorers.co.uk. Offers a good range of sun-protective and other outdoor gear; formerly Outdoor Kids.

Other travel information sources

The Cyclists Touring Club Cotterell House, 69 Meadrow, Godalming, Surrey GU7 3HS; tel: 01483 417217; fax: 01483 426994. Publishes a very nice 28-page information sheet on cycling with children which includes an equipment review.

Expedition Advisory Centre Royal Geographical Society, 1 Kensington Gore, London SW7 2AR; tel: 020 7591 3030; fax: 020 7591 3031; www.rgs.org/eac. Maintains a library of expedition reports and can supply country briefs.

South American Explorers Club 126 Indian Creek Rd, Ithaca, NY 14850 USA; tel: (607) 277 0488; *or* PO Box 3714, Lima 100, Peru; tel: (51) 14 31 4480; *or* PO Box 21-431, Eloy Alfaro, Quito, Ecuador; tel: (593) 256 6076; *or* information via Bradt Travel Guides Ltd, 19 High St, Chalfont St Peter, Bucks SL9 9QE; tel: 01753 893444; fax: 01753 892333; email: info@bradtguides.com; www.bradtguides.com

Stanfords (books and maps) 12–14 Long Acre, Covent Garden, London WC2E 9LP; tel: 0171 836 1321

TALC (Teaching Aids at Low Cost) PO Box 49, St Albans, Herts AL1 5TX; tel: 01727 853869. Sells ORS measuring spoons, and certain books including *Where There Is No Doctor.*

Your local travel agent should have information about special deals and child-friendly tour operators, whilst tourist information bureaux can often provide details of specialist child-orientated holidays in their areas.

Miscellaneous resources

www.DisabledGo.info For access information for push- and wheel-chairs in the UK.

HELP Holidays Endeavour for Lone Parents, 59 Ridge Balk Lane, Woodlands, Doncaster DN6 7NR; tel: 01302 365139. Holidays for lone parents.

National Association for Parents of Sleepless Children Sally Baines (Sec), PO Box 38, Prestwood, Gt Missenden, Bucks HP1 0SZ

World-wide Education Service Waverley House, Penton, Carlisle, Cumbria CA6 5QU; tel: 01228 577123; email: office@weshome.demon.co.uk; www.weshome.demon.co.uk

Breast-feeding and pregnancy advice

Natural Childbirth Trust (**NCT**) Alexandra House, Oldham Terrace, Acton, London W3 6NH; tel: 0870 444 8707; www.nctpregnancyandbabycare.com

La Leche League International Inc 9616 Minneapolis Av, Franklin Park, IL 60131, USA; www.lalecheleague.org; www.laleche.org.uk

Nursing Mothers Association of Australia PO Box 230, Hawthorn, Victoria 3122, Australia or look in the phone directory for the nearest counsellors.

Books

Renfrew, Mary, Chloe Fisher and Suzanne Arms *Bestfeeding: Getting Breastfeeding Right for You,* Celestial Arts, 2000.

Royal College of Obstetricians and Gynaecologists *Travelling in Pregnancy* available from the RCOG bookshop; 27 Sussex Place, Regents Park, London NW1 4RG, for £1.50 + 30p postage.

Resources for young travellers with special requirements

Anaphylaxis Campaign PO Box 275, Farnborough, Hants GU14 6SX; tel: 01252 542029; www.anaphylaxis.org.uk

British Allergy Foundation Tel: 020 8303 8583; www.allergyfoundation.com. Website has good advice on flying with allergies.

British Epilepsy Association Tel: 0113 210 8800; www.epilepsy.org.uk

Contact a Family 209–211 City Rd, London EC1 1JN; tel (helpline): 0808 808 3555; www.cafamily.org.uk. Provides advice and information on a wide range of issues for families with disabled children.

Council for Disabled Children 8 Wakley St, London EC1V 7QE; tel: 020 7843 6000; fax: 020 7278 9512; www.ncb.org/cdc. Do not organise holidays themselves but provide information on travel health; probably the best signposting organisation for further resources.

Holiday Care Service Tel: 0845 124 9971. Offers advice on holidays for people with problems and has lists of sympathetic insurers.

Medic Alert Foundation Freepost, 1 Bridge Wharf, 156 Caledonian Rd, London N1 9BR; tel: 0800 581420 or 020 7833 3034. Supplies bracelets alerting medics to medical conditions; allow 28 days; also **MedicAlert Foundation International** Turlock, CA 95380-1009, USA; tel: (209) 668 3333 or (800) 344 3226.

Mencap Optium House, Clippers Quay, Salford Quays, Manchester M5 2XP; tel: 0161 877 5858. Offers a service of respite care breaks and holidays for children with learning disabilities.

National Asthma Campaign Providence House, Providence Place, London N1 0NT; tel: 020 7226 2260. Information on travel insurance for families who have asthma; the National Asthma Campaign Helpline (01345 010203) offers advice.

Bradt Travel Guides is a partner to the 'know before you go' campaign, masterminded by the UK Foreign and Commonwealth Office to promote the importance of finding out about a destination before you travel. By combining the up-to-date advice of the FCO with the in-depth knowledge of Bradt authors, you'll ensure that your trip will be as trouble-free as possible.

www.fco.gov.uk/knowbeforeyougo

Appendix

FURTHER READING

The Book Trust 45 East Hill, London SW18 2QZ; tel: 0208 816 2977; www.booktrust.org.uk. A superb resource to help you find local books on particular areas or subjects. There is also a dedicated children's book site.

For adults
Books

Bezruchka, Stephen *Altitude illness, prevention and treatment*. The Mountaineers, 1011 SW Klickitat Way, Seattle, WA 98134; Douglas & MacIntyre, Vancouver V5L 2H1; Cordee, Leicester LE1 7HD, 1994

Green, Christopher *Toddler Taming: a parent's guide to (surviving) the first four years* Doubleday, 1984. Excellent book written by a down-to-earth paediatrician

McCluskey, Karen Cunon (ed) *Notes from a travelling childhood: readings for internationally mobile parents and children*. A Foreign Service Youth Foundation Publication, Australia, 1994

Wilson, Jane *Lemurs of the Lost World: Exploring the Forests and Crocodile Caves of Madagascar* Impact Books, London, 1995. Travel narrative highlighting dangers of scorpion sting and crocodile attack; available for £5 from 33 Hartington Grove, Cambridge CB1 7UA

Wilson-Howarth, Jane *Bugs, Bites and Bowels* Cadogan Books, London, 2002. Authoritative health guide for anyone travelling anywhere

Articles and reference

Brouwer, M L, Tolboom, J J M & Hardeman, J H J Routine screening of children returning home from the tropics: retrospective study. *British Medical Journal*, 1999 **318** 568–9 with comments in **319** 121

Centers for Disease Control in Atlanta, Georgia (published annually) *Health information for international travel*. Single copies are available from CDC (Attention Health Information), Center for Prevention Services, Division of Quarantine, Atlanta, GA 30333; best English-language publication for up-to-date international disease-risk information, but very scary. Information is also at www.cdc.gov/travel.

Chadwick D *A Textbook of Epilepsy* (eds) Laidlaw J, Richens A & Chadwick D; Churchill Livingstone, Edinburgh, 1993

Chiodini, P L A 'new' parasite: human infection with *Cyclospora cayetanensis*. *Transactions of the Royal Society of Tropical Medicine and Hygiene* 1994 **88** 369–71

Conlon, C J, Peto, T & Ellis, C J Post-tropical screening is of little value unless the traveller feels unwell. *British Medical Journal* 1993 **307** 1108

Eastaugh, J & Shepherd, S Infectious and toxic syndromes from fish and shellfish consumption. *Arch Intern Med* 1989 **149** 1735-40

Ellis, M, Manandhar, N, Shakya, U, Manandhar, D S, Fawdry, A & Costello, A M de L Postnatal hypothermia and cold stress among newborn infants in Nepal monitored by continuous ambulatory recording. *Arch Dis Child* 1996; **75**: F42–F45

Foyle M J Expatriate children: selection, preparation and typical needs. *Travel Medicine International* 1994 **12** (3) 93–7

Howarth, Jane Wilson Hazards of trekking in Nepal. *Travel Medicine International* 1997 **15** (3) 82–7

Howarth, Jane Wilson and Ellis, Matthew Illness in expatriate familes in Kathmandu, Nepal. *Travel Medicine International* 1997 **15** (4) 150–5

Hughes, C, Tucker, R, Bannister, B & Bradley, D J Malaria prophylaxis for long-term travellers. *Communicable Disease and Public Health* 2003 **6 (3)** Sept 200–8

Manandhar, N, Ellis, M, Manandhar, D S, Morley, D & Costello A M de L Liquid crystal thermometry for the detection of neonatal hypothermia in Nepal. *J Trop Pediatr* 1998; **44**: 15–17

Morley, C J et al Field trials of the *Baby Check* score card. *Archives of Disease in Childhood* **66** 1991 100–120.

Pennington, E & Pennington, S Modifying chickenpox *British Medical Journal* 1991 **303** 164

Shann, F How often do children cough? *Lancet* Sept 14 1996 **348** 699–700

Taubman, B Clinical trial of the treatment of colic by modification of parent–infant interaction. *Pediatrics* 1984 **74** 998

Visscher, P K, Vetter, R S & Camazine, S Removing bee stings. *Lancet* August 3 1996 **348**.

Weerasooriya, M V Comparative efficiency of house curtains impregnated with *permethrin, lambdacyhalothrin* or *bendiocarb* against the vector bacroftian filariasis ... in Sri Lanka. *Trans. R Soc Trop Med Hyg* 1996 **90** 103–4

For children

Most of these books are for younger children because older children will find books to their own tastes in public libraries. They should not pall (too much) on frequent re-reading, but convey a flavour of an exotic destination. Penguin children's '60s' series are mini books that are excellent emergency entertainment when boredom strikes.

General ideas

Brookes, Mona *Drawing with Children: a creative teaching and learning method that works for adults too* Putnam, Berkeley, 1996

Silverman, Goldie *Backpacking with babies and small children* Wilderness Press, Berkeley, 1999

Travel

Boyne, W J *The Smithsonian Book of Flight for Young People* Athenum, New York, 1988

Johnstone, M *The I-Spy Guide to Aircraft* Michelin, 1996

Verne, Jules *Around the World in Eighty Days*, Brimax, 1995

Walters, B M *Look Inside Cross-sections: Planes* Dorling Kindersley, 1994

General

Dorling Kindersley publish excellent illustrated children's reference books on various natural history themes: zoology, geology, meteorology, etc.

Durrell, Gerald *The Fantastic Flying Journey* Conran Octopus 1987. Packed with exotic natural history facts in wonderfully quirky Durrell style. Ages over five years.
How Animals Live Usborne 2003. From four years; full of information although with a more traditional style.
Kerven, Rosalind *Legends of the Animal World* Cambridge University Press 1986. From four years.
Kipling, Rudyard *Just So Stories* Pavillion 1987. Five years upwards.
Legg, Gerald *Minibeasts* Belitha Press. From four years; about invertebrates; attractive.
Legg, Gerald various titles on scary animals Franklin Watts 2003
Parker, Steve *Dinosaurs and How They Lived* Dorling Kindersley 1988. Draws parallels between dinosaurs and the habits of surviving large animals. Children who are already enthusiastic about dinosaurs will be inspired by this.

Africa
Allen, Judy *Elephant* Candlewick, 1993. From five years.
Doherty, Paul *The Mask of Ra* Headline, 1998. From ten years.
Geraghty, Paul *The Hunter* Red Fox, 1996. Five to eight years.
Grindley, Sally *Little Elephant Thunderfoot* Orchard Books, 1996. From five years.
Hadithi, Mwenye & Kennaway, Adrienne, Picture Knight/Hodder and Stoughton have produced a series of delightful picture story books about African animals: *Greedy Zebra* 1987, *Crafty Chameleon* 1988, *Tricky Tortoise* 1990 and *Hot Hippo* 1987. Good for ages three to seven years.
Jacq, Christian *Ramses: The Son of Light* Simon & Schuster, 1997. Young Adult
Malone, Geoffrey *Kimba* Hodder, 1998. About wild lions. Eight to ten years.
McCaughrean, Geraldine *Plundering Paradise* Oxford, 1996. Pirates in Madagascar. Ten to 14 years.
Morpurgo, Michael *Butterfly Lion* HarperCollins, 1996. Story starts in Africa. Eight to ten years.
Price, Willard *African Adventure* 1963 and *Safari Adventure* 1993, Red Fox. Eight to 13 years.

Asia
There are plenty of wonderful locally published tales to be found in India and also comics of the Ramayana and other epics.
Allen, Judy *Tiger* Candlewick Press 1994. From five years.
Bailey, Jill *Save the Tiger* Heinemann, 1990. From five years upwards.
Das, Prodeepta *I is for India* Frances Lincoln, 1996. Five to eight years.
Desai, Niru *The Raja's Big Ears* Storytellers*/also from Roy Yates Books 1986. From three years.
Hergé *The Adventures of Tintin* eg: *Tintin in Tibet*. Mammoth/Reed 1990. From five to adulthood.
Khan, Khodeja *The Radish Thief* Storytellers*. From three years.
Kipling, Rudyard *The Jungle Book* Pavilion 1991. Over six years; includes delightful images of domestic Asian animals in Rikki-Tikki-Tavi, especially the tailor bird and mongoose which are commonly seen in Indian hotel gardens.
Kipling, Rudyard *Kim*. Older children and adults.
Price, Willard *Tiger Adventure, Cannibal Adventure*, etc Red Fox, 1993. Eight to 13 years.
Stone, Susheila *Mitthu the Parrot* Storytellers, 1995*. From three years.

South America and the Caribbean

Durrell, Gerald *The Whispering Land* Penguin, 1964. Ten plus years.

Geraghty, Paul *The Great Green Forest*. Red Fox, 1994. From three years.

Gissing, Vera *Joshua and the Big Wave* MacDonald/Simon & Schuster, 1989. From four years.

Hergé *The Adventures of Tintin* eg: *Tintin in the World of the Inca* and *Prisoners of the Sun*. Mammoth/Reed 1984. From five to adulthood.

Ibbotson, Eva *Journey to the River Sea* Macmillan 2001. From five years.

Australia

The Australians are masters of producing excellent natural history books for children, but you may need to wait to get there before buying any. Some nice examples for four to eight-year-olds include:

Atkinson, Kathie *A is for Australian Animals* Omnibus Books, South Australia, 1994. From five years.

Baker, Jeannie *Where the Forest Meets the Sea* Walker, 1989. From five years.

Reilly, Pauline *The Tasmanian Devil* Kangaroo Press, NSW, 1988. From five years.

Price, Willard *Diving Adventure* Hodder & Stoughton, 1970. Eight to 13 years.

Reference books useful for answering older children's questions

Collins Guide to Tropical Plants by Wilhelm Lotschert and Gerhard Beese (Collins, 1983). Marvellous book with lots of colour photographs covering the vast majority of ornamental and economic plants and crops you are likely to want to look up.

The Penguin Concise Columbia Encyclopaedia 1987 (950pp). Excellent if rather biased towards the American view of the world.

Encyclopaedia of Indian Natural History Bombay Natural History Society, 1986. Good coverage of all sorts of biological topics from how leeches copulate, through methods of seed dispersal, to the territorial behaviour of langurs. A must for anyone running a home school in Asia.

★Available from Jennie Ingham Associates Ltd, 64–68 Camden High St, London NW1 0LT

Appendix 3

GLOSSARY OF TERMS

Acetaminophen or Tylenol is called *paracetamol* outside North America; it is the *generic* drug name for the best standard medicine for reducing fever and pain in children; common trade names in Europe are Calpol and Paramol.

Bacteria Microbes which can cause a range of disease which can be treated with the appropriate antibiotic.

Contagious A disease which can be spread by touch. See also *infectious*.

Dehydration Lack of fluid in the tissues and blood.

Generic The generic name of a medicine is less memorable but more informative than the trade name. In the book all generic names are in *italics* and if you are likely to buy medicines abroad find out the generic name, which usually remains similar throughout the world; trade names can differ hugely.

Haemorrhage Blood loss or bleeding.

Incubation period Time between being exposed to (catching) an infection and developing the symptoms of the illness.

Infant Doctors call children under one year infants, although – confusingly – airlines call children infants until their second birthday.

Infectious A disease spread directly in the air (without touch) from person to person, eg: the common cold.

ORS Oral rehydration solution (pages 134–5).

Paracetamol Acetaminophen or Tylenol.

Primary course of immunisation The first course of immunisation that anyone receives against any given disease. Most people's primary course of tetanus immunisation will be in infancy whilst for Japanese encephalitis it will not be until required for travel so could be at the age of 60.

Prophylaxis Means prevention and often implies medicines taken to prevent malaria. Strictly it refers to any preventative measures so malaria prophylaxis also really includes measures taken to avoid mosquito bites.

Stool Bowel motion.

Subcontinent The geographical region comprising India, Pakistan, Bangladesh, Nepal etc, otherwise called the Indian subcontinent.

Viruses Microbes which can cause disease but cannot be treated with antibiotics. The common cold and many of the childhood diseases causing rashes are viral and so antibiotics are useless: the treatment is a little *paracetamol* to keep the fever down.

Whinge A complaining noise made by young children designed to attract parental attention. It is a nagging whining sound which takes much practice to perfect to make it maximally annoying and effective.

Appendix

COMMUNICATING MEDICAL PROBLEMS
French • Spanish • German • Indonesian • Japanese

This section is clearly not a comprehensive medical dictionary. In fact, the first question is probably the most helpful. In the event of an emergency, however, our aim is to help you to communicate the essentials as simply as possible, along with the judicious use of sign language.

Although English is so widely spoken and understood, the languages featured here should help you to communicate in most other areas of the world. Spanish is spoken in most of Central and South America as well as in Spain; French is understood in much of Africa; while German is often the 'common' European language in Mediterranean countries such as Turkey – the Germans themselves, like the Dutch and Scandinavians, frequently speak impeccable English. Indonesian can be used all over Indonesia, including Bali, and also in Malaysia, while Japanese is essential in Japan. The likelihood, however, is that many doctors will have at least a basic knowledge of English, so don't be afraid to ask.

Does anyone speak English?
F   Est-ce qu'il y a quelqu'un qui parle anglais?
S   ¿Hay alguien que habla inglés?
G   Spricht hier jemand Englisch?
I   Ada orang yang bisa berbicara Bahasa Inggris?
J   どなたか英語を話せますか？

Where is the best/closest hospital/pharmacy/doctor?
F   Où se trouve l'hôpital/la pharmacie/le médecin le/la plus proche d'ici?
S   ¿Donde está el hospital/la farmacía/el médico mejor/más cercano?
G   Wo ist hier das/die/der beste/nächste Krankenhaus/Apotheke/Arzt?
I   Dimanakah rumah sakit/apotik/dokter anak terbaik/terdekat
J   どこの病院/薬局/医者が一番いいですか
    ここから一番近いですか？

My child has opened her bowels/vomited 12 times in the last 24 hours.
F   Mon enfant a dérangement intestinal/a vomis 12 fois en 24 heures.
S   Mi hijo/a tiene descomposición/ha vomitado 12 veces en 24 horas.
G   Mein Kind hat Durchfall/hat sich 12 mai in 24 Stunden übergeben.
I   Anak saya mangalami muntah/berak* dua belas (12) kali dalam dua puluh
    empat (24) jam terakhir.
J   私の子供はこの 24 時間に 12 回も下痢をしています/
    はいています。

He/she passed/vomited/urinated blood.
F   Il/elle a excrété/vomis/uriné (pissé) du sang.
S   El/ella ha excretado/vomitado/orinado sangre.
G   Er/sie hat Blut ausgeschieden/gebrochen/uriniert.
I   Dia ada darah dalam tinja/mutah/kencing.
J   彼/彼女は出血しました/吐血しました/血尿をしました。

He/she has a fever/has been ill for 3 days.
F   Il/elle a la fièvre/est malade depuis 3 jours.
S   El/ella tiene fiebre/lleva enfermo 3 días.
G   Er/sie hat Fieber/ist schon 3 Tage krank.
I   Dia deman/sakit sudah tiga (3) hari.
J   彼/彼女の熱/病気は３日前から続いています。

He/she is allergic to...
F   Il/elle est allergique à...
S   El/ella es alérgico/a a...
G   Er/sie ist allergisch gegen...
I   Dia alergi terhadap...
J   彼/彼女は～（薬名）にアレルギーがあります。

It seems to hurt here.
F   Il me semble que ça lui/la fait mal ici.
S   Parece que duele aquí.
G   Es scheint hier weh zu tun.
I   Rasa sakit disini.
J   ここが痛そうです。

We need *paracetamol*/antihistamine syrup for this child.
F   Je voudrais du *paracétamol*/du sirop antihistamine pour cet enfant.
S   Necesitamos *paracetamol*/jarabe antihistamínico para este/a niño/a.
G   Wir brauchen *Paracetamol*/antihistaminischen Saft für dieses Kind.
I   Kita memerlukan *parasetamol*/antihistamin sirup untuk anak ini.
J   この子供にはパラシタモール/抗ヒスタミン・シロップ
    を飲ませたほうがよいです。

How often does he/she take this medicine?
F   Combien de fois doit il/elle prendre ces médicaments?
S   ¿Cada cuanto tiene que tomar los medicamentos?
G   Wieviel mal am Tag muss er/sie die Medizin einnehmen?
I   Berapa kali sehari obat ini harus diminum.
J   何時間おきに彼/彼女にこの薬を飲ませますか？

Does he/she really need an injection or can he/she take medicine?
F   Est-ce qu'une piqure est indispensable, ou peut-il/elle prendre des
    médicaments?
S   ¿Es necesaria una inyección o es posible que el/ella tome los medicamentos?
G   Ist eine Spritze notwendig, oder kann er/sie das Medikament einnehmen?

I   Apakah dia perlu sekali untuk mendapatkan suntikan atau cukup obat saja.

J   彼/彼女は本当に注射が必要ですか？

      彼/彼女は薬を飲むべきですか？

Notes on Indonesian

c is pronounced ch in Indonesian, so *kencing* (urine) is pronounced kenching and *cukup* (enough) is pronounced chookoop; g is always hard, as in *alergi*. The Indonesian for and is *dan*.

* *muntah-berak* means vomiting and diarrhoea; *muntah* means vomiting only and *berak* means diarrhoea only.

Index